LANDMARK

Do____

Richard Sale

A West-Countryman by birth, Richard Sale has been visiting Dorset for as long as he can comfortably remember, drawn by its glorious mix of scenery and the Coastal Path which, he maintains, offers the finest coastal walking in Britain.

A research scientist who concentrates on writing and photography, he has written several guide books including Landmark titles on the Cotswolds, Italian Lakes, Provence & the Cote d'Azur, and Tuscany & Florence. His other books include a series of essays on Dorset.

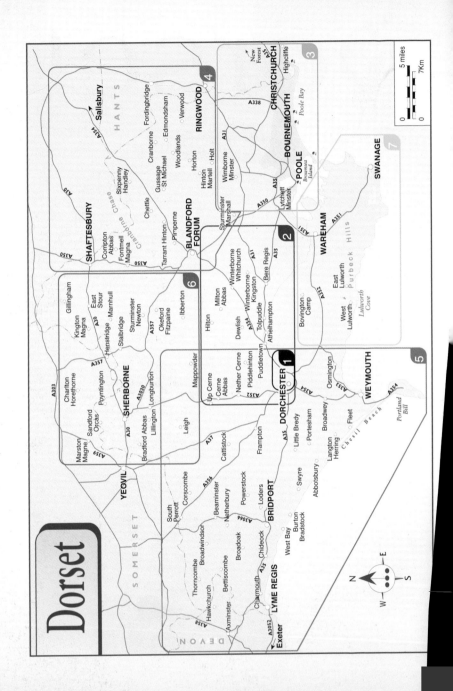

Dorset

SOMERSET

DEVON

HANTS

Salisbury

SHAFTESBURY

Gillingham
Kington Magna
East Stour
Marnhull
Henstridge
Stalbridge
Sturminster Newton
Okeford Fitzpaine
Ibberton

Compton Abbas
Fontmell Magna
Tarrant Hinton
Pimperne
BLANDFORD FORUM

Chettle
Sixpenny Handley
Cranborne
Fordingbridge
Edmondsham
Verwood
RINGWOOD

Gussage St Michael
Woodlands
Horton
Hinton Martell
Holt
Wimborne Minster

New Forest
Highcliffe
CHRISTCHURCH
BOURNEMOUTH
Poole Bay
POOLE

Charlton Horethorne
Poyntington
YEOVIL
Marston Magna
Sandford Orcas
Bradford Abbas
Lillington
Longburton
SHERBORNE
Leigh

Mappowder
Up Cerne
Cerne Abbas
Nether Cerne
Piddlehinton
Puddletown
Athelhampton

Hilton
Milton Abbas
Dewlish
Winterborne Whitchurch
Winterborne Kingston
Tolpuddle
Bere Regis

Sturminster Marshall
Lytchett Minster
Brownsea Island

WAREHAM
Purbeck Hills
East Lulworth
West Lulworth
Lulworth Cove
SWANAGE

Thorncombe
Hawkchurch
Axminster
Exeter
Broadwindsor
Bettiscombe
Charmouth
LYME REGIS

South Perrott
Corscombe
Beaminster
Netherbury
Powerstock
Broadoak
Chideock
West Bay
Burton Bradstock

Loders
BRIDPORT
Swyre
Abbotsbury

Frampton
Cattistock

DORCHESTER

Little Bredy
Portesham
Langton Herring
Chesil Beach
Broadway
Fleet
Osmington
WEYMOUTH
Portland Bill

Bovington Camp

0 5 miles
0 7Km

N
W E
S

LANDMARK VISITORS GUIDE

Dorset

CONTENTS

*I*ntroduction

Dorset, one of England's smallest counties, is also one of its richest, both for its scenic beauty and its historical interest. Within boundaries it crams 'old-fashioned' seaside resorts such as Weymouth, Bournemouth and Swanage. There is dramatic cliff scenery, beautiful coves and bays like Lulworth and Kimmeridge and lovely old ports such as Lyme Regis and old Poole. Inland Dorset has fascinating old towns – Dorchester, Sherborne, Shaftesbury and Wimborne – and scenery every bit as beautiful as the coast – the downland of Cranborne Chase and the famous Dorset heathland. There is the history of England – Maiden Castle, where the Romans fought the Celts, Wareham where the Saxons met the Vikings, and Monmouth's rebellion which ended in the infamous Bloody Assizes of Judge Jeffreys. The county has a unique natural history, for Dorset is the final stronghold of rare reptiles, birds and butterflies.

And there is Thomas Hardy's Wessex. No English county has been captured as completely as Hardy's evocation of Dorset in his Wessex novels.

Dorset has something for everyone, and in this guide all aspects of this most delightful of counties are explored. Also included are a few trips over the border. Dorset's position – close to the New Forest, to Salisbury and the great country houses of Wiltshire – means that even the most ardent lover of the county will sometimes be tempted to leave it, if only for a day.

A SHORT HISTORY

The history of the county is explored at the relevant places within the book, but here a brief overview of Dorset's fascinating past is given.

It is likely that man first trod on Dorset soil about 150,000 years ago, but the treading has not been continuous since that time, as successive ice ages pushed the settlers southward. The last Ice Age finished about 10,000 years ago, and the retreating ice was followed northward by Mesolithic, Middle Stone Age hunters, the first permanent county residents. In the wake of the ice the county was swampy, hardly hospitable, but by the time the Neolithic farmers arrived from the Mediterranean, the chalk downlands of middle Dorset were dry, the poor soil capable of sustained agriculture. The Neolithic residents left their mark, the long barrows, as did those

TOP TWELVE TIPS

All visitors to Dorset will create their own list of the best that the county has to offer, but as a starter, here – in no particular order – are my **Top Twelve:**

Dorchester

The best small town in Britain. Wander the streets, visit the County Museum, walk the ramparts of Maiden Castle just outside the town – or try one of the teashops. (See page 18)

Old Harry Rocks

Walk to Foreland Point to see the chalk stacks. (See page 196) Lulworth Cove/Durdle Door The tortured rocks of an almost circular cove, one of the most beautiful in Britain and, nearby, the place where the sea has punched a hole through the cliff. (See page 210)

Lyme Regis

Famous for fossils, the place where Jane Austen wrote part of *Persuasion*, the setting for *The French Lieutenant's Woman*, and one of Britain's prettiest old ports. (See page 152)

Sherborne Abbey

A display of the stonemason's art which is breathtaking. (See page 174)

Gold Hill, Shaftesbury

As steep a hill as exists in the county, with a fine row of houses and views of Dorset downland. (See page 139)

Hardy's Cottage, Higher Bockhampton

Dorset will always be Hardy's county. Though he lived most of his adult life in Max Gate, Dorchester, it is at Higher Bockhampton that Hardy's Wessex has its roots. (See page 37)

Forde Abbey

A marvellous house, incorporating the remains of an old monastery, and beautiful gardens. (See page 147)

Athelhampton

Some say it is the finest stone-built manor house in England, and it stands in magnificent formal gardens. (See page 61)

World of Toys, Arne

A delightful, fascinating collection. (See page 193)

Brewer's Quay, Weymouth

The past brought to life in Timewalk, set within a converted Victorian Devenish brewery, now complete with shops, café and bar, and with regular art and craft exhibitions. (See page 168)

Corfe Castle

A beautiful village, the wonderful ruins of the old castle – where dreadful deeds really did take place. (See page 198)

who followed them, the Bronze Age round barrow builders. These latter folk evidently found Dorset much to their liking, as the county is littered with a large number of their barrows.

Next came a people that an ancient book in the Dorset County Library (quoting Genesis 10:2 as the source) claims were descended from Gomer, son of Japheth. These were the iron-using Celts. The Celts were a tribal people, and the tribe that settled in Dorset gave their name to the county. They were the people near the tidal water, *Dwry Triges*, or Durotriges as the Romans called them. So Dorset is named from its tidal water, the sea. What could be more appropriate?

The Romans fought the Celts, most famously at **Maiden Castle** where the battle for Britain was effectively won. There are few Roman remains within the county, but many of its towns were founded by the new occupiers. When the Romans left, the Saxons took over, leaving their mark with some lovely churches, but they also founded more towns, including the fortress town of **Wareham** where the conflict between the Saxons and the Vikings was fought out. Dorset was the land of the West Saxons, a tribe that has given us the name for which Dorset will always be known – **Wessex**. Even without Thomas Hardy, Wessex would be Dorset's heritage. But with Hardy it is the cornerstone of its being, and its lasting appeal to the visitor.

The Normans built churches and founded abbeys as they did everywhere in England. Dorset's history was now England's, but there were local events that had national significance. In 1685 the **Duke of Monmouth** landed at Lyme Regis. His intended overthrow of James II failed quickly and violently, but the aftermath was longer and almost as painful, **Judge Jeffreys' Bloody Assizes** becoming a byword for cruelty. After Monmouth's rebellion Dorset was quiet, but there was to be one more incident which placed the county at the forefront of English history: at the quaint village of **Tolpuddle** six men were arrested after starting an association for farm workers. What at first seemed a local dispute escalated when the men were transported to Australia. Protests led to questions in Parliament, to the pardoning of the men and, eventually, to real Trades Unions.

NATURAL DORSET

Amazingly for such a small county – it measures only about 60 by 40 miles (95kms by 65kms) – within the borders of Dorset there is a representative selection of almost three-quarters of the landscapes of England. Dorset has chalk downland and valleys based on clay, it has heathland and limestone hills. In addition, the lack of mineral ore and large cities has meant that the landscapes of Dorset have remained unspoilt: **Cranborne Chase** and **Blackmoor Vale** look much the same now as they have for centuries.

The coastline too represents the geography of England's coast. It cannot boast the granite of nearby Cornwall, but it has the hard rocks of **Portland** and **Purbeck**, these producing cliffs as high and angular. And within walking distance of the hard Purbeck cliffs it has others of that softest of rocks, chalk, with formations that rival the more famous cliffs at Dover. It has black oil

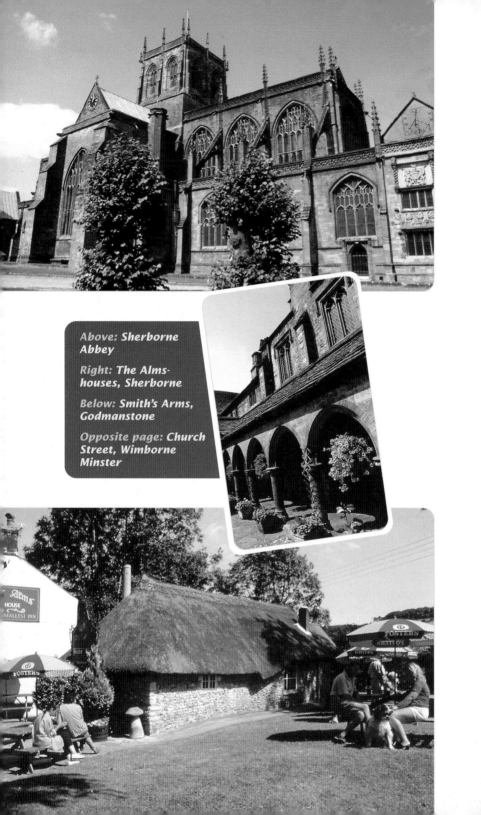

Above: **Sherborne Abbey**

Right: **The Alms-houses, Sherborne**

Below: **Smith's Arms, Godmanstone**

Opposite page: **Church Street, Wimborne Minster**

shale, its oil content high enough to be extracted commercially near Kimmeridge; there is the crumbling blue Lias of **Lyme Regis**, packed with fossils; and there is a unique feature – **Chesil Beach**.

This rich diversity of landscapes gives Dorset a wonderful range of habitats and a correspondingly good range of wildlife. The chalk downlands, especially those of Purbeck, are home to an enviable range of butterflies, some very rare. The Lulworth skipper butterfly is named from the first place it was recorded, and still the only place where it flourishes. Dorset's famous heaths are the last stronghold of the colourful, but elusive, Dartford warbler, and also of two of Britain's rarest reptiles, the smooth snake and the sand lizard. Ironically, the main food of the very rare smooth snake is the equally rare sand lizard.

The Dorset coast is good for sea birds, but is also surprisingly good for dolphins and porpoises, identification charts at the **Durlston Country Park** near Swanage helping lucky visitors with naming what they have just seen.

VISITING DORSET

The M27 motorway and then the A31/A338 dual carriageways reach the east Dorset border and Bournemouth. To the west the M5 traverses Somerset, but gets no closer to Dorset than a dozen miles, though reasonable roads connect with it. From the north there are A class roads from Salisbury and Bath. The lack of the most up-to-date roads means it takes time to reach the county, but the lack also mirrors the absence of industrial development: Dorset remains an agricultural county, one still served by a road network that has survived – give or take the odd widening scheme – for centuries. The roads within the county are good, but often single carriageway – the county is forcing you to slow down, to accept it at its own pace. But it is such a small county, everything is so close, no journey will ever be that long: by the end of your stay you will be grateful for the slower pace – Dorset is a stress-free zone.

It is also a place for visiting at all times of the year. The seaside holidaymaker and sun-seeker will come in summer – the highest temperatures are found from June to September, with the lowest rainfall from April to June – but there is plenty to do at all times of the year. In spring the show of bulbs at the famous gardens dotted throughout the county are worth a journey of many miles, while in autumn the trees in the same gardens and in the country hollows are the colour of old gold. Even in winter there is much to do: **Dorchester** is still a wonderful place to visit, as are Sherborne and Shaftesbury, Wimborne and Christchurch. The walk along **Bournemouth**'s promenade on a clear winter's day is as bracing as a summer stroll is relaxing, while the **Dorset Coastal Path** offers a view of raw nature. Even in the snow there is beauty in the county: try a walk on Maiden Castle, its ramparts picked out in the drifts.

THOMAS HARDY, MAN OF DORSET

Though he lived into the second quarter of the twentieth century, Thomas Hardy was born in 1840, about the same time as James

Places to Visit

National Trust in Dorset

Brownsea Island, Poole Harbour

Famous for its association with Baden-Powell and the Scout/Guide movement, the island also has a fascinating history and is a wildlife reserve. (See page 99)

The Cerne Abbas Giant

Enigmatic chalk-cut figure notable for its absence of censorship! (See page 56-8)

Cloud's Hill, near Bovington

The home of TE Lawrence (of Arabia) while he was serving at Bovington, and with the RAF under the name of TE Shaw. It was close to the house that Lawrence died in a motor cycle accident. (See page 77)

Corfe Castle

The ruins of an historically interesting castle, positioned to defend a gap in the Purbeck Hills. The place where the young King Edward was murdered in 978. (See page 194)

The Hardy Monument, near Portesham

The curiously-shaped memorial to Dorset's other Thomas Hardy, the one who cradled the dying Nelson at Trafalgar and may have been asked for a last kiss. (See page 160)

Hod Hill, near Stourpaine

One of Dorset's most impressive Iron Age hill forts. (See page 129)

Kingston Lacy, near Wimborne Minster

A 17th-century house with an important collection of paintings and artefacts and an estate which includes two villages little changed since medieval times. (See page 105)

Lodge Farm, near Kingston Lacy

A late 14th-century farm house.

Max Gate, Dorchester

The Victorian house designed and occupied by Thomas Hardy for over 40 years until his death in 1928. (See page 32)

Studland Beach and Nature Reserve

One of Dorset's safest beaches and an excellent nature reserve at the edge of Studland Heath. (See page 192)

White Mill, near Sturminster Newton

An 18th-century mill on the site of one mentioned in the Domesday Book.
(see page 118)

In addition to the above, the Trust also owns land at Coney's Castle, Lambert's Castle and Pilsdon Pen – the highest hill in the county – in rural west Dorset, and Golden Cap on the coast of west Dorset; Win Green Hill – actually in Wiltshire, but the best viewpoint to see Cranborne Chase; and Spyway Farm and Ringstead Bay near Purbeck.

Foreland Point, Purbeck

Chesil Beach

Lyme Regis Harbour

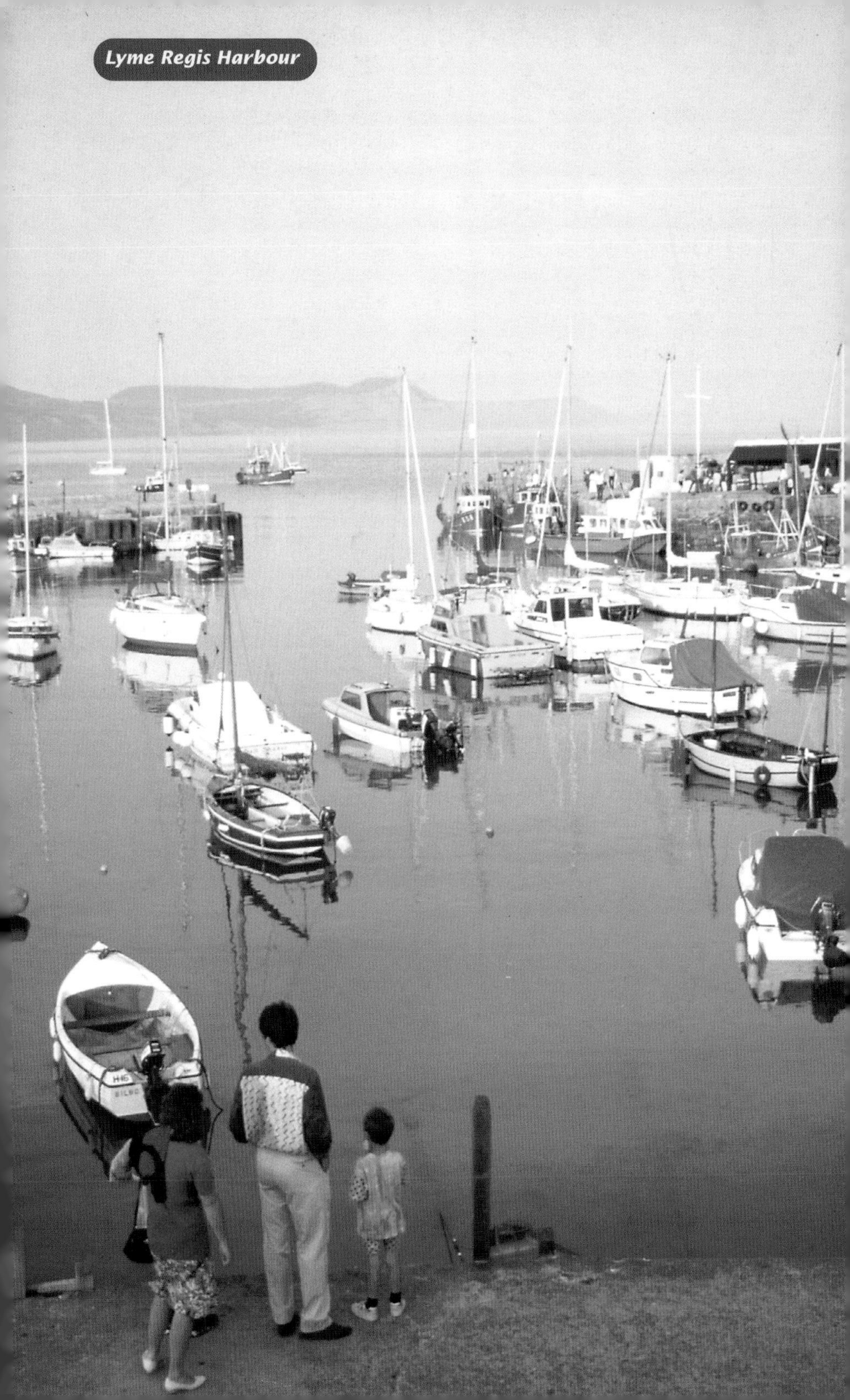

Hammett, one of the martyrs, arrived back in Tolpuddle. Hardy was born at Higher Bockhampton and raised in a rural community, but he was not from a labouring family. Visitors to the family home can see at a glance that this was not the cottage of a farm labourer, but of a craftsman, one of the middle class, for Thomas's father was a stone mason and master builder. But the young Hardy was in touch with the elements of the countryside: **Puddletown** and **Duddle Heaths** were as barren and desolate as any of the Dorset heaths, the perfect model for Egdon.

There were also the little touches that mould the character of the sensitive young. Hardy recalled in later life the shock of seeing the body of a young farm labourer, a boy of his own age, lying in a ditch having died of starvation. He also recalled with pain watching another labourer of his own age being publicly hanged. Hardy maintained that nothing his father ever taught him 'drove the tragedy of life so deeply into my mind'. That such events could cause Hardy grief is understandable, because he had the sensitivity of all precocious, yet fragile, children.

Precocious the boy most certainly was: it was said he could read before he could walk, and it is certainly true that his present from his mother on his ninth birthday was Dryden's translation of Virgil. He was also, at least in his early years, what was then termed 'delicate'. At his birth the attending doctor maintained he was stillborn: his survival appears to have been assured by the midwife who refused to accept this verdict.

Thomas went to the local village school at first but was then transferred to a school in Dorchester, the daily walk to and from which seems to have corrected his health. It may also have helped him develop his attachment for the countryside, for the shy and lonely boy often went for long walks across the heath and local farms. At Dorchester he also met **William Barnes**, the famous Dorset dialect poet, and formed a friendship that was to be both life-long and influential.

At 16 Hardy left school and, in keeping with the family tradition, became an assistant to a **Dorchester architect**, John Hicks. Although by this time Hardy was writing poetry, he was clearly impressed with his chosen career. In later years he maintained that there could be no more satisfying life than that of an architect in a county town. With that objective in mind he left Dorchester in 1862 to continue his training in London. The big city did not agree with him. At that time London was an unpleasant place, the rich leaving it for country retreats in the summer months to escape the stink and the flies that rose from the sewage-laden Thames. In time the foulness affected Hardy's health and he was happy to return, in 1867, to Dorchester as Hicks' assistant.

The following year was significant, for in that year he met Emma Gifford, later to be his wife, while working on a church in Cornwall, and, at the insistence of William Barnes, offered a book for publication. The book was not published, but certain passages received enthusiastic comments, and although this curate's egg type of praise could have depressed many an author it seems to have spurred Hardy on, for he dismembered the book and produced *Desperate Remedies*, which was published anonymously, in

1871. This was followed by *Under the Greenwood Tree*, published, also anonymously, in 1872.

These first two books made Hardy little, if any, money, but he was encouraged enough to put his name on his third novel, *A Pair of Blue Eyes,* in 1873. The following year *Far from the Madding Crowd* appeared. The book made his reputation, and in the same year he married Emma Gifford and gave up architecture to concentrate on writing. At first the couple lived at Sturminster Newton, but in 1885 they moved to **Max Gate** in Dorchester. Hardy personally supervised the building of the house and it was to remain his home for the rest of life. Almost all his major novels, including *The Mayor of Casterbridge* which is based on Dorchester, and *Tess of the D'Urbervilles*, his most famous work, were written here.

By the turn of the century Hardy's fame had brought not only total financial security, but a workload that was putting a great strain on both himself and Emma. He therefore stopped writing novels, though he continued to write verse and short stories. In 1912 Emma died, and a year later Hardy married again, his bride Florence Dugdale, his secretary. During this period of his life Hardy received many honours, enormous public acclaim and was the 'grand old man' of English literary life. He was awarded an honorary degree of Doctor of Letters by Cambridge University in 1913, and by Oxford University, the Order of Merit in 1920 and the freedom of Dorchester in the same year. He liked honours and praise, loathing and attacking his critics, and was very disappointed that he was never awarded the Nobel prize.

Hardy died on 11 January 1928. His heart was removed and buried with his first wife at Stinsford: Higher Bockhampton was a hamlet in the parish of Stinsford and generations of his family already lay in the churchyard. His ashes were laid in Poet's Corner in Westminster Abbey after a state funeral.

The entrance to the Antelope Walk, Dorchester

Following the Roman conquest of the Celtic tribesmen of Maiden Castle, a town was established where the centre of Dorchester is now found. The town was called *Durnovaria*, a name deriving either from Durotriges, showing a grudging respect for the men who had defended Maiden Castle; or from *durno*, a fist, which Maiden Castle resembles from some angles.

To supply the town with water, the Romans built an aqueduct from the River Frome at Notton. Tracing the line of this supply, an open channel, shows it to have been 12 miles (19 kms) long – the longest known example in Britain. It was a mighty feat of engineering, but since a river runs just 75 ft (23m) below the Roman town the aqueduct is also a mystery – why not build the town by the river instead? A section of the aqueduct can still be viewed to the west of the Poundbury hill fort (itself a short distance to the north-west of the town centre and prob-

Execution of a Poisoner

On 21 March 1705 a crowd estimated to be almost 13,000 strong gathered to see the execution of 19-year-old Mary Channings. Mary Brookes was born of well-to-do parents who sent her to London to finish her education as a young lady. Unfortunately, on her return Mary had some rather unladylike habits, spending time in ale houses (and buying her own drinks) and being over friendly with the opposite sex. Her horrified parents forced her into marriage with an older man, Thomas Channings, a local grocer. Mary spent Channings' money extravagantly and then poisoned him by putting mercury in his milk and wine. Her execution was postponed so she could bear and feed a baby which, she confessed, had been fathered by a lover rather than her husband. When the child was weaned she was brought to the Rings, proclaiming her innocence to the last, to be strangled and burned.

ably contemporary with the larger Maiden Castle).

Much is known of the Roman town and some of its dwellings: periodically remains have been uncovered by building works, most noticeably a hoard of 22,000 coins, mostly of the third century AD, found in South Street. Sections of the town wall have also been discovered. The earliest wall was an earth bank and ditch, but a stone wall was built around 300AD. This wall was almost 6ft (2m) thick and 13ft (4m) high and enclosed an area of roughly 80 acres. Sections of the walls can still be seen, and their line is followed by a series of avenues of horse chestnut and sycamore trees forming **The Walks**.

In keeping with their general policy of utilising anything – buildings, customs, whatever – that was handy in order to 'Romanise' and pacify an area, the Romans used **Maumbury Rings**, to the south of the town, as an amphitheatre. The Rings were a Neolithic henge site, old at the time of the conquest, but sufficiently theatre-like for the Romans' purposes. Their use for entertainment rather than religious ceremonies lasted down through the centuries, and it was here that the last witch to be burned in England was brought, just three centuries ago.

Because of its position, the largest town in old Wessex, Dorchester fell foul of Danish raiding parties, including an army under Sweyn, who came 40 years before Edward the Confessor reigned. The town's walls were destroyed and its fortunes declined. There was a further decline after the Norman Conquest when Hugh FitzGrip demolished many houses to make way for his castle: the **Domesday Book** states that the town had only 88 houses, a hundred fewer than before the Conquest. But charters granting the town three annual fairs and its position as the local market town led to prosperity, as did a woollen cloth-making industry. Dorchester's position, on the road between the port of Weymouth and London, also aided its fortunes.

The increased prosperity was

stopped in 1613 by a fire which began in a candlemaker's shop, destroyed 300 houses and damaged the town's churches, though remarkably no one was killed. Rebuilding began almost immediately, the town having recovered by the time of the **Civil War**. During the War it was claimed that no town in England was more staunchly Parliamentarian than Dorchester. To defend the county against the Royalists, over £15,000 was spent on defences. With these and the town being packed with a hardy folk well used to fire, it might be thought that a difficult battle awaited the king's army, but Dorchester surrendered without a shot when ordered to do so.

As the tide of war washed over Dorset the town changed hands several times. In 1644 the Parliamentarians took command: the victors took eight prisoners, Irish Royalists, and these they decided to execute. Only seven were hanged, the eighth man acting as hangman. Was he elected for the job or the drawer of the long straw? There was more bloodshed during the Bloody Assizes in the wake of Monmouth's rebellion, but after this the town settled down to a quieter, more peaceful existence, its later building suggesting a genteel prosperity.

Thomas Hardy describes Dorchester (his Casterbridge) as being as 'compact as a box of dominoes'. It is a delightful description and wholly accurate; the visitor need only walk a mile or two to savour all its delights and, if a Hardy reader, to become acquainted with many places familiar from the books.

A WALK AROUND DORCHESTER

A good place to start an exploration of the town is the 'Top O' Town' car park at the western end of the main street. It is also the proper place to start, as an exposed section of the **Roman town wall** and a statue of **Thomas Hardy** are close by. The wall is to your right as you head towards the main street, while Hardy's statue is opposite. The statue in bronze, the work of Eric Kennington, was erected in 1931. It depicts Hardy in old age, hat on knee and seated on a tree stump. His expression seems slightly quizzical, perhaps because he faces the modern confusion of a roundabout rather than the county library which lies beyond his right shoulder.

From the statue, our exploration of Dorchester heads along High West Street, but first go in the opposite direction, following Bridport Road for a short distance to reach the **Keep Military Museum** housed in a building dating from as late as 1879 when it was the entrance-way and munitions store for the Dorset Regiment's main depot. The Keep records 300 years of military history in Dorset and Devon, with collections of weapons, uniforms and medals and some excellent modern displays. There is also a regular programme of special exhibitions.

HIGH WEST STREET

From the statue, continue along High West Street. To the right is the **Tutankhamun Exhibition** which reproduces the famous tomb of the Egyptian boy king, including the fabulous gold face mask. Just beyond the Exhibition, a detour to the left follows the curiously-named

21

Judge Jeffreys Restaurant

Opposite St Peter's and the County Museum is the **Judge Jeffreys Restaurant**, the only half-timbered building now existing in the town. The building dates from the early seventeenth century, the name reflecting a legend that it was here that the judge lodged during the Bloody Assize. The building has two fine Jacobean panelled rooms (on the first floor), and Tudor fireplaces on the ground floor which are still used.

century, but most being seventeenth and eighteenth century. Soon, to the left, is one of Dorchester's most charming groups of buildings. The first is **Holy Trinity Church**, built in 1875. Further on is the splendid **County Museum**, built in the early 1880s, but in medieval style. Such fictions can be a disaster, but here the building, with its elegant windows and battlements, is a complete success. Inside there are superb collections on the history and natural history of the county – including excavated remains from Maiden Castle – and exhibitions on Thomas Hardy and William Barnes. The natural history section includes an excellent collection of fossils, including dinosaur footprints, while the section on Hardy includes a reconstruction of the great man's study.

Beside the Museum is St Peter's Church which, unusually, has its entrance porch on the pavement. Close by is a bronze statue of **William Barnes**. Barnes was born at Bagber, near Sturminster Newton, in 1801, the son of a farm labourer. His intelligence was recognised by his vicar who persuaded him to become clerk to a local solicitor. Barnes educated himself, learning – it is said – over 60 languages and dialects. He became a schoolmaster, first in Wiltshire and then in Dorchester, setting up his own school in the house next door to the architect John Hicks under whom Thomas Hardy studied. Barnes obtained a degree in theology in 1850, and after the unfortunate closure of his school, he became vicar of Winterborne Came (just south of Dorchester) living out his years there. He died in 1886.

Barnes was a great friend of

Glyde Path Road past the fine seventeenth-century Colliton House to reach **hangman's Cottage**, a delightful thatched cottage whose attractiveness belies its old residents' occupation. Reputedly one occupant kept his rope under the eaves – away from prying eyes. The Roman walls lay close to the site of the cottage and nearby are the remains of a Roman town house, one of very few two-storey houses to have so far been discovered in Britain.

Back in High West Street, the next house on the left, on the corner of Glyde Path Road, is the **Old Shire Hall**, built in 1796 and housing the old Crown Court and Cells. It was in this Court that the Tolpuddle Martyrs were tried on 17–19 March 1834, and the room has been refurbished to look as it did at the time. Beneath the Court are the cells in which prisoners, including the Martyrs, were kept before trial.

Continue down into the town, passing an array of fine houses, the earliest dating from the sixteenth

Dinosaur Museum

A turn left beyond the Antelope (into Durngate Street) allows a detour to Dorchester's **Dinosaur Museum** – in Icen Way, on the corner of Durngate Street – one of the county's best indoor children's sites, with computerised displays, videos, hands-on exhibits, fossils and skeletons, not only of dinosaurs but more recent prehistoric animals – mammoths, sabre-toothed tigers etc. There is a shop called (what else?) the Dinastore.

Left: Keep Museum, Dorchester

Right: William Barnes statue, Dorchester

Hardy who admired him both as a man – once producing a wonderful pen portrait of the old clergyman in cloak, knee-breeches and buckled shoes – and as a poet. The vicar must have been stimulating company: in addition to his knowledge of languages he played several musical instruments, was an expert woodcarver and knowledgeable on local history and geology. Barnes' verse was written in the Dorset dialect which he considered the true English, but unlike Scotland, where Robbie Burns' dialect verse is revered, England has less time for such things and it is left to scholars to see Barnes as Burns' English equal.

St Peter's is the only surviving church from medieval Dorchester. Built in the early fifteenth century it was restored in 1856 by local architect John Hicks and his young assistant, Thomas Hardy, then aged 16. Hardy drew (and signed) the plan of the church that hangs in the south chapel. The church is in Perpendicular style – apart from the Norman south doorway – and has a simple, but beautiful tower. Inside there are some fine works. The pulpit is Jacobean and was almost certainly used by John White, the vicar from 1606 to his death in 1648. White was a staunch Puritan **Continued on Page 29**

I t may seem impertinent in a book such as this to look at Hardy's
work, but some comments on its significance in shaping the Dorset
that the visitor sees are justified. Wessex has become a growth industry:
there are more books on Hardy and Hardy country than were ever
written by the man himself; the Dorset telephone directory has more
entries under Wessex than can be comfortably counted, and certainly
some that cannot be read without a wince.

Hardy's Wessex was, in fact, larger than is usually credited. It is
natural, because of his birth, life and death near Dorchester, that Wessex
should be associated with Dorset. But Dorset was only South Wessex to
Hardy. His North Wessex extended to Christminster (Oxford); Upper
Wessex went as far east as Quartershot (Aldershot); and Lower Wessex
included Cliff Martin to the north and Tor-upon-Sea to the south (Combe
Martin and Torquay). Even those with only a passing interest in Hardy's
books will know that Casterbridge was Dorchester, Sherston was
Sherborne and Port Bridy was Bridport. Hardy needed a strong, real
framework on which to hang his books, for even the subject matter itself
is based on truth, anecdote and legend of the local countryside.

Two quotes from Hardy,
as man not as writer, help
us to understand his craft.
Once, in old age, he noted
that 'it is better for a writer
to know a little bit of the
world remarkably well than
to know a great part of the
world remarkably little.'
Also in old age he argued
that some of Chekhov's
stories could not be
justified as they contained
nothing unusual and were
peopled by characters of
little interest. The latter
comment is, in itself, hardly
reasonable, but coupled
with the first, it throws
light on Hardy and his
stories.

**Thomas Hardy Statue,
Dorchester**

He was born into a land where the people, the agricultural folk, had a great understanding of their world and were keen, when they were being entertained, to be removed from it into a world of strangeness and the unusual. And this world, to an extent, they carried with them in their legends of ghosts and fairies, of witches and the supernatural. This love of the unusual is what made Hardy have Tess swear an oath on a standing stone, to the northwest of Abbot's Cernel, and to speak her final words at the 'heathen temple' of Stonehenge. The menhir is real, the weird Cross and Hand stone to the north-west of Cerne Abbas; it is, therefore, something with which the reader, and particularly the local reader, could identify. Even the name of that particular book is taken from reality. Until the middle of the fifteenth century, one village of the Piddle Valley was Pidel Turberville, but at that time the name changed to Briantspuddle to commemorate a specific member of the family, Brianus de Turberville.

In his striving for the unusual and the strange, Hardy exaggerates the tragedy of his books. Before the reader starts out on a novel he knows that the chief characters will come to a bad end, occasionally on the gallows. As GK Chesterton said, Hardy invented 'the extravagance of depression'. It must also be admitted that some of his prose is ugly, contrived and stilted, and that his portrayal of women is superior to his portrayal of men.

But read Hardy to gain an insight into a world, gone for ever, of country folk who rarely left their own valley and were at one with their environment, and to wonder at his insight into that environment, the beauty of his description of the natural landscape and its changes with season. As to his portrayal of people – that is like trying to speak of Hardy the man. He once wrote the truth of such attempts: 'Nay, from the highest point of view, to precisely describe a human being, the focus of a universe, how impossible!'

At other places in this book – at Lyme Regis where he landed and Holt Heath where he was captured – the rebellion led by the **Duke of Monmouth** will be considered. The most unpleasant aspect of the Rebellion – the trials and sentencing of the rebels and those who had offered tacit support – became known as the Bloody Assizes and the man who commanded them infamous, his name a byword for savagery.

George Jeffreys was born in Shrewsbury in either late 1644 or early 1645 He was the son of John Jeffreys, head of a prosperous old Welsh family. He went to Shrewsbury Grammar School, and then on to St Paul's School, London and to Westminster. He went to Trinity College, Cambridge in 1662, but did not finish his degree, being admitted to the Inner Temple in 1663 as a gifted lawyer.

As a barrister he acquired a considerable reputation as a skilled cross-examiner and by 1671, at the age of about 26, he was Common Sarjeant of the City of London. By then he was also married. In 1677 he was knighted and in 1678 he became Recorder of the City of London. In 1683 he was made **Lord Chief Justice** and, later, Lord Chancellor, being created Baron Jeffreys of Wem.

Following the **Monmouth Rebellion,** Jeffreys became a close ally of James II in his plan to convert England to Catholicism, and sat as president of the Court of Ecclesiastical Commission. This is odd as Jeffreys was both a staunch Anglican and far too clever not to have seen James for what he was, a sadistic bully.

When James fell and William of Orange landed in Torbay, Jeffreys was imprisoned in the Tower where he died in 1689. His death was almost certainly due to kidney failure, as he had suffered for years with kidney stones. Rumours at the time had him poisoned in the Tower, with his body being returned to Dorchester and walled up in the courtroom.

Jeffreys was a man about whom, in later life and after his death, much was said and none of it complimentary. It was claimed that he was a drunkard, a womaniser, a frequenter of brothels, but he appears to have been a devoted family man, having six children by his first wife, Sarah, although after her death he had a less happy second marriage. He was said to have gloated over the deaths of men he had condemned, to have executed them himself and to have claimed to have sent more men to their deaths than any judge since the Norman Conquest. While some of this seems unlikely, his reputation remains: 'Judge Jeffreys? He'll rip yer guts out and show them to yer aiderwards.'

All the ugly rumours were, of course, due to the **Bloody Assizes**. While there can be little to justify the violence of the Assizes, it may help to place them in context. When Jeffreys was born, judicial cruelty was the norm. Nor was such cruelty becoming a thing of the past – far from it. Not until 1810 was the last man hanged, drawn and quartered in England, and the quartering

Continued overpage

of dead bodies continued until 1870. If you were lucky enough to be a woman you were instead burned alive. Executions were public until 1868 even though hanging by strangulation as distinct from hanging by dropping through a trap door stopped around 1830. In 1833 a boy of nine was hanged for stealing ink worth 2d. There were punitive executions following rebellions both before and after Monmouth.

At each Assize, Jeffreys headed a five-man commission: himself, Barons Montague and Wright, and justices Wythens and Levinz. They started in **Winchester** and went on to **Salisbury**, but the real work did not start until the commission reached **Dorchester**.

There, on the morning of Saturday, 5 September 1685, 30 men were tried, all of whom pleaded not guilty. Jeffreys then made an offer to the rest. Anyone pleading not guilty and being found guilty would hang for sure, but anyone pleading guilty would have his sentence decided on the severity of his treason. This speeded the procedure up considerably: 103 men were tried on the Monday. As to honouring the offer – of the first 30 who pleaded not guilty, 29 were found guilty and hanged. The last man, William Saunders, was found not guilty. Of the other 233 who pleaded guilty, 80 were hanged. By 9 September, Judge Jeffreys was leaving Dorset, but two men were still at work, **Jack Ketch**, a bungling executioner and his assistant, a butcher named 'Pascha' Rose.   To ensure that all the county had a taste of the penalty for rebellion, the executions were held in various places – after Dorchester, twelve died at Lyme Regis, twelve at Weymouth, eleven each at Sherborne and Poole, ten at Bridport and five at Wareham.

After Dorchester the commission sat at **Exeter** and then moved on to **Taunton** where the largest number of rebels, 526, were tried. The death sentencing rate of one in four that Dorchester had seen was maintained, with 139 being so sentenced. There has been much speculation about the actual number of men involved, again with many legends growing up around the Assizes. One story had 800 sentences in one day, with 700 executed and 'many were not given a minute's time to say their prayers'.   It is likely that, of the men who were found guilty, 480 were sentenced to death, 850 transported, 260 whipped or fined and 80 pardoned.

In 1685 Judge Jeffreys was a hero, at least to those outside the West Country, and to loyalists within it, and no great protest against the Assizes was heard until the fall of James II.

That Jeffreys was largely responsible for the outcome of the Assizes cannot be denied. That James II was the real culprit is also beyond doubt. Jeffreys was probably not as evil as he has been painted, but acted on the instructions of an evil superior. But, as the Nuremberg trials demonstrated, carrying out orders is not an acceptable excuse.

who helped his fellow Dorset Puritans emigrate to found Massachusetts in America: he is buried under the porch.

There are also several fine monuments: in the south chapel are two fourteenth century effigies of knights. But the best pieces are later: that of Sir John Williams and his wife dates from 1617. In it the pair kneel on opposite sides of a shrine that stands beneath an arch. The monument to Denzil, Lord Holles was erected in 1699, 20 years after his death, and represents him as a (well-fed) Roman senator reclining below a pair of *putti*.

CORNHILL/SOUTH STREET

From just beyond St Peter's Church, North Square turns left to reach the town prison built in 1884 (but incorporating parts of an eighteenth century building) on the site of Dorchester's castle. On the corner of North Square and High Street is the Town Hall/Corn Exchange built in 1847. The elaborate clock turret was added later and apparently there was much speculation about how long it would be before the unsupported turret fell down. It is still intact. The Hall houses the chair in which Judge Jeffreys is reputed to have sat as he 'laboured so hardly on that occasion to reconcile the hearts of Dorset-shire families to their king'.

Turn right opposite North Square, following Cornhill, which soon becomes South Street. The ball-topped obelisk is the old town water pump. Just beyond, on the right, is the **Antelope Hotel**, a lovely, early eighteenth-century building. It was in the Antelope that the Bloody Assize was held, tradition maintaining that the courtroom was hung with scarlet cloth.

In Antelope Walk is **Teddy Bear House**, an exhibition of life-size teddy bears 'inhabiting' the rooms of the house and 'manufacturing' smaller bears – fun for children and nostalgic for parents. Almost opposite the hotel was the Treves cabinet-maker's shop where Thomas Hardy bought his writing desk. The desk was made by William Treves whose son, Frederick, a pupil of William Barnes, became one of the best known physicians of his day. He was personal surgeon to four monarchs – performing a life-saving appendicitis operation on Edward VII, at that time a very new procedure – but is most famous as the doctor-friend of John Merrick, the 'Elephant Man'.

Continue along South Street for about 150 yards to reach Napper's Mite, to the left. Built by Nathaniel Napper in the early sixteenth century – to fulfil the requirements of his father's will – as an almshouse for ten poor Dorchester men (who also received £5 per year, paid monthly), the Mite is now a tiny shopping precinct. The Mite's frontage was rebuilt in 1842, following the original design. A little further on, to the right, are Nos 39 and 40 South Street. William Barnes lived in No. 40, while Thomas Hardy worked in John Hicks' architect's office at No. 39. Hardy Arcade across from the houses, has nothing to do with Thomas, being named after another Thomas (probably a distant relative) who founded a grammar school on the site in 1569. Continue along South Street to reach South Gate near a hexagonal post box dating from about 1870.

Above: Kingston Maurward House

Below: Stinsford Church

Opposite page: Antelope Walk, Dorchester

SOUTH WALKS ROAD

South Walks Road, to the left, is a lovely avenue following the line of the old Roman walls – whose course can also be followed to the right. Ahead, a short distance along Weymouth Avenue, is the **Eldridge Pope Brewery**, built in 1880 and one of the most distinctive buildings in the town with its red and cream bricks. The brewery, begun by Charles Eldridge, one time landlord of the Antelope, but acquired by the Popes in 1874, was badly damaged by fire in 1922 but beautifully restored. It still brews a collection of sought-after ales and lagers. Beyond the brewery and the police station, **Maumbury Rings** will be found on the right. Thomas Hardy visited the Rings when he was in his eighties to watch the filming of *The Mayor of Casterbridge*.

Turn left along the South Walks, crossing Acland Road to reach a group of three statues. These life-size bronze figures are by Dame Elisabeth Frink and represent an executioner confronting two condemned prisoners, a memorial to Dorset folk martyred for their religious beliefs. Nearby there is a list of martyrs. The figures convey both the sense of humanity of those involved and the inhumanity of the process: the group stands on a site once occupied by Dorchester's gallows.

Cross Icon Way and continue along South Walks Road to High Street Fordington. To the right here is **St George's Church**, of Norman foundation but completely restored (and doubled in size) in about 1910. Thomas Hardy, who was on the restoration committee, resigned in disgust at their proposals, but the work does not seem to have been too dreadful. Thankfully it retained a great treasure from the earliest church, the tympanum above the south doorway, a fine relief sculpture of St George in battle. The style is very similar to that of the Bayeux tapestry and is dated around 1100. Many claim the work to be one of the finest of its type in Britain.

MAX GATE

Continuing along High Street Fordington leads – eventually (it is over half a mile away and many will prefer to drive) – to Max Gate, designed by Thomas Hardy and his home from its completion in 1885 to his death in 1928. The curious name derives from the house's position, at a gate, or toll booth, of a turnpike road which was operated by a man known only as 'Mac', a man Hardy refers to in *The Dynasts*. The house, symmetrical but with a few architectural flourishes, is a little dull, and it is known that Hardy himself was not happy with it. Some have described it as ugly, but that seems too harsh. Whatever the shortcomings of the house, the garden conveys the peace and timelessness of Hardy's Wessex.

Part of the house can be visited: as might be expected it has a wealth of memorabilia, though the study where Hardy worked has had all its furnishings removed to the replica in the County Museum. From Max Gate, Hardy would head south-west across the fields to the fine thatched rectory at Winterborne Came where William Barnes lived. The house is now owned by the National Trust who were presented with it by Hardy's sister after the death of his second wife, Florence.

HARDY'S DORCHESTER

Those who are students of Hardy's books will want to buy a copy of a booklet published by the Thomas Hardy Society and to carry out a thorough exploration of Dorchester. For less ardent readers, a short stroll at the centre of the town passes some fascinating places mentioned in the better-known books.

North Square, which runs between St Peter's Church and the Town Hall/Cornmarket soon reaches a large square which Hardy calls Bull Stake Square in *The Mayor of Casterbridge*. Interestingly, in this case Hardy did not invent a new name, but used an old one that had slipped from common usage many years previously. Head back to the High Street. Here during the annual fair described in *Far from the Madding Crowd*, Gabriel Oak looked for work. On the far corner to your left – diagonally opposite St Peter's Church, itself noted in several books: in *The Trumpet Major* Hardy notes that its tenor bell was the finest in the district – is where Hardy set High Place Hall in *The Mayor of Casterbridge*, though his model for the Hall was Colliston House which stands in Glyde Path Road.

Turn left along High East Street, soon reaching the King's Arms Hotel, on the left, into which Farmer Boldwood carried Bathsheba after she had fainted (on hearing Troy was believed drowned) in *Far from the Madding Crowd*. The hotel is also featured in *Under the Greenwood Tree*. Opposite the hotel is All Saints' Church from which Bob Loveday heard the service while waiting for a wagon, after failing to meet Matilda on the coach in *The Trumpet Major*.

Return to Cornhill/South Road and turn left along it, soon reaching the Antelope Hotel, called The Stag in *The Mayor of Casterbridge*. Further on, on the left, Barclays Bank now occupies the house on which the Major of Casterbridge lived. Finally, the delightful clock on Napper's Mite, further on, on the left, is mentioned in both *Far from the Madding Crowd*, during the journey of Fanny Robin's coffin, and in *The Mayor of Casterbridge*.

WINTERBORNE CAME

From Max Gate, Thomas Hardy would take field paths to visit his friend William Barnes. The rectory sits close to the A352, half a mile north-east of the village. It is possible to walk to the village, as Barnes sometimes did: a visit by car involves the need for thoughtful parking. The church where Barnes was rector until his death in 1886 is a delightful, mostly fifteenth century building tucked away among trees that are a reminder of lines from *Linden Lea*, the dialect poet's most famous work:

> *'Ithin the woodlands,*
> *flow'ry-gleaded,*
> *By the woak tree's mossy*
> *moot,*
> *The sheenen grass-bleades,*
> *timber sheaded'*

Within the church there are some interesting monuments. That of John Miller and his wife, dating from 1611, has the pair in effigy on a tomb chest decorated with members of their family. Less visual is that to Colonel Dawson Barnes who fought with the Russians during Napoleon's retreat from Moscow and had two

Continued on Page 42

33

A short distance to the south of Dorchester is the ancient hill fort of Castle. The name is from maidun, the big hill. Many experts believe this to be the finest and most important fort of its type in Britain. It is certainly among the most spectacular, and is also readily accessible. So important is the site, both in the context of Britain's history and also as a visitor site in Dorset, that a very full investigation of its origins and construction are given here. There are other hill forts in Dorset, including the important Badbury Rings site and one on top of Pilsdon Pen. The description of Maiden Castle will also be of interest to visitors to those sites.

Neolithic Times

We do not understand the lifestyle of Neolithic man, despite the finds that have been made and the classifications that have been created around him. Stone tools and flint arrowheads offer the bare bones of a civilisation, and though from them it is possible to gain insight into life and culture, it is not possible to add the flesh. But happy or sad though their lives may have been, the Neolithic people lived with a background of fear – a fear of their neighbours, or of alien invasion, that caused them to construct, at great expense of labour and, presumably, time, fortified camps within which a group of families could safely withstand attack. And if you wanted to be safe, and to feel secure, where better than on top of a hill, with a good view of the surrounding countryside.

To the ancients securing a living on the flat land between the River Frome and the South Winterborne stream, the twin hillocks of land that stand island-like must have seemed a gift from the gods. The Neolithic folk occupied the eastern hillock only, lacking the numbers or technology to take over the whole site. They carved a ditch to separate their hillock from the other half of the island, creating a rampart with the excavated rubbish. They may have cut further ditches to strengthen the sloping sides of their island on its other three sides. The completed site covered 10 acres certainly, perhaps as many as 15, and is classified as a **causeway camp**. The word 'camp' is well chosen as it can never be certainly shown that the ditch and rampart were purely defensive. This is chalk country – cut the turf, dig down and flint is exposed in chunks. Axes, knives and scrapers for animal hides have been found in the ditches: the workings were quarries as well as a defensive measure.

At a late stage in their occupation by Neolithic folk, the twin hillocks saw a construction which in its way was as remarkable as the later defensive works. Indeed, if we recognise that the later work was a matter of life and death, then this earlier work, which was concerned only with death, is the more remarkable. Extending from the centre of the eastern, occupied, hillock to the end of that at the west, the Neolithic farmers constructed a burial tomb – a **long barrow**. The funeral mound is 500 yards (400m) long, and though nothing that the lay eye can detect has survived the site's subsequent occupation by the Celts, excavation has revealed enough to leave the visitor in awe.

Walk the camp between its eastern and western ends – the mound filled that space: it was almost 65 ft (30m) wide, and though the height can only be guessed at, at other sites similar barrows are 10 ft (3m) high, sometimes more. Over 100,000 tons of earth were moved using antler spades. And who, we may ask, did our ancient ancestors revere so much that they would go to such extremes to honour him in death?

For a long time it was believed that the answer to that question had, in part, been discovered when a skeleton was unearthed at the barrow's eastern end. The skeleton is that of a man about 30 years old and about 5 ft 4 ins (1.63m) tall, and the manner of his burial was remarkable. Before interment his arms and legs were broken, and three crude attempts were made to extract his brain through holes smashed in his skull. It is almost idle to speculate why, and yet as the visitor stares down at the remains, displayed in an 'as-found' grave in Dorchester Museum, it is difficult not to wonder. Interestingly, many experts now believe the burial post-dates the long barrow, although they do believe the man lived before the arrival of the Celts.

Bronze Age Spear

Following the burial of the broken man at the eastern end of the site, Maiden Castle was abandoned. It is not clear why Bronze Age man lost interest, though it is probable that a change of climate made it difficult to farm the chalklands efficiently. From time to time the ghosts of those who lay in the barrow were disturbed: a Bronze Age hunter came this way, following game on to the overgrown ditches and ramparts of the castle. He stalked his prey, threw his spear and missed. His spear landed in the undergrowth and was lost. The shaft rotted away, the spear point remaining for an inquisitive historian to find 30 centuries later.

The Iron Age

Apart from chance visits, the site remained quiet for over a thousand years, until a new tribe of farmers moved on to the chalklands. The newcomers, mid-European Celts, are technically known as Iron Age A people. They brought iron tools and weapons with them, and also an enthusiasm for tribal conflict which, in later years was to cost them dear. The Celtic propensity to fragment, to form around minor princes and to fight each other lost them their lands to the Saxons and, later, the Normans and the English. Here at Maiden Castle it resulted in the construction of the first recognisably **defensive earthworks**.

The Iron Age farmers were better equipped to dig and move earth than their Neolithic predecessors, and so took up the challenge of the twin hillocks, constructing their defences all the way round the island. Their defences also consisted of a ditch and rampart, but the advance in technology and, perhaps, a more warlike eye meant more controlled building, to a specific plan. The ditch was V-shaped and deep. On the village side there was a platform, a berm 8–10 ft (2.5–3m) wide, and then a rampart perhaps 8 ft (2.5m) high and 10ft (3m) wide. The earth of the rampart was held back by a wooden wall to give the extra defence of a vertical climb for the attacker. As the retaining wooden wall of the rampart decayed it was replaced with a dry-stone wall of limestone slabs brought from a quarry at Upwey 2 miles (3kms) to the south.

After the work, the people of the area could either live within the fort, or escape to it in the event of invasion. Unless a radical change in the water table has occurred in the last two thousand years there was no source of water within the fort, though this does not appear to have troubled the locals. Clearly war involved an assault which resulted in the fort being taken or not. If not, the marauding army grumbled its way back to its own territory. Presumably the cost of keeping an army in the field was too high for a siege, or armies were too small and could not adequately watch the entire perimeter of the big forts: Maiden Castle is almost a mile (1.5km) long – the defenders could wait for nightfall and sneak out for water.

By extending the defensive structure to include the western hillock, the **castle** had its living area increased to 45 acres, an open space 800 yards long and over 300 yards wide at its widest. Within it, eventually, was a village of four to five thousand people, an ancestor for every true-bred Dorset man living today. The fort dwellers lived in timber huts standing by roads that may even have been metalled with crushed chalk or pebbles.

Archaeological Finds

The village had a large number of **pits**, each some 11 ft (3.5m) deep, so many that perhaps each hut had its own. The pits are filled with a mixture of rubbish, ash and chalk debris, which could mean that there were alternate layers of debris and in-fill, in much the same way as on municipal rubbish dumps today. More likely, the chalk pits were communal, for storing grain or even water, and were only used for rubbish when they had gone sour and a new one had been opened. The debris from the pits has, as all good debris does, provided the archaeologist with valuable material and allowed him to paint a compelling picture of life in the village. One pit contained a dead dog and a dead baby. Another contained the body of a young woman of about 20.

The Celts

At some stage in the later Iron Age occupation of the fort, a European advance in the art of warfare made the defences of the castle useless. In Brittany the Veneti tribe of Celts perfected the art of **slingshot warfare**, a particularly potent form for seaborne engagements, the Veneti being a sea-trading people. The sling was a phenomenal weapon, better then than the bow. A skilled user could hurl a $^1/_2$ –2 ounce (15–50g) pebble 200 yards, though the effective distance was probably only half that. At 50 yards a good slinger could hit a stick or a man's head. The slinger could fire his pebbles far more quickly than the archer could loose his arrows, and so a large number of men could create a hailstorm of stone. An army of slingers could now decimate the defenders of a hill fort without even approaching the ditch and ramparts. The answer to the sling was obvious enough – wider defences. But the Celts did not blindly enter into a phase of furious digging. What was needed was that a defender, with the advantage of the slope, should be able to hit the attacker, while the attacker, working against gravity, should consistently fall short. That a scientific approach was used can be seen in the dimensions of other Dorset forts. At Pilsdon Pen where the natural slope is steep the defences are narrow, but at Badbury Rings the slope is less steep and the defences are wider. Here at Maiden Castle we have an intermediate statement on the science of slinging.

The weak point of any defended structure is its gateway. Ramparts and ditches could be made virtually impregnable, but the villagers needed to be able to walk in, and even perhaps to drive their cattle in, or to ride in on grain-filled carts. It was therefore imperative to defend in depth this easy access to the village. To do this, the castle had at each end, but with the west

*Aerial photograph
of Maiden Castle*

being more elaborate than the east, a complex **jumble of ramparts**, topped with defended battlements through which the enemy had to weave in order to arrive at the final wooden gate. In general, the ramparts and battlements were arranged so that the attacker presented his left, his unshielded, side to the defender as he advanced through the maze.

The Celts came not only in search of new land, but to escape a menace that was thrusting northward into their European homeland. That menace was the **Roman army**. Britain had already seen such an army, if only briefly, when Julius Caesar had landed in 55BC. A century later another army came, not with exploration but with conquest in mind. The Roman historians, speaking of the invasion of 43AD, noted that the army of the 2nd Augustan legion under Vespasian, overcame 'two very formidable tribes and over twenty towns, together with the Isle of Wight'. One of those 20 towns, the strongest of them all, was Maiden Castle.

The Roman Era

The Romans landed in south-east England and pushed westward, overcoming some fierce opposition. They crossed the River Frome at the ford, a spot we now call Dorchester, and must have been astonished to see before them the huge ramparts of the castle. **Vespasian** was a good general and would have recognised from his experiences in north Europe that the multiple ditches and ramparts meant slingers. He would have seen the western gate, recognising the strength that the maze of alleyways between the ramparts gave it. He would have noticed that the peace which had fallen on the countryside had allowed a few huts to be built very close to the eastern gate. A man destined to be emperor would most definitely not have missed such a tactical blunder.

The defenders of the castle must have known that the Romans were coming and would have been prepared. All the farmers from outlying crofts would have gone inside for safety. The water contain-

"Famous Victim"

The Roman soldiers had artillery, ballistae – *stone-* or spear-throwing engines which the defenders may not have seen before. Many would have been killed by these engines. The museum in Dorchester has the famous remains, as excavated, of a famous skeleton with the metal head of a Roman *ballista* arrow embedded in his spine. The spinal cord was probably severed.

ers would have been ready, the piles of sling pebbles placed at points along the walls. When the Romans approached they would have kept their distance, wary of the sling, perhaps marching a small reconnaissance band around the castle. The Celts, in time-honoured fashion, would have hurled the odd pebble and a vast quantity of abuse at the band of men in their body armour and uniforms.

The Romans fired the untidy group of huts near the eastern gate, perhaps using the confusion caused by the smoke to outflank the defenders. But though the castle was taken, the defenders must have fought hard: the Romans, perhaps incensed by the unexpectedly bold, resistance went wild inside the fort, attacking women and children as well as the menfolk. The soldiers destroyed the two gates, then withdrew to a camp below the castle, leaving the survivors to the night and their dead. The survivors laid the dead in shallow graves, evidence of a hasty burial, though none was interred without the food and drink they needed on their journey to the afterworld. In some graves a small gift was added, perhaps a family heirloom, or the present from a young widow or an orphaned child.

Sixty years ago the war cemetery was discovered and the graves were opened. The report of the excavation includes photographs of the remains and is chilling. One woman had her hands tied behind her back and three sword slashes to the head: a man was hit ten times across the head.

Following the Roman conquest, the castle was still occupied for a decade or two by the survivors of the slaughter. Then the people moved out and north to the new town of Dorchester. The wind-blown soil filled the ditches and grass regained the ramparts.

After the Romans

Three hundred years later a group of heretics to the authorised religion, Christianity, built a small temple near the old east gate. There was a two-roomed house for priests: four of them lie buried near the spot. Relics unearthed near the temple indicate a return to paganism. After a short time the site was abandoned again, this time for good.

Today, Maiden Castle is a pleasant place on a sunny afternoon in late summer. The grass is lush, with wild flowers poking through, the ditches and ramparts alive with the noise of children: what were defences are now an adventure playground.

horses shot from beneath him at Waterloo. William Barnes, the village's beloved rector, lies below the 'Celtic' cross in the churchyard.

Close to the church stands the mid-eighteenth century **Came House**. Pevsner calls the house a masterpiece, noting that the memorial to the architect/builder, Francis Cartwright, in Blandford St Mary church inc-ludes an image of Came, a recognition that it was his finest work. The house was built for John Damer whose elder brother created Milton Abbey, but is sadly not open to the public.

STINSFORD AND HIGHER BOCKHAMPTON

Just off the main A35/A354 which heads north-east from Dorchester after bypassing the town to the south, lies the village of **Stinsford**. Stinsford is Mellstock in *Under the Greenwood Tree*, a village remembered with great affection by Thomas Hardy. Hardy's grandfather started a small group of musicians who played in church's gallery to accompany services and his father (also Thomas) assisted with the group (usually four, a cello and three violins). Young Thomas also played violin in the group, though by that time it only played at weddings. In later life Hardy was agnostic, but records the group and the church with great affection when writing about Mellstock.

Hardy's first wife Emma was buried in the churchyard of **St Michael's Church** and it would have been a fitting resting place for him too, but great men of letters go to Poet's Corner in Westminster Abbey. That is where Hardy's ashes lie, but

his heart was removed before cremation and now lies beside his wife. His second wife Florence also lies in the churchyard.

Were it not for Hardy's grave, St Michael's would attract few visitors. It is thirteenth century, but suffered at the hands of Victorian restorers, though it does retain two interesting features: on the outside of tower, on the west side, is a Saxon relief carving of St Michael with outstretched wings, probably reset during the restoration work; and inside, look for the memorials to William and Susanna O'Brien.

Earl's daughter marries actor...

Susanna O'Brien was the daughter of the Earl of Ilchester, destined to play a role in English aristocratic society, but unfortunately she married an actor, a marriage that so enraged the Earl that he threatened to disinherit her. William agreed to leave the stage to avoid the loss, the pair having a happy marriage with the grudging blessing of the Earl. The story, with its clear, and somewhat dubious, messages delighted Thomas Hardy who used it as the basis of several stories and passages.

Just to the east of Stinsford lies the hamlet of **Kingston Maurward**. The famous house here was built for George Pitt, a cousin of William Pitt the Elder. In its original form (it was completed in 1720) it was red-brick, but legend has it that during a visit George III is said to have questioned its looks – 'Brick,

Places to Visit

Dinosaur Museum

Icon Way
Open: May-October, daily 10am-5pm.
☎ 01305 269880

Dorset County Museum

High West Street
Open: All year, Monday–Saturday
10am–5pm. Also open Sundays
10am–5pm in July and August
☎ 01305 262735

Eldridge Pope Brewery

Weymouth Avenue
Open: All year, guided tours Monday-
Friday during the day and evening.
Please ring for details of times and
for pre-booking (which is advised).
No booking is required for tours on
Wednesday at 11am and 1pm.
☎ 01305 251251

Hardy's Cottage (National Trust)

Higher Bockhampton, to the north-
east of Stinsford.
Open: Easter-October, Sunday–
Thursday 11am–5pm. Also open
Good Friday.
☎ 01305 262366

Keep Military Museum

Bridport Road
Open: All year, Monday-Friday
9.30am-5pm. Saturday and Bank
Holidays 9.30am-1pm, 2-5pm.
☎ 01305 264066

Kingston Maurward Gardens, Farm Animal Park and Nature Trail

Near Stinsford, to the east of
Dorchester
Open: Mid-March-23 Decmber, daily
10am-5.30pm
☎ 01305 264738
Please note: Dogs are not allowed on
the site.

Max Gate (National Trust)

Alington Avenue
Open: Easter–September, Monday,
Wednesday and Sunday 2–5pm
☎ 01305 262538

Old Crown Court and Cells

Old Shire Hall, Stratton House
High West Street
Open: Court: All year, Monday–
Friday 10am–12noon, 2–4pm. Closed
on Bank Holidays.
Cells: mid-July–August, Tuesday–
Friday 2.15–4.15pm. Also open on
Wednesday 10.15am–12.15pm.
☎ 01305 252241

Teddy Bear House

Antelope Walk
Open: All year, daily 9.30am-5pm.
☎ 01305 263200

Tutankhamun Exhibition

High West Street
Open: All year, daily 9.30am–5.30pm.
Closed 24–26 December.
☎ 01305 269571

Mr Pitt, only brick'. The mortified owner promptly encased the house in Portland stone. The house, beautiful when seen across the large lake in its grounds, is now an agricultural college and is not open to the public. The grounds are, however, and are well worth the visit. They are in English style, that is natural, with lawns and water meadows as well as the lake. There is also a fine Edwardian garden with stone terraces and yew hedging.

Within the grounds there are a Farm Animal Park with unusual breeds (children can help feed the younger animals) and a nature trail. The house's coach house is a restaurant, and the complex also includes a late Elizabethan Manor House saved from dereliction and restored in fine style.

From Kingston Maurward, head east, soon reaching Lower Bockhampton, then turn left (north) to reach **Higher Bockhampton** and **Hardy's Cottage**. It was here that Thomas Hardy was born on 2 June 1840, in the centre of the three bedrooms. In later life Hardy described the cottage: 'It faces west and round the back and sides, high beeches bending hang a veil of boughs and sweep against the roof'. Over a hundred years later it is still a valid description. The cottage was built in 1800 by Thomas' great grand-father, a simple two-storey thatched cottage at the end of a long lane, on the edge of Puddletown Forest. Some might find the situation gloomy, but many, like Hardy, find it peaceful and inspirational.

In summer, when the cottage garden is filled with colour and the trees are in full leaf, it is a beautiful place. The cottage has some lovely features: it is said that the narrow porch opening allowed Thomas' grandfather to watch for Excise men in comfort, the old man not being above a little brandy smuggling; note the low-beamed ceilings of the upper rooms; and the way the thatched roof wraps itself around the upstairs windows. The somewhat grim memorial stone in the garden (of granite, one of the few British rocks not found in Dorset) was erected by American Hardy enthuiasts in 1932.

I n this chapter we explore the central part of the county –
the Valleys of the Piddle and Winterborne rivers and the
Devil's Brook, and the land between the A35 and the A352.
This area might seem an artificial creation, but as is often
the case in Dorset it is held together by reference to Thomas
Hardy's Wessex. The land between the two main roads is
Egdon Heath and the Valley of the Great Dairies, while the
villages of the Piddle Valley are Hardy's Longpuddle,
Athelhall and East Egdon.

FROM DORCHESTER TO CERNE ABBAS

Leave Dorchester northwards along the A37, but soon bear right on the A352 towards Cerne Abbas and Sherborne. The road passes close to **Charminster**, a large, somewhat straggling village of excellent cottages and houses. The River Cerne cuts through the village: on the western bank sandwiched between the water and the main road stands the church, by far the village's most interesting building.

The main building is twelfth century, but it is completely overshadowed by a magnificent sixteenth-century tower, square and sturdy, but softened by buttresses, a small round tower, clever gargoyles and elegant pinnacles. The tower was built by Sir Thomas Trenchard, a man who clearly had no time for false modesty, a number of stylised T's being carved both on the outside and inside. The south chapel was the Trenchard family mausoleum, though the fact that Trenchards lie in the Purbeck marble tombs is conjecture as the tablets have disappeared. The memorial to Grace Bale, her kneeling figure restored to its coloured glory, cherubs staring down from the clouds above her, is also Trenchard: Grace was Sir Thomas' daughter.

Sir Thomas was the resident of **Wolfeton House**, to the south of the village, beside the River Cerne. The house was built around 1500, but only the gatehouse and a small section of the main house are original, the rest being lost during a massive

Wolfeton House

Wolfeton House was also the site of one of those curious incidents that make English history so appealing. In 1506 Archduke Philip of Austria and his Spanish wife were returning to Spain through the English Channel when their ship was wrecked in Weymouth Bay. The duchess spoke only Spanish, the language her husband had adopted out of respect for her. Not surprisingly, no one in Weymouth spoke Spanish, but the regal bearing of the bedraggled pair caused them to be brought to Wolfeton. Sir Thomas Trenchard did not speak Spanish either, but probably seeing the possibility of advancement in entertaining royalty, sent for John Russell of Berwick House, Swyre who did speak the language. Russell took the pair to London to meet Henry VII. Trenchard's hope that something good come out of the shipwreck was then realised, but hardly in the way he had imagined – Henry VII was so impressed by Russell's abilities he made him the first Earl of Bedford.

rebuilding programme in the nineteenth century. The gatehouse with its two round towers is detached from the main house and is curious in having towers of different sizes and an off-centre arched gateway. The house itself has surviving sections of the Great Hall, an octagonal tower and much of the magnificent carved woodwork from the original house. The doorway to the East Drawing Room is a remarkable piece of work, worth the visit on its own. The staircase is also superb: legend has it that one member of the Trenchard family drove a coach and horses up it, and it is said that a ghostly carriage is occasionally seen repeating the feat, surely one of the most dramatic hauntings of any house in Britain.

Beyond Charminster the main road closely follows the River Cerne. The site of a Roman villa – of which there is virtually nothing to see – is passed before is reached. The main interest here is the Smith's Arms, a flint-built, thatched inn, once the village blacksmith's shop, that is now claimed to be the smallest inn in England. The village church is also of flint, supplemented with stone.

There is a flint and stone church in the next village too. **Nether Cerne** is set close to the river beneath a hill that shows evidence of strip lynchets, the early medieval terracing method of working hillsides. The church, now redundant, was once ministered by monks from the Benedictine Abbey at Cerne Abbas.

CERNE ABBAS

Some 1400 years ago St Augustine came to Dorset as a missionary from Rome to spread the word among the tribes who had gained control of the land in the century since the Romans had departed. He walked up the valley of the river we now call the Cerne, and preached to the folk of a hamlet beneath a spur of the valley ridge. They were unimpressed,

and so that the good man should be left in no doubt about their feelings they tied cows' tails to his cloak, pelted him with mud and sent him on his way up the valley. The saint stumbled to the base of the spur and stopped at a spring to clean himself of his humiliation. He washed: then he looked skyward and saw God.

The spring is now enclosed by St Augustine's Well, and the spot became holy, a **monastery** being built here probably no later than the ninth century. This building did not survive, and in 987 Ethelmaer, the Earl of Cornwall, refounded the monastery as an abbey of Benedictine monks.

This story of the original founding of the abbey is told by Gotselin, a French monk of the eleventh century, who mentions St Augustine by name and refers to the hamlet as Cernel. The name is significant for its sacred associations: Cernunnos was a Celtic god with antlers and a magic snake. The second syllable could also derive from *Hele*, which gives us Heel Stone at Stonehenge and Hell Stone near Abbotsbury, from the ancient word for sun. The story of the founding was picked up and retold by William of Malmesbury in the early twelfth century, by which time the abbey was well established.

To the abbey, in the spring of 1471, came Margaret of Anjou, one of the most formidable women in English history. Finding herself married to a madman, Henry VI, she fought like a tigress to protect the interests of her son, Edward, Prince of Wales. Defeated at Towton, she retreated to France, but landed at Weymouth to fight yet again. Margaret and Edward came to Cerne Abbas to rest and heard the news

A refreshing cup of tea

Outside the church are the old village stocks. One man in Cerne's history is recorded as having been installed in the stocks for being drunk. It was a long, hot day and the man's wife was frequently seen feeding her man from a teapot. The teapot was filled with beer, however, and by the end of the day the man was much drunker than he had ever been before. History does not, unfortunately, record whether the authorities impounded him again or threw up their hands in despair.

that Warwick had been defeated and killed at Barnet and that Henry was in the Tower. The obvious thing to do was to go back to France, but instead she rallied her army to meet the Yorkists at Tewkesbury. Her army was defeated, she and her son were captured and he was murdered. Her battle was over and she was allowed to return to France.

When it was dissolved by order of Henry VIII a century later, there were 16 monks at the abbey. The town had depended on the continued existence of the monks and their departure led to a decline which was only arrested in the nineteenth century when Cerne became prosperous again as a market town and a centre for leatherworking (it was an ancient trade, Cerne having provided leather boots for Sir Walter Raleigh: the new trade included boot making for George III and the young Queen Victoria) and malting. It was a short-lived prosperity as the railway bypassed the town and by the end of the century the population had halved. The main road also bypasses the town, but today that is an advantage, and Cerne Abbas is a precious old world gem held pearl-like on the string of the river, tourism bringing new prosperity.

All that remains of the abbey lies

behind Abbey Farm at the end of **Abbey Street**, a cul-de-sac. To reach the remains, walk the length of the street. To the right is the **church**. It is a beautiful building with a fine tower in Perpendicular style. In a niche in the tower, above the porch, there is a statue of the Virgin and Child, a rare survival of the purges carried out by the Puritans. Inside there is a stone screen, an unusual feature, and a memorial brass to John Notley, one of a local family some of whom moved to the USA where, in the seventeenth century, they bought land which now forms Capitol Hill in Washington DC.

Opposite the church is an elegant row of timbered houses complete with overhangs. Such buildings are, to us, wonderfully evocative of the bustle of Middle Ages life, the community spirit. Of course, the overhang was so that your thrown refuse and sewage landed in the road rather than on people's heads. There was stench and flies, kites like vultures and rats in plenty. The Black Death came this way: it had not travelled far from Melcombe Regis where it landed in England. The first house in Abbey Street is The Pitchmarket, so called because here the local farmers pitched their corn sacks on

Continued on Page 52

The Smith's Arms at Godmanstone,
said to be the smallest pub in Britain

St Augustine's Well

Further along Abbey Street, to the right again, is the village duckpond, a pretty spot. Next again is the churchyard where the abbey itself was sited. By the trees at the far corner is **St Augustine's Well**. The legend of its creation as the saint washed himself is only one of several. In another, the saint was told by local shepherds that the village was dry of both water and beer but that they, being godfearing folk, would prefer water. St Augustine struck the ground with his staff and the spring gushed out. Since there is a river just a few yards away, this story is doubtful, and the washing tale could apply to any of several springs that lie along the valley side. It was here, however, that the locals brought their newborns to be washed, a Dorset custom being that babies immersed in cold spring water grow healthy.

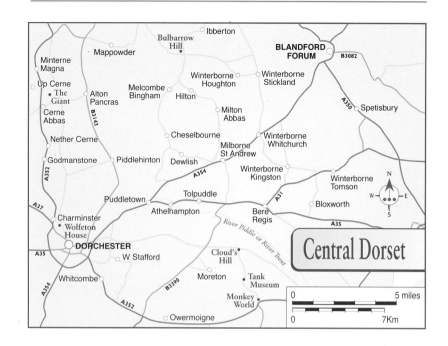

Central Dorset

Abbey Street, Cerne Abbas

market day ready for buyers to inspect. Behind the house there was once a memorial to the wedding of Thomas Washington and Maria Randall. Many have speculated that Thomas was the uncle of George Washington, famous as the man who, as a child, could not tell a lie – and equally famous as the first President of the USA.

At the end of Abbey Street is **Abbey Farm**, one of the most perfect manor houses in Dorset, or in England: the front garden, running directly from the roadside with no formal boundary; no wall to block the view; the lack of symmetry in the gables and windows; the colour of the walls and roof.

At the rear, reached beyond the honesty box, there is a courtyard, enclosed on two sides: cross the lawns beyond to reach all that remains of the abbey, apart from some stonework in the churchyard. Here is the porch to the Abbot's Hall, sadly decayed, but still recognisably built by masons working for the glory of their god. On the front is a magnificent two-storey oriel window. There is another oriel on the guest-house, the other surviving abbey building, closer to the Farm. The name is tentative as there is no firm evidence that this was indeed the guest-house. If it was, then it was here that Margaret of Anjou stayed on her way to Tewkesbury.

Cerne Abbas has little else to compare with the treasury of Abbey Street, but there are things worth seeing. The oldest inn sits in Long Street and is called, inevitably, the New Inn, though it has a strong rival for the title of oldest, the Royal Oak, also in Long Street. Both were once coaching inns, and each had its own forge for the shoeing of coach horses. Also of interest is a **tithe barn** (a short distance to the south-west of the village centre) which rivals, in appearance if not size, the famous one at Abbotsbury. Interestingly the link with Abbotsbury is maintained by Cerne Abbas also having a St Catherine's Chapel, to the east of the town, up a hill. The hill is Cat and Chapel Hill, which seems very likely to have been a mis-saying that became a misprinting. There is a legend that a secret underground passage leads from the old abbey to the old chapel site.

To complete the scan through Cerne's built history, the workhouse to the north of the village is a link with Victorian times. The size of this barracks-like building reflects Cerne's old status as a valley town rather than a village. The sombre appearance and hard lines of its structure reveal an uncompromising attitude to the inmates and their situation. The workhouse was a point on the road from feudalism to democracy, and Cerne Abbas boasts a link with another significant point on that road.

An Ancient Children's Rhyme

The fits of giggles of modern young visitors to the Piddle Valley is no new thing. Many years ago the valley children would sing:

Hey diddle, Hey diddle, Hey diddle; I live on the banks of the Piddle.

But if it should flood there is no doubt I would be in a Piddle right up to my middle

Ann Winzer

In Piddlehinton churchyard lies Ann Winzer, who preceded Florence Nightingale by 40 years, nursing some of the many thousand casualties in the rain and mud of Waterloo. It would be interesting to know how the nurse would have viewed some local remedies. The *Piddle Valley Book of Country Life* notes that to cure whooping cough you must catch a shrew, then bore a hole in an ash tree, insert the shrew and plug up the hole. The shrew and disease then die together. This remedy may explain the name Shear Ashes – shrew's ashes – near Piddlehinton.

Denzil Holles, born in 1599, the son of the first Earl of Clare, married a Cerne widow and lived in the Abbey Farm, part of her willed property. It was Holles who, in 1629, held the Speaker of the House of Commons in his chair when he tried to rise and so force the house to answer the king's summons rather than their own. 'God's wounds,' shouted Holles, 'you shall sit till we please to rise.' And sit the Speaker did. Holles had a stormy career as MP for Dorchester and had the distinction of being imprisoned, at different times, by both Charles I and Oliver Cromwell. A man of honesty, his qualities were recognised by all, it would appear, and he was created baron at the Restoration and became a member of Charles II's privy council. On the death of his wife he moved to Dorchester, where his tomb can be seen in St Peter's Church.

But excellent though Cerne Abbas is, the village's most famous object lies outside the village, a short distance to the north (see page 54). Most reach the **Giant** by car, stopping at the viewpoint and notice board beside the main road, but it can also be reached on foot: go through the churchyard and head northwards. The close approach to the figure is exciting, but access to it is closed and the closer the visitor is, the more difficult the detail is to grasp. Overall it is better to view the Giant from the road.

UP CERNE AND MINTERNE MAGNA

The River Cerne rises as a pair of streams, one springing from the side of East Hill, the other from Little Minterne Hill. Under East Hill lies **Up Cerne**, an achingly pretty hamlet with a church built of flint and stone bands standing beside a seventeenth century manor house.

Minterne Magna, Hardy's Great Hintock, also lies in a hollow, though the main road ensures it is neither as quiet nor as secluded as Up Cerne. The church is a handsome building, despite its curious origin of having been started in about 1620, but then left for almost two centuries before completion. Inside there is a fine monument to Sir Nathaniel Napier whose father Sir Robert was responsible for Napper's Mite in Dorchester. The names Napier and Napper were clearly interchangeable at the time, Sir

Continued on Page 59

**Opposite page:
Abbey Farm,
Cerne Abbas**

Left: Cerne Abbas

Piddletrenhide

It is interesting to speculate that the god which the mud-spattered St Augustine saw when he looked up was the Cerne Abbas Giant, a chalk-outlined man. It is not clear when this figure was cut, or by whom, or why, but one thing is certain: that however primitive the outline, however 'vulgar' the pose, the figure has a presence beyond its physical existence: it is a work of art. The figure is 180 ft (55m) tall, the overall outline – including the club, itself 120 ft (37m) long – largely fills a rectangle 230 ft (70m) high and 170 ft (52m) wide. The figure is outlined by trenches cut into the chalk beneath the turf, each trench being 2 ft (60cm) wide deep.

The giant faces west on the sloping side of Giant Hill. He also faces the viewer, but is striding to the left, holding a knobbed club in his right hand, his left hand extended. His facial features are picked out, eyes and eyebrows in outline, nose in relief. He has bold nipples and ribs and, boldest of all, an erect penis. It is, as much as anything else, this latter feature which has made the figure so famous – or infamous? As archaeologist Jacquetta Hawkes put it, that feature is the one that is 'the source of so much interest and so little open comment'.

The first record of the Giant was published only a little over 200 years ago, in the *Gentleman's Magazine* of 1764. Considering the now claimed antiquity of the figure, this is remarkably late. All dates suggest a first cutting 1,800–2,000 years ago, so why did it take 1,600 years before someone thought it worthy of comment? The recent history of the Giant suggests that if it is not looked after, its trenches periodically scoured, it disappears into the grass of the hillside. The drawing of 1764 shows a navel in addition to the existing features and this has disappeared completely.

So how did the figure manage to survive and remain unnoticed? During a long part of its existence, 500 years at least, a Christian monastery sat under the Giant's feet. Did the abbot and his monks never once consider that this naked, heathen object should be veiled for ever? On the evidence of the navel the figure must have been scoured a great number of times during the abbey's existence, and it is hard to imagine that the abbot was enamoured of such a ritual cleaning of a pagan god. It really is very intriguing.

It is now generally agreed that the figure was cut either just before or just after the Roman invasion. Evidence for a pre-conquest construction lie in similarities with other known

Celtic works. Especially significant is a skillet handle found at the hill fort of Hod Hill only a dozen miles or so from the Giant. Although the Romans occupied this fort after the conquest of Dorset, the object is definitely Celtic. It is a superb piece, bronze and delicately styled with the heads of birds as the pan holders. On its shaft it bears a representation of a Celtic god, believed, from evidence gathered elsewhere in Britain, to be Nodons. There are similarities between the 4-inch bronze figure and the Cerne Abbas figure, including the stance, looking outwards but striding off to the side; a knobbly club held in one hand; and the stylised face. Nodons was a hunter god, and in his other hand the skillet-hand figure carries a hare. It is possible that the Cerne Giant also once had something in his left hand, but that inadequate scouring allowed it to be lost. A Celtic origin would also explain the overt masculinity, as the Celts were a liberal folk.

But there are those who argue that the Giant is not purely Celtic, but Romano-British. This makes it younger, moving it from the first century AD at latest, to the second century AD at earliest. If it was indeed a figure carved by a team with a Roman foreman, then who does it represent? The accepted answer is Hercules. Interestingly, Emperor Commodus, of the later second century, campaigned in Britain and believed he was the reincarnation of Hercules.

Evidence from other sources suggests that representations of Hercules had him holding a knobbed club in one hand, the other (sometimes) holding a bow. The arm of the bow hand was invariably draped with a cloak, often a lion's skin. Certainly the Cerne figure has its left arm extended in a manner that could easily accommodate a draped cloak. And the obvious masculinity? Perhaps Commodus believed his godlike abilities extended into fields other than fighting and commerce. Perhaps that aspect shows an amalgam of ideas from Rome and the Celts.

Without a clear indication of the reasons for the figure's construction, it is idle to speculate, other than with abstract phrases – fertility rites and the like. It is nicer to just look in wonder, and to enquire how the locals coped with their gigantic neighbour. Legend has it that there was once a real giant who regularly walked into the valley to steal sheep. One day he was tired and lay on the hillside to sleep. As he slept he was killed by local shepherds, who then drew round him so that after the body had gone the outline would recall the story for future generations. Another story has it that the Giant is only sleeping and that those who are brave enough can watch him come down the hillside to drink in the stream as Cerne Abbas church bell strikes midnight.

One fertility rite which is still maintained to be true is that the Giant can help childless couples produce heirs. The usually published version of the legend is that the woman in question must sit on the figure. The more bold writer suggests that the women need to sit on the penis. The real version is that the couple must copulate on the penis for the Giant's power to work.

Another fertility rite associated with the Giant was maypole dancing, a maypole having been set up above the figure. Despite its current image – junior-school children and Morris dancers – maypole dancing is very ancient and very pagan. Originally the pole was a tree, a poplar, birch or fir, the bark flayed to ribbons. The dancers progressed in leaps and jumps in the direction of the sun's movement, and the tree was burned on mid-summer's day. The Cerne maypole on Giant Hill was taken down in 1635: the Puritans who were soon to govern England would have no truck with such heathen rubbish and it was not replaced.

Robert's name invariably being given as Napper in pieces on Dorchester, but the tombs here clearly having it as Napier. There is also a monument to General Charles Churchill, the brother of the Duke of Marlborough. Churchill was the local squire, a title that eventually passed to the Digby family who built the excellent Minterne House, tucked away behind trees at the southern edge of the village. The house is not open to the public, but its gardens are, a vast array of woodland together with stands of acers, azaleas and rhododendrons which can be explored along a network of paths. With the lake, streams and neat bridges, the gardens are excellent.

THE PIDDLE VALLEY

Leaving Dorchester along the A354 the visitor reaches Puddle-town, the largest of the villages in the Piddle valley.

But to explore the valley properly it is first necessary to go north. The river rises in Soggy Wood near Alton Pancras. The Saxons named the first settlement Awiell Ton, the farm near the source, and named the stream Piddle – clear water. In time the Saxon term for a stream of clear water received lavatorial acclaim, and now no self-respecting nine-year-old can be taken to the valley and hear the name without dissolving into a giggling heap.

As if to anticipate this effect on the nation's youth, **Alton Pancras**, the valley's first village, is suffixed with the name of the saint to whom its church is dedicated – St Pancras, an orphaned boy martyred at the age of 14 by the Emperor Diocletian and once the patron saint of children, a patronage now taken over by St Nicholas. All parts of the story came together in the late seventeenth century when Alton seemed to be a favoured spot for drunkenness. The story is told of Henry Spinter, that 'one saboth daye a littel before the eveninge prayer he went up into the tower and at a trappe dore did pisse downe upon theor heads in the belfry that they could not stand there

The Piddle Valley

nor neare itt to the great offence of those that were present.'

From Alton Pancras a fine walk crosses West Hill – from where on clear days Glastonbury can be seen and where the tway-blade orchid grows – to **Plush**, a secluded hamlet. Plush was never a parish, its church being visited by the local travelling vicar. One, in the mid-seventeenth century, does not appear to have found favour with the locals. He had to clear the pulpit of chickens before he could even contemplate starting the service, and then turned to the congregation to ask, 'Would ye please remove this bag of ferrets before I begin my sermon?'

By road the hamlet is reached from Piddletrenthide, a straggling place, but in many ways the nicest of the Piddle villages. At this point the valley is narrow and steep-sided, cut deep into the bare chalk upland. The village name is probably French: this is the Piddle village of *trente hide*, thirty hides, the *hide* being an ancient measure of land area. There is an alternative suggestion that the *trent* is just another ancient word for a winding river, and indeed the river has been called the Trent, a name preferred by the puritans if not the purists.

Legend has it that King Ethelred, the elder brother of Alfred the Great, lived in the village, a legend supported by Kingrove to the west and Kingcombe to the east. Queen Emma – wife of a later and better known Ethelred, the Unready – was French, giving us a French connection, and she gave the manor to her monastery at Winchester. In Domesday it is noted that 'one knight and a certain widow' owned two ploughs in the parish. A plough is about 120 acres of land, the acreage that could be worked by one ox team in one year, but much more interesting is who was the 'certain widow'?

The village church is claimed by many to be the most beautiful in Dorset, being not only a lovely building but also well positioned. The western wall of the tower has a Latin inscription by a former vicar which includes the date 1487 written just that way, probably the earliest example of Arabic numerals on a building in England.

The next valley village is **Piddlehinton**, a manor given by Robert, William the Conqueror's brother, to his abbey at Mortain in France. During the Hundred Years' War, Henry V suddenly realised that this situation had never been rectified and that the peasants of the valley were paying taxes to the French for the maintenance of their resistance to his army. He promptly gave the manor to his son, who later gave it to Eton College. The college continued to 'own' the village until this century.

Further down, the valley broadens out and here is Waterston Manor, an excellent seventeenth-century manor house, and Hardy's Weatherbury Farm, the home of Bathsheba Everdene in *Far from the Madding Crowd*. Weatherbury itself was Puddletown, the first valley village to have changed the name from Piddle to Puddle, a change which appears to have been a straightforward censorship, reinforced in the 1950s when the local council decided they did not want their town to be Piddletown even if it was the more historically accurate rendering. From here to the sea the Piddle flows through or near villages that are Puddles.

The town is finely observed in *Far from the Madding Crowd,* a book which, behind the story, breathes the scent of a village of cottages with brick floors and thatched roofs. Hardy speaks of the effects of the Enclosure Acts, and of the annual hiring fair where labourers were re-engaged for another year's labour. There are hints at the darker truths of the life in those times: of labourers not taken on who were evicted from their cottages; of the old, too tired to work; of moving house annually, to cottages the farmers would not keep their dogs in; of the winters where half-starved, sick children froze.

Now only the better cottages remain, the town being largely new. In the church there are several fine memorials to the Martyn family of nearby Athelhampton, but the most interesting is the alabaster effigy of a knight wearing a Yorkist collar of suns and roses, a very rare representation. This was once thought to be of Sir William Martyn, but he died in 1503 while the effigy cannot be later than 1470. However, the knight does have an ape chained to his feet and an ape was the symbol of the Martyns, leading some to speculate that the effigy was carved for Sir William, but before his death.

To the east of the church, **Ilsington House,** though remodelled externally, has much original seventeenth-century wood panelling and eighteenth-century furnishings. Much of the work on the house was carried out by General Garth who was probably the father of an illegitimate son born to Princess Sophie, the daughter of George III for whom Garth was equerry. If, as is likely, this is true, the event was so scandalous that it was hushed up at the time and even now difficult to verify. The boy was brought up by Garth as his son. At present the house is not open to the public.

To the south of Puddletown, the river runs east, passing the squire's house at **Athelhampton** before reaching the labourer's village of Tolpuddle. Athelhampton Hall was Hardy's Athelhall and is the reputed site of the palace of King Athelstan. The name reflects this association with the king, who was killed by the Danes at Portland. The house was started in 1485 (the same year as the Battle of Bosworth) for Sir William Martyn, Lord Mayor of London in 1493 and a member of a famous local family. The name Martin is said to be synonymous with the ape, in the same way that Brock is a badger, and Reynard is a fox, and this led the family to take the strange motto – 'He who looks at Martyn's ape, Martin's ape shall look at him'.

To the east of Athelhampton, and spoiled by the main road, is **Tolpuddle,** the village of the Martyrs (see page 78). At the entrance to the village the TUC has erected six memorial cottages and a small museum. Elsewhere, there is James Hammett's grave with a plain, dignified headstone engraved by Eric Gill – the Martyrs' Tree and shelter, and the Methodist chapel. There is little else of note, though the village is a pretty place for all its sombre overtones.

Beyond Tolpuddle the river thankfully leaves the main road. **Affpuddle,** the next valley village is a quiet place whose church has a fine tower. North of the church the Piddle is not one river, but several streams which meander through water meadows. Next is

Continued on Page 64

F ollowing the enclosing of some six million acres of common land between 1770 and 1830 under the Enclosure Acts and the release of additional men onto the work market at the end of the Napoleonic Wars, conditions in the 1820s for the labouring man were harsh. Where there had been a stable situation with each farm labourer having his own plot of land, now there was a landless workforce competing for jobs and wages.

By 1830, the situation in **Tolpuddle** was rather worse than elsewhere in the country. The general wage was 10 shillings per week for a labourer, but at Tolpuddle it was only 9 shillings. Led by **George Loveless**, the labourers met the farmers at a meeting witnessed by Dr Warren, the Church of England vicar, and an increase to 10 shillings was agreed. Then the farmers went back on their agreement and decided instead to reduce the wage to 8 shillings.

The infuriated labourers sought assistance from the local magistrate, William Morden Pitt, who set up a meeting between farmers and men at Dorchester. There Dr Warren denied all knowledge of the 10 shilling agreement and the men lost their case. Indeed their wage was cut to 7 shillings, with a threat of 6 shillings if peace was not forthcoming. Such behaviour – the Church siding with the Establishment – led many to join the Methodists (George Loveless was himself a Methodist lay preacher).

Trade unions had been made legal in 1824 and so, when George Loveless formed a **Friendly Society of Agricultural Labourers** in Tolpuddle in 1833, he was legally entitled to do so. The society was established, following many meetings under the tree, now the (replacement) **Martyrs' Tree** on the village green, after a meeting with representatives of Robert Owen's Grand National Consolidated Trades Union. The society maintained an active secrecy. There were passwords to get into meetings in the upstairs room of Thomas Standfield's cottage and, most significantly in view of future events, oath-taking ceremonies for new members. The ceremony was quasi-religious: the new man blindfolded at first; George Loveless in a long white smock; swearing on a Bible. At one fateful ceremony, a certain Edward Legg was invested in the presence of George Loveless, his brother James, Thomas Standfield and his son John, and James Brine. There may also have been another present, as we shall see.

Following the meeting, Edward Legg turned informer. On 24 February 1834 George Loveless and the other men were arrested together with James Hammett who, though he was almost certainly not at the meeting, never protested his innocence. It is thought that he may have stepped in for his brother John, whose wife was pregnant.

Since the society itself was legal, the pretext for the men's arrest was administering an illegal oath, a charge brought under an Act of 1797 designed to deal with the Spithead and Nore

The Martyr's Memorial Tolpuddle

mutinies. The Tolpuddle men were all found guilty and a sentence of seven years' transportation was passed.

In sentencing, the judge noted that *'The object of all legal punishment is not altogether with a view of operating on the offenders themselves; it is also for the sake of offering an example and warning'*. The sentence was necessary, the judge added, for the security of the country. The men were manacled, transferred to the prison hulks at Portsmouth and thence to Australia.

Robert Owen and William Cobbett started organising a campaign for their release, noting that all the secret orders, Masons, Oddfellows, etc., took oaths. Eventually, on 14 March 1836 the men were pardoned, though it was some time before they returned home. George Loveless was first to arrive, in January 1837. The Standfields, James Loveless and James Brine came back in March 1838, with James Hammett not returning until 1839. At first all the men went to Essex as tenant farmers, but Hammett returned to Tolpuddle as a builder. He died in 1891 and is buried in Tolpuddle churchyard. The other five emigrated and never returned.

Briantspuddle which has a elegant war memorial by Eric Gill and a fifteenth-century cruck-built cottage. To the south-west of the village, **Culpepper's Dish** is a huge swallow hole – caused by rainwater eating away the chalk. There are many such holes locally, but Culpepper's – over 100 yards across and 40ft (12m) deep – is by far the largest. The last Piddle village to bear the river's name is **Turner's Puddle**, an attractive little hamlet.

AROUND MILTON ABBAS

The whole of central Dorset, from the western county boundary to Blandford Forum in the east, is a designated Area of Outstanding Natural Beauty (AONB) the southern boundary of which takes a line close to (but not reaching) the A354. Parts of the AONB have already been explored in the trip north of Dorchester to Minterne Magna, and in the upper reaches of the Piddle Valley. Heading east from Dorchester, passing Puddletown, the visitor on the A354 soon reaches Milborne St Andrew. A turn left here, for Milton Abbas, allows the eastern end of the AONB to be explored.

Milborne St Andrew lies in the steep valley of a tributary stream of the River Piddle, its church set among trees and with a pretty array of cottages and houses that do their best to take the edge off the fact that the main road cuts right through the heart of the village. The church houses the monuments of several members of the Morton family whose fine mansion lay to the south-east. The house was demolished in 1802, but a pair of big stone gateposts marks the old entrance.

To the south of Milborne a hill fort with a pair of ditches and ramparts tops Weatherby Hill. Within the fort, in 1761, Edmund Morton Pleydell erected a brick obelisk, apparently just for the joy of doing so. The obelisk is now completely obscured by trees.

Turn left from the main road in Milborne St Andrew, following a minor road through pleasant country to reach **Milton Abbas**. In 935 King Athelstan founded an abbey in the secretive but picturesque Delcombe Valley, legend having it that he camped in the valley on his way to battle and had a vision of his coming victory which he interpreted as a sign from God. This first abbey, home to 40 monks, was extended by the Normans who built a larger church, but the entire complex was destroyed by fire in 1309.

Rebuilding began soon after, but was very slow, eventually stopping altogether towards the end of the fifteenth century. By the time of the Dissolution only the chancel, tower and transepts of the church had been completed, together with the cloisters, some scattered buildings for the monks and the Great Hall, one of the last buildings to be finished (under the guidance of Abbot Middleton, one of Milton's greatest Abbots). The Dissolution was peaceful: there were only 12 monks and the last abbot, John Bradley, accepted the position of Bishop of Shaftesbury. The estate was bought by Sir John Tregonwell, though the abbey church became the parish church of Milton Abbas, the large town which had grown up around the abbey. Tregonwell converted the monastic buildings into a house and here his son, also John, was born.

Morton's Fork

One member of the family was John Morton, born in 1420. This brilliant lawyer and theologian was vicar of Bloxworth, but became Archbishop of Canterbury in 1486 and Lord Chancellor in 1487. As Lord Chancellor he worked hard for an increase in royal authority by making private armies illegal and reducing the wealth of the nobility. The latter he achieved by demanding voluntary' contributions to the royal exchequer. His approach to collecting money become known as **'Morton's Fork'** because of its deadly two-pronged thrust: if the noble had a lavish lifestyle he could clearly afford to pay, but if his lifestyle was more modest, impoverished even, then this was clearly because he had salted his cash away. King Henry VII grew rich on these voluntary donations and ensured that Morton became a Cardinal. In later life Morton was responsible for the extraordinary roof of Bere Regis church.

At the age of five young John slipped out of the house and began an exploration of the church. He somehow made his way to the top of the tower and across to its unguarded edge, from which he fell. The tower has a full drop to the ground on one side only: that is the side down which John fell, but in the style of the day, the young boy was dressed in petticoats and these, acting as a parachute, allowed him to land unharmed. Taking full advantage of his luck, the younger John lived a further 77 years, enjoying rude good health until his death in 1680.

For 70 years after the younger John's death Milton Abbey remained in the Tregonwell family, but in 1752 the husband of the last heiress sold the estate to a local man, Joseph Damer. Damer married the daughter of the Duke of Dorset and was made Lord Milton and, later, the Earl of Dorchester.

At first Damer and his wife lived in the old house, but in 1771 he decided that a new, larger house was required. The monastic buildings, apart from Abbot Middleton's hall, were demolished and a new house erected. Soon after its completion Damer, by now accustomed to his role as local squire and forgetting his origins as local man, decided that Milton Abbas was too close and set about driving the townsfolk away and demolishing their houses. This may be a harsh judgement, for eventually Damer had a new village built in a side valley and moved what remained of the population to it. It is also not clear how many townsfolk were left in Milton Abbas when Damer began his clearance: the loss of the Abbey had affected the town's prosperity and it had almost certainly been shrinking. After Damer's death the new house remained in private hands until 1954 when it became a public school for boys.

The **Abbey Church** is a massive structure. Its construction was clearly an ambitious project: some chapels at the eastern end were demolished after the Dissolution, and the nave was never started, so the intention was to build something at least half as big again. The size is emphasised by the relatively modest height of the school. Stylistically, the church is very much of its

• ATHELHAMPTON HOUSE •

Athelhampton Hall has been claimed as the finest stone-built manor house in England. It stands in magnificent, formal gardens which give it an undeniable majesty. When approaching, the effect of the crenellations, authoritative to the front, and the gables, domestic to the side, is spectacular. Inside, the hall is beautiful, with a magnificent roof, ancient glass and marvellous panelling. The main bedroom, with its original fireplace and wood panelling, is superb. Also of interest is the dovecote on the lawns beyond the house, a circular building with the nest holes reached by a ladder suspended from a revolving roof, which allows the holes to be visited without having to descend and move the ladder. The site has a licensed restaurant, and there is a regular programme of events.

Althehampton House

period (early to mid-fourteenth century), elegant, but straightforward. Entry is through a porch added in 1865 during restoration work by Sir George Gilbert Scott, the lack of a nave taking the visitor immediately into the heart of the building. Inside, Milton is more beautiful and interesting than outside, with fine vaults and buttresses, impressive windows and some excellent monuments. Sir John Tregonwell lies beneath a Purbeck marble tomb, but the best work is the white marble tomb of Caroline Damer, the wife of Joseph. Designed by Robert Adams and sculpted by Agostino Carlini, the tomb has the Countess and the Earl reclining on a chaise longue, the recumbent Countess being watched by her husband who supports himself on his elbow.

Finally, look for the tabernacle or pyx-shrine, a huge oak 'cupboard' (almost 10 ft – 3m long) for storing the Host. This would originally have been suspended in the chancel and is a unique survival in an English church, others having been destroyed by the Puritans.

The house beside the church was constructed around a central quadrangle to a design by Sir William Chambers. The idea was for a house which was at one with the church, but Chambers' pseudo-Gothic does not seem to have succeeded. Though elegant, the façades are too low and the details just do not soar. Even Chambers himself is on record as having referred to it as 'this vast, ugly house in Dorset'. Inside, the best part is Abbot Middleton's Great Hall with its rich woodwork and fine roof.

Outside the house, Damer had **Capability Brown** create fine parkland, its centrepiece a lake, an enlargement of the abbey's fishpond, which covered a section of the old town of Milton Abbas. From the park a series of over 100 turf-cut steps flanked by yew hedges once led up to St Catherine's Chapel. The steps are closed to visitors – though still visible – but the chapel can be easily reached by another path. It is Norman, dating from the Norman Abbey's construction, and was perfectly aligned with the abbey church. But there was an earlier, Saxon chapel, probably marking the site of Athelstan's vision. The chapel, now engulfed in trees, was once a pilgrimage site for local women-folk anxious to find a husband, just as at St Catherine's Chapel above Abbotsbury.

From the Abbey a walk through Capability Brown's parkland leads to the 'new' village of Milton Abbas. Despite Damer's dubious behaviour, it has to be admitted that the village he created is very pleasant, though the accommodation was small. What are now single cottages were then pairs, each two-up, two-down. They were also overcrowded, the remnant town population being larger than could be comfortably accommodated. It is said that one cottage was home to 36 people. Despite this, author Fanny Burney, during a visit in 1791, thought the houses far too good for their inhabitants. Today the regularity of the cottages and the gentle curve of the village road make Milton Abbas seem idyllic, if over-organised. The new village church was by James Wyatt: opposite is an almshouse, built to accommodate six poor folk. The almshouse pre-dates the village, having been moved from the old town rather than be demolished, a fact which explains why the poor had rather better living standards than some of the villagers.

To the west of Milton Abbas – take the road to the left as the lake of Milton Abbey is reached and turn right at the T-junction – **Long Ash Farm** is home to a rare breeds collection, with all the species of

British domestic pig and many breeds of poultry. There is a children's corner with the usual pets as well as goats and piglets.

BULBARROW HILL AND MELCOMBE HORSEY

The road past Milton Abbey leads to **Hilton**, a quiet village ringed with wooded hills. The church has several features brought here from Milton after the Dissolution, most notably the north aisle windows. There is also a series of 12 large paintings of the Apostles which owe more to enthusiasm than artistry, but are nonetheless interesting for their period (around 1500). From the village a straightforward path heads north to Greenhill Down where Dorset Wildlife Trust have a Nature Reserve. The reserve can also be reached from the north, but the Hilton approach is easier. The reserve covers 30 acres and was set up to preserve a typical chalkland habitat. There are no rarities, but the plant and animal life does include some good species – pyramidal orchid and wild basil, several types of dragonfly and damselfly, brown argus and green hairstreak butterflies, dormice and all three species of newt.

From Hilton, continue northwestwards to Ansty Cross. To the right from here is – **barrow Hill**, the second highest point in Dorset (all of 6ft – 2m lower than Pilsdon Pen) and one of the county's best viewpoints. From the masts, on clear days, Somerset's Quantock Hills are visible. Just a short distance from the summit (head north-westwards) is Bul Barrow, the prehistoric burial mound which names the hill.

Turning left at Ansty Cross takes the visitor into one of the least visited areas of the county, the Melcombe hamlets and the high chalk downland that stretches back to the Piddle Valley, an area falling in the parish of Melcombe Horsey. **Melcombe Bingham** village, laid out along its only road, is now almost a mile from its church and manor house (to the east) and almost the same distance from the house which names the parish. To add to the confusion, the former is called Bingham's Melcombe and the latter Higher Melcombe, despite its having been the seat of the Horsey family. Bingham's Melcombe church and house can be reached on foot along a private road. The house (not open to the public, but seen from the church) dates from the fifteenth century, but has been renovated and rebuilt over the centuries. Beside it stands St Andrew's Church, earlier than the house. The porch has graffiti dated 1589, an indication that vandalism is not only the modern plague many believe it to be, and a pulpit which, a parish record notes, cost £10 in 1723 when bought from the Bastards of Blandford – presumably the famous firm of builders rather than those responsible for the graffiti. The land on which the Bingham family built their house was sold to them by the Horseys whose house at High Melcombe was built a little later. The house is rarely open to the public.

To the west of Higher Melcombe lies excellent walking country, the hills of Lyscombe and Bowdens forming a small horseshoe around the picturesque Lyscombe Bottom, to the south. To the north is Nettlecombe Tout where a hill fort was started, but never completed. The hills, particularly Bowdens Hill, show evidence of a Celtic field system, with ditches across the hill ridge, probably part of the defensive system of the fort.

To the south of Melcombe Bingham a return to Milborne St Andrew can be made through Cheselbourne and Dewlish. **Cheselbourne** is a long village laid out beside a meandering chalk stream, while **Dewlish** has an equally picturesque setting on a larger stream ominously called the Devil's Brook. The church houses a large monument to Field Marshal Sir John Michel who died in 1886. Close to the church is a splendid manor house dating from the early seventeenth century. Dewlish House, a short distance downstream of the village, is equally good.

Dewlish

Curiously for a chalkland village, there was once a sand pit in Dewlish, village lore insisting that it was discovered, in 1814, when a local noticed a woodmouse throwing sand out of a tunnel it was digging. The sand was a source of minor wealth for a few years. Interestingly, about 70 years later, another local digging in the chalk found the remains of several prehistoric animals which had apparently fallen into a wide crack in the bedrock.

THE WINTERBORNE VALLEY

Continuing along the A354 towards Blandford Forum, the next village is Winterborne Whitechurch. Dorset has two groups of 'Winterborne' villages, and it would be good to report that those to the west of Dorchester are spelt with a 'u' (Winterbourne), whereas those to the east are spelt without. Sadly, the western group of villages use both spellings! The derivation of the name is from streams that only flow in winter, summer rain being readily absorbed by the chalk, 'borne' or 'bourne' being an old word for a stream, a usage that is not restricted to Dorset.

Winterborne Whitechurch is barely large enough to support its name, a pleasant village just off the main road that was the birthplace of George Turberville, a minor Elizabethan poet, but one whose name was to become famous. The flint church has some interesting arches carved with strange heads and odd foliage probably dating from the thirteenth century. Do not be deceived by the splashes of colour, however, because although some of it is undoubtedly medieval, there is a story that much of it dates from an enthusiastic restoration in the late nineteenth century by the vicar's wife. The pulpit is said to have been brought here from Milton Abbey.

To the south of the A354 there are three more Winterborne villages. The first is **Winterborne Kingston** which lies on the line of a Roman road which linked Dorchester to the Badbury Rings hill fort. The church here is a neat building, sympathetically restored by GE Street, one of

Continued on Page 72

• DORSET HEATH •

What is a heath? Technically, heathland is created where there is a sand or gravel soil that allows water to percolate downwards relatively quickly. In time this percolation removes the nutrients from the top soil, leaving it grey and barren: only a thin dark surface layer containing the humus of recently decomposed plants can support life. That surface layer is highly acidic, and this poor acid soil gives the country its typical plant cover. In England, where such conditions exist on mountains or upland there is moorland: at lower levels there is heathland. In Dorset a belt of heathland extends across the county, from east of Dorchester towards the New Forest.

The heath has never been continuous, at least not in recorded history, but has existed in pockets. It is estimated that in the early years of the last century there were around 75,000 acres of Dorset heath. Today there is barely one fifth of that acreage left, and some of that is under threat. Some of the heath has been lost to forestry, the great plantations north of Bovington Camp, and the expanse of Wareham Forest to the east, though even the forests have been unable to eradicate the heath totally: dotted throughout the plantations there are still boggy areas where some, at least, of the precious heath plants still flourish.

Studland Heath

Milton Church

the better Victorian restorers.

Now head east, passing Winterborne Muston, a tiny hamlet, to reach the hamlets of **Anderson** (formerly Winterborne Anderson) and **Winterborne Tomson**. Anderson consists of little but a charming early seventeenth-century house with later additions and a tiny, now redundant church. Winterborne Tomson is little bigger, but has the distinction of a church saved with money raised by the sale of some of Thomas Hardy's letters. The church is a delight, little more than 30 ft x 20 ft (9m x 6m) and with a tiny belltower. But it is twelfth century and did not deserve a fate that apparently involved being used as an ad hoc 'home' by pigs and chickens. In 1931 AR Powys, the brother of the novelist John Cowper Powys, recognised its worth and began a restoration. The work soon ran into financial problems, but was rescued when Hardy's letters to the Society of Protection of Ancient Buildings were sold. The details of the sale and restoration are inscribed on a tablet of Purbeck marble.

Turn left at Red Post to reach **Winterborne Zelston**, the last village on this stretch of the River Winterborne. The village lies to the north of the main road, a pretty, secluded place with a neat bridge over the river, a fine pond and fine little church.

Turning left at Winterborne Whitechurch follows the river back into the chalk downland. Whatcombe House, built in the mid-eighteenth century, is passed, on the left, before **Winterborne Clenston** is reached. Little more than a scattered hamlet, Clenston has a delightful little church, built in 1840, and a fine manor house, probably dating from the sixteenth century, but much remodelled and then very well restored in 1955.

Next is **Winterborne Stickland**, with some fine old thatched cottages, but a number of recent, less sympathetic, additions. The church is worth visiting for two monuments. One, to Thomas Skinner, who died in 1756, is a sarcophagus with a beautiful polished beach marble lid, while the other is a real curiosity. Raised in 1653 to Rachel Sutton it is a black column with a

Botany Bay Barn

From Winterborne Tomson the road turns away from the river to reach the A31 at **Red Post**. The curious name is related to that of the barn just a short distance along the road opposite, towards Bloxworth. This is **Botany Bay Barn**. In the days of transportation of prisoners to Australia, those condemned at Dorchester Assize were force marched to Portsmouth and spent their first night on the walk at this barn. The red post was the indicator to a possibly illiterate guard that he should turn off the main road here to reach the barn. Until the early years of the twentieth century the central post in the barn, to which the prisoners were chained, still existed.

base and capital, and a long Latin inscription which tells the reader that the whole is a *Statua Sepulchri*.

At Stickland the River Winterborne executes a right-angled bend. Turning with it, the visitor reaches the final village, **Winterborne Houghton**, close to which the river rises. There are pretty thatched cottages here and a flint and stone church, built in 1861 to replace an earlier one from which the fine font was retained. On the downland above the village, a high arc of land, there are a large number of round barrows suggesting a well-established Bronze Age community, and evidence of Iron Age or Romano-British houses and field systems.

EGDON HEATH

Dorset is synonymous with English heathland for, although heath is not unique to Dorset, the county – or more precisely the Hampshire Basin, a geological area that covers both Dorset and Hampshire – contains some of the finest examples. Thomas Hardy uses the characteristics of the then existing Dorset heathland for **Egdon Heath**, which appears as a sombre, if not sinister backdrop to many of his novels. Hardy made his Egdon harsher and larger than the real ones, exaggerating its wildness for dramatic effect and coalescing the many small patches of Dorset heathland to form one large tract.

THE FROME VALLEY

To the south of Egdon Heath, Hardy placed his **Vale of Great Dairies**, using as his model the farmland of the River Frome's valley, made fertile by the silt deposited by the flooding river, together with farmland created by ploughing and enriching the heathland margins. Today the valley farms remain, the area being no more populated than it was when Hardy was writing, with a few well-scattered villages. Our exploration of the Piddle Valley has already encroached on Egdon Heath, but here we shall visit the area on a meandering west-to-east journey.

Leave Dorchester along the A352 towards Wareham. Soon, a left turning can be taken to reach the village of **West Stafford**, prettily sited in the Frome Valley and with an array of thatched cottages – even the bus shelter is thatched. The church is probably sixteenth century, and has a striking memorial to one vicar, Canon Reginald Southwell Smith, who was the minister here almost throughout Queen Victoria's reign. Canon Smith is shown in a recumbent effigy: he clearly needed the rest. To the east of West Stafford, on the road for Woodsford, is Talbothays Lodge, built in 1894 for Henry Hardy, Thomas' brother, and designed by Thomas himself. The name is interesting: Thomas called West Stafford 'Talbothays' in *Tess of the d'Urbervilles*. It has been speculated that Hardy also designed Talbothays Cottages opposite the Lodge.

Continue along the road towards **Woodsford** to reach Woodsford Castle, claimed to be one of the oldest continuously occupied castles in the country. The castle began life as a mansion, but in 1335 the owner, William de Whitefield, was granted 'permission to crenellate' by Edward III. This permission allowed the fortification of the mansion, with five

Continued on Page 76

• BOVINGTON CAMP •

Bovington Camp was established during the 1914-18 War and has remained in military hands since that time. It was at Bovington that TE Lawrence served as a private soldier in the Royal Tank Corps. There is a museum at the camp which has a collection of memorabilia of Lawrence – uniforms, medals etc. But this is the **Tank Museum**, its main interest being the history of mechanised warfare. The collection, over 300 tanks and armoured vehicles from all over the world, starts with Britain's first tank, 'Little Willie' built in 1915, then progresses through the 1914–18 War, the inter-war years, the 1939–45 War and through the modern battle tanks, including a section on the Gulf War. There are videos and visitors can have rides in some of the vehicles. On special days, there are battle re-enactments, and a timetable tells visitors when modern tanks can be seen in action at the Lulworth range. The museum has a licensed restaurant and a picnic area, and an assault course for children. There is good disabled access.

Bovington Tank Museum

Above: Winterborne Tomson Church Below left: Village cross, Winterborne Zelston Below right: Red Post

round towers being built. Only one survives and the detail of the rest of the castle is obscured by a vast thatched roof. The castle is not open to the public. Beyond is the village of Woodsford and further on Moreton is reached by a minor road that passes the now forested Hurst Heath before crossing the B3390.

Instead of turning left to West Stafford the visitor can continue along the A352, passing the turning to Winterborne Came, on the left, to reach **Whitcombe**, a small group of thatched cottages, a large thatched barn and a pretty church. When William Barnes was made vicar of Winterborne Came, the living included Whitcombe. It was in this church that he took his first service in 1847 and also where, in February 1885, he took his last. Years later the church became redundant, but is lovingly maintained as a memorial to Barnes, and in order to preserve its medieval frescoes. The best is that of St Christopher on the east wall. The saint is shown with a staff, wading through water, out of which he lifts his robe, carrying the infant Jesus on his shoulders. The mermaid holding a mirror and combing her hair is a homely touch.

BROADMAYNE AND OWERMOIGNE

Continue along the main road to **Broadmayne**, which has some pretty cottages, now somewhat lost in new development. West Knighton, to the north, is similar. Around both villages, but particularly to the south-west of Broadmayne, there are numerous round and bowl barrows, a continuation of the huge numbers to be found on the downland to the east: this area was clearly very

popular with Bronze Age folk.

Now ignore the B3390, heading off to the left towards the Piddle Valley, continuing to **Owermoigne**, which lies just off the main road. This village, too, has pretty thatched cottages amongst the modern development. The church has an ancient tower, reputedly once used by local smugglers as a contraband store, presumably because the excise men would not have dreamed of such a sacrilege. A little way north of the village is Moigne Court, a thirteenth-century manor house which, though having no crenellations or towers, was fortified with a moat and can claim to be Dorset's oldest fortified mansion. It is not open to the public.

Further north, the **Mill House Cider Museum** is open. It has a collection of old cider presses, some still in working order and used each winter to produce cider which is on sale in the museum shop. A video explains the process of cider making. There is also a collection of clocks (mostly long-case and turret) some of them Dorset made, all of them antiques; and a bed from early nineteenth century China.

MORETON AND BOVINGTON

From the museum, continue northwards, forking right to cross Moreton Heath and the railway line to reach **Moreton**. In the cemetery here – the new cemetery a short distance from the church – is the grave of **TE Lawrence** (Lawrence of Arabia), his dignified headstone the work of his friend Eric Kennington. The grave attracts many visitors, drawn by the romantic legend of Lawrence. Some make a pilgrimage from here to Cloud's Hill, his home for the last years of his life, taking the track by the church northwards, crossing the surprisingly long and narrow bridge over the River Frome (the river bank here is a favourite spot with picknickers in summer) and continuing through woodland to reach a road close to the house.

Beside the churchyard the Moreton Gardens offer a moment's seclusion. there are flower beds and woodland, a pond and a meandering stream. There is also a plant centre.

Moreton church should not be missed: it is a masterpiece of Georgian Gothic architecture and has one of Dorset's outstanding art treasures. The church was built in 1776 by James Frampton of Moreton House, and enlarged in the nineteenth century in excellent style. In 1940 a bomb fell in the churchyard severely damaging the north side of the church, but the restoration work was brilliant, all but the most trained eye failing to spot the repairs. The bomb blast destroyed all the church's glass, which was replaced, over time, with engraved glass, the work of **Lawrence Whistler** who most experts claim to be the greatest engraver of the twentieth century. Whistler's first work, and many would say the finest in the church, were the five windows in the apse which were completed in 1955, five years after the church had been reopened. Later, over a ten-year period from 1974, Whistler engraved the remaining windows. One of the most poignant is in the Trinity Chapel, a memorial to a pilot killed in 1940 during the Battle of Britain. As with all the windows, the theme here is light.

After inspecting Whistler's windows, look for the memorial to Mary Frampton, James Frampton's first wife who died in 1762. The epitaph is in a frame of flowers and is a moving message of love and friendship. There is also a good brass of a kneeling knight, a memorial to an earlier Frampton, also James, who died in 1523.

From Moreton, turn right (southeast) and take the road beside the River Frome, passing the Winfrith Atomic Energy Research Establishment on the right. At the main road, the A352, near Wool, turn left then, soon, left again to head back towards Egdon Heath. A left turn leads to the vast Bovington Camp, but a short distance ahead is **Monkey World**, an ape rescue centre. The centre was set up in 1987 to rescue chimpanzees from exploitation, but now has many species of monkeys and apes in a natural setting. There is a café, and indoor and outdoor play areas for children.

To the north of the camp – along a road which also allows occasional glimpses of armoured vehicles in action, speeding their way over earth mounds of improbable steepness – is **Cloud's Hill**. It was here that TE Lawrence lived, while not on duty, from 1923 and where he was intending to live permanently after his retirement from the RAF in 1935. It is a tiny cottage, delightfully set among rhododendrons on the edge of the heathland forest. Above the door is a Greek inscription which Lawrence maintained could be translated, in the vernacular, as 'why worry?' Inside there are collections of books and records, the latter played on a vast player. There is also a large number of photographs, of Lawrence or taken by him. The cottage is very small and can be crowded, but if it is not the visitor may be struck by the lack of domestic items. Lawrence, the would-be great writer, had catered for his artistic side well, but seems to have all but neglected his bodily needs. The making of a meal seems to have taken very much second place in his life.

At the T-junction just beyond Cloud's Hill, turn right to follow a road which explores some of the last heathland of Hardy's Egdon Heath. This is great country for gentle exploration, the unfenced roads allowing short walks on to Bere, Higher Hyde, Stoke and South Heaths. After an exploration of the heath, a visit should be made to Bere Regis, one of central Dorset's most historically interesting large villages. From Cloud's Hill turn right, then first left, approaching Bere Regis by crossing the shallow and ominously named Gallows Hill, and then crossing the River Piddle.

BERE REGIS

Today's Bere Regis is a pleasant, but not overly pretty place whose main interest lies in its church. There was almost certainly a church in early Saxon times (most definitely if Queen Elfrida's nunnery really did exist), and certainly one in the eleventh century. This was modified and enlarged by the Normans, and houses some interesting monuments in Purbeck marble, probably to members of the Turberville family, and the most extraordinary roof of any church in Dorset. The roof was probably the bequest of John Morton (whom we have already met at Milborne St Andrew) who definitely left money for the Morton Chapel. Certainly the roof dates from the time of Morton's death

(1500) and has one or two features that suggest his involvement, including a boss that may be a portrait. The roof is intricately made and has some good carvings (and some not so good it must be said), but its chief interest lies in the representation of the twelve apostles, full size and gazing down at the congregation from their position on the hammer-heads. These vividly coloured figures alone make a visit to Bere Regis worthwhile.

Also of interest in the church are the fire hooks in the porch. Medieval villages, with their thatched roofs and open fires, were always at the mercy of fire: Bere Regis suffered devastating fires in 1633, 1717 and 1788. These fire hooks were used to haul burning thatch off roofs to stop the blaze spreading.

In the churchyard are several tombs of the Turbervilles, the local family whom Thomas Hardy immortalised as the d'Urbervilles. It was at Bere Regis (Hardy's Kingsbere) that Tess was buried beside her ancestors. It is likely that the Purbeck marble tombs in the church are also from the family, though the Turberville vault lies beneath the south aisle. There is also a memorial brass to Sir Robert Turberville, the manorial lord in the reign of Henry VIII.

A short distance to the east of Bere Regis is **Woodbury Hill**, called Greenhill by Thomas Hardy in *Far from the Madding Crowd*. As with many other Dorset hills this was also the site of an Iron Age hill fort. In medieval times it was the site of an annual fair which lasted five days. Each of the first four days had a different main theme for the sale, and on the fifth day everything unsold was offered at knock-down prices.

Athelhampton Hall

Nr Puddletown
Open: March-October, daily except
Saturday 10.30am-5pm. November-
February Sunday 10.30am-dusk. The
house opens at 11am.
℅ 01305 848363

Cloud's Hill
(National Trust)

Open: Easter-October, Wednesday-
Friday, Sunday and Bank Holidays
12noon-5pm or dusk
℅ 01929 556363

Mill House Cider
Museum/A Dorset
Collection of Clocks

Owermoigne
Open: April-October, daily 10am-
5pm. November-March, daily except
Monday 10am-4pm. Closed Christmas Day-mid-January.
℅ 01305 852220

Milton Abbey

Milton Abbas
Open: The abbey house (the school)
and park are open at Easter (Good
Friday-Easter Monday daily 10.30am-
5pm) and during the summer school
holidays (usually second week of
July-end of August daily 10.30am-
6pm). The abbey church is open all
year, daily 10am-6pm.
℅ 01258 852489

Minterne Gardens

Minterne Magna
Open: Open: Easter-early November,
daily 10am-7pm or dusk
℅ 01300 341370

Monkey World

Nr Wool
Open: All year, daily 10am-5pm
(open until 6pm in July and August)
℅ 0800 456600

Day Five sounds as though it was the
medieval equivalent of a car boot
sale.

And finally in this exploration of
central Dorset we continue east, beyond Woodbury Hill, to **Bloxworth**
where John Morton, who probably
paid for the church roof at Bere
Regis, was once vicar. Morton might
not recognise the church today as it
has undergone many refurbishments
since his time. It is most memorable
for an old hour glass, a large egg-
timer close to the pulpit, which dates
from a time when sermons were required to be at least an hour long. It
is said that if, when the sands had
run out, the vicar turned the glass
over rather than drawing to a close,
the congregation would sink lower
in their seats, resigning themselves
to another hour at least.

The old village outside the church
has now almost disappeared among
modern developments, though several red-brick, thatched cottages survive. Bloxworth House, a short distance north, is also red brick. It is a
fine house, dating from the early
seventeenth century and is occasionally open to the public. The house
was used as the centrepiece for the
film version of *Far from the Madding Crowd*.

Moreton Gardens and Plant Centre

Moreton
Open: March-October daily 10am-5pm

Rare Poultry, Pig and Plant Centre

Long Ash Farm
Nr Milton Abbas
Open: Easter-September, daily except Wednesday 10am-6pm. October Sunday 10am-6pm.
% 01258 880447

Tank Museum

Bovington Camp
Open: All year, daily 10am-5pm. Closed for a week at Christmas and for 4 days at New Year.
% 01929 405096

Tolpuddle Martyrs Museum and TUC Memorial Cottages

Tolpuddle
Open: April-October, Tuesday-Saturday 10am-5.30pm and Sunday 11am-5.30pm. November - March, Tuesday-Saturday 10am-4pm and Sunday 11am-4pm. Open Bank Holiday Mondays except Christmas.
% 01305 848237

Wolfeton House

Charminster, nr Dorchester
Open: Mid-July-mid-September, Monday, Wednesday and Thursday 2-6pm. Gropus by appointment throughout the year.
% 01305 263500

Bere Bere Regis

I t is said that Queen Elfrida, filled with remorse over the murder of King Edward in Corfe Castle in 978, built a nunnery at **Bere Regis** and retired to it, easing her years of torment with ecumenical prayer. But the Queen is not responsible for the royal addition to the name. That dates from early medieval times when the village was often used as a stop-over by kings on their way to the south-west. King John, who used the village when visiting local hunting reserves, is said to have built a house here, though no firm evidence for one has ever been discovered. Legend also claims that Simon de Montfort, the founder of the English Parliament (and one of history's foremost defenders of the rights of Englishmen, despite being a Norman lord) had a house here.

3 Bournemouth, Poole and East Dorset

In this chapter we visit the eastern end of the county, the towns of Bournemouth and Poole together with Poole Harbour, and the superb churches of Wimborne Minster and Christchurch. We then head north, exploring the eastern county as far as Cranborne Chase, before looking at the possibilities for day trips over the border into Hampshire's New Forest.

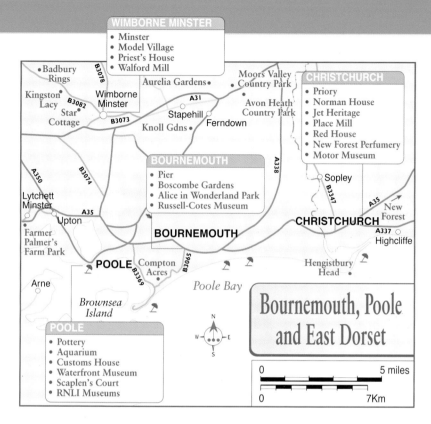

WIMBORNE MINSTER
- Minster
- Model Village
- Priest's House
- Walford Mill

- Badbury Rings
- Kingston Lacy
- Star Cottage

Wimborne Minster

Aurelia Gardens •
Stapehill
Knoll Gdns • Ferndown

Moors Valley Country Park
Avon Heath Country Park

CHRISTCHURCH
- Priory
- Norman House
- Jet Heritage
- Place Mill
- Red House
- New Forest Perfumery
- Motor Museum

Sopley

Lytchett Minster
Upton

Farmer Palmer's Farm Park

Arne

BOURNEMOUTH
- Pier
- Boscombe Gardens
- Alice in Wonderland Park
- Russell-Cotes Museum

BOURNEMOUTH

CHRISTCHURCH

New Forest
Highcliffe

POOLE Compton Acres

Brownsea Island

Poole Bay

Hengistbury Head •

Bournemouth, Poole and East Dorset

POOLE
- Pottery
- Aquarium
- Customs House
- Waterfront Museum
- Scaplen's Court
- RNLI Museums

0 — 5 miles

0 — 7Km

BOURNEMOUTH

Until the county boundary changes of 1972, Bournemouth was in Hampshire, and there were many, on both sides of the old border, who fought hard to keep it that way. But bureaucracy prevailed and Bournemouth is now Dorset's largest town, a fascinating statistic, as prior to 1810 the town did not exist at all.

At that time the River Bourne (a somewhat exaggerated name as the river is never more than a stream) flowed to the sea through a gap in the crumbling cliff line. This gap was a boon to smugglers, the Bourne's

Mouth being a favourite haunt of one particularly active gang. The gang was run by Isaac Gulliver, a man of ample proportions and, it would seem, a sense of humour as he was responsible for naming the Lilliput district of Poole.

It has been speculated that the smuggling gang's operations were known to Captain Lewis Tregonwell who was in charge of the Dorset Yeomanry guarding the cliffs from Hengistbury Head to Sandbanks (the early nineteenth century being a time of fears over a Napoleonic invasion). It does seem unlikely, given the nature of his job, that Tregonwell could have been unaware of Gulliver's activities.

In 1810 Capt Tregonwell brought his wife Henrietta, a lady of wealth, to visit the western end of his 'beat'. She was entranced by the dunes and cliffs near the Bourne's Mouth, and the pair soon built a house by the river, a house now incorporated into the Royal Exeter Hotel (in Exeter Road, a short distance inland from the pier).

Bournemouth grew relatively slowly, taking 60 years to amass a population of 6,000. At that time, in 1870, the railway arrived: by 1900 the town's population had reached 60,000. Bournemouth's first pine trees were planted soon after Tregonwell's arrival, and the town's salty, pine-scented air was soon being advertised as a cure, or relief, for tuberculosis, that scourge of Victorian England. Robert Louis Stevenson came here for the cure, and wrote *Kidnapped* and *Dr Jekyll and Mr Hyde* in a house in Alum Chine Road. Sanitoria were built, many of the older visitors being moved about the town (which had expanded across the cliffs, making Bournemouth a relatively hilly resort) in bath chairs. The reputation this gave the resort was maintained into the twentieth century: the sanitoria, bath chairs and TB-sufferers were all long gone, but folk still retired to Bournemouth and it became known as a rather genteel place, full of older people seeking peace and quiet.

The town's enthusiasm for beautiful gardens (it is a three-time winner of 'Britain in Bloom' and in 1995 won the 'Entente Floriale – Europe in Bloom' competition) and the old-fashioned feel of the sea front and the chines, merely added to the reputation, particularly at a time when many younger families were jetting off for cheap holidays on the Spanish Costas, leaving Bournemouth to the older generation.

Lately there has been a modest change: the sea front is a little livelier with a scattering of modern attractions, the International Centre is home to rather more than just political party conferences. But it would still be a major surprise to find a whelk stall. Bournemouth may have adapted to the modern family holiday of a couple of days stop and move on, but it still does what it has done best for years, offering a tranquil break in pleasant surroundings, with acres of clean sand and lungfuls of fresh air.

A TOUR ROUND BOURNEMOUTH

A tour of Bournemouth should start at the sea front, perhaps heading east (towards the pier) from **Alum Chine**. The chines are steep sided gullies cut through the cliffs, usually by stream action, though in the case of Alum Chine, the gully is wide and not too steep. On the cliff a tropical garden was planted in the 1920s, at first with evergreen oak, then with palms and yuccas and some curiosities such as sacred bamboo and Australian bottlebrush. At the top of the Chine's road is Skerryvore where Robert Louis Stevenson lived from 1885 to 1888. The house was destroyed during the 1939–45 War but there is a small memorial garden.

From Alum Chine, early morning walkers on the sea front will dodge cyclists and joggers, while later in the day it will be human traffic from the beach huts to the sands and deck chair hire staff. The West Cliff railway offers a quick journey to West

Children's Entertainment

Children are well catered for in Bournemouth, with a variety of organised games on the beach and two fine theme parks a little way north of the town, close to the local airport at Hurn. The **Alice in Wonderland Family Park** is aimed at younger children, and has a huge maze, various rides, indoor and outdoor adventure playgrounds and junior go-karts. There is also a farmyard animal corner and a theatre. All the activities have an Alice in Wonderland theme. The Park also has a shop and a restaurant. Next door (but managed by the same company) is Captain Kid's, a large indoor play centre with rope swings, adventure areas and pool-based activities. Accompanying adults are free at **Captain Kid's**, and combined tickets with the Alice Park are available. Another indoor play area is **The Magic Castle** and **Underground Dungeons** in Boscombe. This site even has a special area for children under three years of age: there is an upper limit of ten years. The play area, on three levels, is fully supervised, so parents can have a quiet coffee in the site café. Finally, there are also several excellent leisure centres in Bournemouth.

Cliff Promenade, but the cliff road is descending rapidly to reach the sea front at the pier, originally built in 1855, but rebuilt in 1880 and regularly refurbished. **Bournemouth Pier** is 890ft (273m) long and a real piece of old English seaside, with a fine theatre at its end.

From the pier, a trip inland sees the best that Bournemouth has to offer, but a continuation of the walk is a delight. About the same distance as Alum Chine to the pier, perhaps a little more, passing the East Cliff railway, brings you to Boscombe Pier, built in 1886. Inland here, to the left, are **Boscombe Gardens**, laid out in 1868 by Sir Henry Drummond Wolff, MP for Christchurch. The flower beds are changed in spring and summer. The brightly coloured shrubs and flowers are charming, and include such eccentricities as a floral 'Thomas the Tank Engine'.

The Boscombe Cliff Gardens, to the right of the pier, have been reorganised since 1993 after years of neglect. Its highlight is an Italianate Garden complete with an array of columns. An interesting sidelight on coastal erosion is thrown by the history of the Gardens, a successful bowling club within its boundaries ceasing in 1924 when much of the green disappeared into the sea during a violent November storm. The groynes on the beach on both sides of Boscombe Pier were a (to date successful) attempt to moderate the power of the sea.

From the pier head inland, going under Exeter/Bath Road to reach the Lower Gardens, next to the **Pavilion Theatre** (on the right). The theatre was opened in 1929, when it was primarily a ballroom, with professional dance partners to help things get under way. Though dancing is still on the programme, the theatre now stages concerts and shows, a Christmas pantomime.

The Lower Gardens, starting with the Town Crest picked out in

Shelley Park

Beyond the Boscombe Cliff Gardens, on the cliff top is **Shelley Park**, named after a one-time lord of the manor Sir Percy Florence Shelley, son of the poet Percy Bysshe Shelley. This garden includes an area of sand dune, specifically stabilised with heather to provide a home for the sand lizard. There are also pines and, in spring, a fine display of daffodils. The younger Shelley lived in Boscombe's manor house in Beechwood Avenue from 1851. The house is now Bournemouth Art College, but there is a small museum devoted to the poet. To the east of Boscombe Pier there is one further garden, Fisherman's Walk, with several dozen varieties of roses.

miniature plants, are Bournemouth's main attraction, the flower beds, rock gardens, trees and shrubs following the River Bourne back to The Square. The Gardens are the venue for art exhibitions in summer and include refreshment kiosks and aviaries with budgerigars and various finches. The Square was once just a bridge over the river, but now, with its clock tower and pedestrianised area, it is the heart of Bournemouth. Beyond The Square are the Central and Upper Gardens, more natural than the Lower Gardens and a delightful mix of trees, shrubs, flower and heather beds. In autumn they are beautiful.

From The Square, bear right along Richmond Hill (with WH Smith on your right). The first turning left, St Stephen's Road, leads to **St Stephen's Church** which Sir John Betjeman claimed was 'worth travelling 200 miles and being sick in the coach' to see. That is debatable, but the church is lovely. It was built by JL Pearson (one of the best Victorian church builders, who also built Truro Cathedral: though quite different, the two have the same simplicity and elegance of line) in the last years of the nineteenth century. The tower, a delightful addition in the style of an Italian campanile, was added in 1907. Inside – it was the interior that Betjeman was really referring to – the church is spacious, with an array of pillars (in Bath stone rather than anything local) and wonderful stone vaulting.

Turn right opposite St Stephen's Road, following Yelverton Road. Now turn left to reach **St Peter's Church**, Bournemouth's original parish church. The first church on the site was built in 1844, but that was replaced in 1879 by what was then described as one of the best churches of its time. Its architect was GE Street, like Pearson one of the best church architects working at the time. The tower/spire rises 202 ft (61.5m), but the surrounding modern buildings have diminished its glory somewhat. Inside, the church is richly decorated, particularly the chancel with its alabaster pillars, brass and iron work. The stained glass in the south wall of the south chapel is by the pre-Raphaelite artists William Morris and Edward Burne-Jones.

Puch and Judy Show Lower Central Gardens, Bournemouth

West Promenade, Bournemouth

Gladstone's Farewell

It was in Peter's Church in 1898 that William Gladstone, the 'Grand Old Man' of British politics took his last communion. It was also in Bournemouth that he made his last public statement. In a poignant story it is told that as Gladstone, very sick and close to death, stepped onto the train at Bournemouth Station for his last trip home. A man in the crowd shouted 'God bless you Sir'. Gladstone turned very slowly, raised his hat and said 'God bless you all, this place and the land we love'.

Finally, the churchyard is worth exploring for its remarkable collection of important burials. Here lie John Keble, founder of the Oxford Movement, the early feminist Mary Wollstonecraft Godwin, author of *A Vindication of the Rights of Women*, and her daughter, also Mary, who was the poet Shelley's wife and the author of *Frankenstein*. Mary Godwin, who died shortly after giving birth to her daughter, and her husband were originally buried in Old St Pancras churchyard in London, but when it was demolished to build a railway in 1851 they were re-interred here, beside their daughter. Mary Shelley was buried here because her (and Shelley's) son lived in Boscombe. Close to her grave lies Shelley's heart allegedly snatched from the flames of the ad hoc cremation on the Viareggio beach where Shelley's drowned body was found. Legend has it that the heart would not burn and was retrieved by Edward Trelawney and Lord Byron and given to his wife.

Continue along Yelverton Road, then bear left along Upper Hinton Road to reach Bath Road. To the left from here, across from the railway station (from where Gladstone took his last train ride) is the Langtry Manor Hotel, named after Lily Langtry, the famous actress known as the Jersey Lily after a famous portrait of that title by Sir John Millais: Lily was born in Jersey. Lily once lived in the house, and it was here that she 'entertained' the Prince of Wales, the future Edward VII.

Across Bath Road is the Royal Bath Hotel, built in 1838 and still one of the finest in town. Behind it – go along Russell-Cotes Road opposite – is the **Russell-Cotes Art Gallery and Museum**. The museum was the home of Sir Merton and Lady Annie Russell-Cotes who gave it, complete with its furnishings and artworks, to the town in 1922. The large house is a paradise for those interested in late nineteenth-century furniture and in curios of all sorts from countries visited by Sir Merton and his wife. There is Italian Renaissance pottery, Siamese swords, oil paintings and soapstone carvings, and much else besides. On the terrace outside is an excellent geological collection including sections of a petrified tree and some very good ammonites. Those fascinated by the geological specimens and curios at Russell-Cotes might also enjoy the Shell House in **Boscombe** which has a vast collection of shells from around the world, arranged throughout the house and garden.

CHRISTCHURCH

To the east of Bournemouth, beyond Boscombe and Southbourne (which nineteenth century entrepreneurs tried unsuccessfully to turn into a major holiday resort to rival Bournemouth) lies Christchurch, its old town almost perfectly preserved despite the size of the modern town that has grown up around it. As with Bournemouth, Christchurch was in Hampshire until 1972, the new boundary between Dorset and Hampshire following the River Avon (more or less) southwards but then losing its nerve and stepping east to move Christchurch and Highcliffe into Dorset. The opposition was just as fierce, but in Christchurch's case, Dorset did gain an old town as lovely as anything they already possessed, rather than, with Bournemouth, something so large it threatened to take over.

Saxon **Twynham** was built at the confluence of the Rivers Avon and Stour, its name deriving from this fine position. It was a small town, built on a ridge of solid ground in the marshland where the rivers met. But it was a strategically important place, the natural harbour formed by the long finger of Hengistbury Head (apparently scratching the nose of Mudeford) offering safe anchorage to an invasion fleet. King Alfred fortified the town and later the Normans built a castle. By the time the Normans arrived Twynham was already an important religious centre, with 24 canons resident at the church.

Twynham was given to Ranulf Flambard, Bishop of Durham and first minister to William Rufus, and he decided to replace the Saxon church with a splendid new building, the legendary construction of which gave Twynham its new name. One version of the legend has the new church being constructed on higher ground, but the builders returning to the site each day to find their materials moved to the present site. This story is told in several places, and seems at odds with the new church being built on the site of the demolished Saxon building.

But all versions of the legend agree on one miraculous happening. One of the roof beams was cut too short, failing to span the distance across the south aisle. The despairing carpenters went home, but when they returned the next day they found the beam had lengthened overnight and now fitted exactly. Convinced that only Jesus the Carpenter could have understood the problem, they attributed the miracle to him and the new church (and then the town) became known as Christ's Church.

In 1150 the church became an Augustinian Priory, with monastic buildings being erected to the north. At the Dissolution these buildings were demolished, but the church became the parish church.

Christchurch Priory is thought by many to be the finest church (as opposed to cathedral) in England. It is also, at 311 ft (95m), the longest, and entry is through one of the largest porches (a porch that overtops the aisle it reaches). From the outside the priory is impressive (if not beautiful) whether viewed from its own grounds or from across either of the rivers. Inside, the great Norman arches of the nave are superb, as is the stonework of the reredos, the chancel (the Great Quire) and the Lady Chapel. Within the choir there are medieval misericords

Christchurch Priory

with excellent carvings. The stained glass windows of the Lady Chapel depict scenes in the life of the Virgin. The reredos is fourteenth century and is virtually complete, a remarkable survival as well as a work of art.

Above the Lady Chapel – reached by 75 steps – is a room housing **St Michael's Loft Museum**. This was the town's grammar school for boys: it now has an exhibition on the priory's history. Beneath the tower there is a memorial to the poet Shelley, originally intended for St Peter's in Bournemouth. The tower itself can be climbed – about 180 steps up a spiral stairway: there is a timetable of ascents, as visitors must be accompanied by a guide – for a fine view of the town and harbour.

One of the Priory's most poignant places is the **Salisbury Chantry**, built by Margaret, Countess of Salisbury, complete with tomb, as her own final resting place. Margaret was the daughter of the Duke of Clarence, Edward IV's brother, and was said by Henry VIII to be 'the most saintly woman in England'. Henry appointed her governess of Princess Mary, but when Margaret's son,

• NORMAN CASTLE •

Just north of the Priory is all that now remains of the **Norman Castle**, a section of the keep's massive walls on top of an artificial mound. The first castle was probably built in about 1100, though the remains date from a century or so later. By the mid-sixteenth century the need for the castle had long gone and the building was used as a cattle pound. Interestingly, during the Civil War the parliamentarians became nervous of the castle's defensives and 'slighted' it, that is destroyed its potential as a fortress. A little further north, the ruins of a hall of the castle, called the Constable's House, can be seen.

The Norman House, Christchurch

Cardinal Pole, attacked Henry's claim to be Head of the Church, Henry imprisoned the Countess. Two years later, at the age of 70, she was tried for treason and sentenced to death. The story is told that Margaret, one of the last of the Plantagenets, refused to put her head on the executioner's block, forcing him to strike at her as she stood tall and proud. Henry ordered her burial in the Tower, her tomb at Christchurch lying empty.

It is sad that Margaret does not lie in her chapel: it would have been a beautiful resting place. Made from Caen stone, a very hard stone, it is still as clean cut as when it was built, a masterpiece of the carver's art. Finally, look for the memorial to Lady Fitzharris who died, in 1815, while her children were still young. She is shown reading to them, one cradled beneath her cheek, the other leaning against her knee.

From the Priory, walk to the car park in Quay Road. Now follow Quay Road to reach the Town Quay and Place Mill. There has been a mill at this point since the time of the Domesday Book at least, though the present building is later. It operated as a corn mill for centuries, until forced to close in 1908 when repair bills finally outweighed profits. It was then used as a boat shed, but has recently been restored. It can be visited during the summer. The nearby quay is a pleasant place for a stroll, but a better walk follows the mill stream from Place Mill to the town bridge, near the castle ruins. Known as **Convent Walk**, this offers a wonderful view of the Priory.

To continue an exploration of the town, return along Quay Road, passing the Priory car park to reach the **Red House**, on the left. Named because of its red bricks, this was once the workhouse but is now a museum of local history with a fine collection of costumes, toys and dolls and other items from Christchurch's domestic and industrial past. There are also displays on local geology and natural history, and the House's art gallery has regular displays of photographs and craftwork. The garden is also worth visiting, a real old English garden with moon daisies and other wild flowers, herbs and roses.

Turn right along Church Lane, then left along Church Street. First right is Castle Street where the **New Forest Perfumery,** in a twelfth-century thatched building, once the town court house, offers fragrances made from New Forest plants. Our walk continues ahead into High Street with its array of eighteenth-century brick buildings. The first turn to the right, Millhams Street, leads to **Christine's Secret Garden,** designed by a local councillor for all visitors, but with the blind and disabled particularly in mind. The wide paths and raised flower beds allow visitors to touch and smell the flowers.

Further along High Street, to the left, is the Tourist Information Office, while ahead again (beyond the A35 bypass – please be cautious when crossing it on foot) is the **Southern Electric Museum.** Housed in an old, tiny power station, the museum displays historical electrical equipment, both for the production and use of electricity. The domestic appliances include a very early washing machine. A final museum, though bearing Christchurch's name, is actually some way from the town, close to the airport at Hurn. The **Christchurch Motor**

Museum has a collection of vintage cars and motoring memorabilia, together with a bar and restaurant, but for many visitors the main attraction is the chance of driving a 1928 $4^1/_2$ litre open racing Bentley around the adjacent circuit. Also at Hurn are the **Alice in Wonderland Family Park** and **Jet Heritage**. The Park is aimed at younger children, and has a huge maze, various rides, indoor and outdoor adventure playgrounds and junior go-karts. There is also a farmyard animal corner and a theatre. Most of the activities have an Alice in Wonderland theme. The Park also has a shop and a restaurant. Jet Heritage, at the airport, is a museum of vintage aircraft lovingly restored and then flown. The collection includes a Hunter and a Meteor as well as a MiG 21.

HENGISTBURY HEAD AND HIGHCLIFFE

To the south of Christchurch lies Hengistbury Head, a plateau of high land linked to the mainland by a narrow causeway of much lower ground, and backed by a sand spit that almost closes off the mouth of Christchurch Harbour. The lower-lying land between the Head and Southbourne is cut by **Double Dykes**, a pair of defensive ditches dug in last century BC. It is thought that the dykes were not part of the Iron Age settlement on the Head (itself a continuation of man's long use of the Head's position as a fortress, Bronze Age, Neolithic and much earlier remains having been unearthed) but to protect a port which, finds indicate, traded with continental Europe: Italian *amphorae* (wine or oil jars) have been unearthed at the site.

Today the Double Dykes keep out cars, but not people. Visitors can take the land train from the car park or follow the paths across the headland. The view of Christchurch – beyond the sand spit with its vast array of chalets – is superb. The lakes in the foreground are water-filled pits, the remains of ironstone mining, the ironstone being taken along the coast to Buckler's Hard where the iron was used in the construction of wooden naval ships.

To reach Highcliffe, cross Christchurch's bridge (following Castle Street into Bridge Street) into Purewell. To the right here is **Stanpit Marsh**, a nature reserve protecting many marshland plants and birds. Further on, also to the right, is the **Two Riversmeet Leisure Centre and Arena**, the latter a venue for numerous events.

Next is **Mudeford**, once a popular landing spot with smugglers who favoured the Haven Inn, on the Quay. The Inn was the scene of a famous battle between smugglers and Excisemen during which the latter's leader was killed and, reputedly, a cannon was fired, its ball landing in Christchurch Priory's grounds. The smugglers won the day, their haul being safely spirited away. It is an apt expression, the contraband including 120,000 gallons of spirits as well as 30 tons of tea.

Highcliffe, the most easterly town in the new Dorset, is a pleasant place with a good beach between the array of groynes set up to limit erosion of the cliffs. From the beach there are fine views of the eastern end of the Isle of Wight. **Highcliffe Castle**, at the western end of the town, was built in the early

Britain's First Airshow

In July 1910 the first airshow ever to have been held in Britain took place on the flat land to the west of the Double Dykes. The show attracted many of flying's earliest pioneers including Wilbur Wright, Louis Blériot, Col. Sam Cody and the Honourable Charles Stuart Rolls, the Rolls of Rolls-Royce.

Rolls was the first Britain to have flown across the Channel, and the first man to have completed a double crossing. On 12 July he was demonstrating the manoeuvrability and handling ability of his plane by landing on a target. His first try overshot the bullseye and he decided to make a second attempt. As he approached the target he realised that he was going to undershoot the bull and he attempted to pull out of his dive. His plane, a bi-plane, broke up under the strain, falling to the ground from a height of about 50 ft (15m). When Rolls was pulled from the wreckage he was dead, the first fatal victim of an air crash in Britain.

nineteenth century in suitably romantic style. The quotation above the upper windows is from the Roman poet Lucretius. Translated, it extols the virtues of being on land during a great storm at sea, watching the struggles of the seafarers! The castle is not open to the public but its woodland and garden are, a path leading through this parkland to a sandy beach.

POOLE AND POOLE HARBOUR

The area between Bournemouth and Poole is almost wholly urbanised, the point at which one stops and the other starts being a matter, it seems, for the residents. Bournemouth's seafront continues beyond Alum Chine, passing other chines – most famously Branksome Chine. Sir John Betjeman wrote a poem comparing the chine's pine-scented air to Greek wine but, in sharp contrast, it was here, in 1946, that the body of Doreen Marshall was found.

Neville Heath was convicted of her murder in a trial that both horrified and fascinated postwar Britain: he was subsequently executed. Beyond further chines **Sandbanks** is reached, the spit of land which, with Studland across the water, almost closes off Poole Harbour. A ferry links the two headlands.

Inland from the road that runs to the Sandbanks ferry is **Compton Acres**, a series of formal gardens set among pines and heathland. The gardens were created by TW Simpson around his neo-Tudor house (built in 1914) during the 1920s. The gardens had become badly neglected when the property was acquired by Stanley Beard who restored it and opened the gardens to the public. There are now an Italian Garden, Japanese Garden (claimed to be the only genuine one in Britain), rock, heather and water gardens, and many others, all linked by paths and little bridges. There is also a woodland walk and some inspiring views of Poole Harbour. The

NEXT BOAT

Visit
BROWNSEA ISLAND
A National Trust Property
NATURE RESERVE • SAFE BEACHES
WOODLAND WALKS • PICNIC AREAS
RESTAURANT • GIFT & TUCK SHOP
STUDY CENTRE

BOAT FARES & ADMISSION FEE

Adults	£3·70	£2·30
Sen. Cit.	£3·45	£2·30
Child	£2·60	£1·10

Half hourly service weather & tides permitting

TICKETS HERE

*Above and right:
Poole Quay*

gardens are superb at all times, but especially good in spring when the bulbs are magnificent. Refreshments are available and special provision has been made for disabled visitors.

Compton Acres stands between **Lilliput**, named after Bournemouth's smuggler, and **Canford Cliffs** which is a steep chine and **Martello Towers**, a fantastic Scottish-like mansion, a late nineteenth-century folly. To the north is **Branksome**, the district from which the chine gets its name, an area of fine residential houses, and with a good park. To the west is Parkestone, another residential district of Poole, and then **Poole** itself.

Poole Harbour

Poole Harbour, with a shoreline of 50 miles (80km) is the world's second largest natural harbour (after Sydney, Australia) and was valued by fishing and trading folk from earliest times. The Celtic Durotriges lived close to the harbour, as the finding of a third century BC boat off Brownsea Island shows. The boat, one of only a handful found in Europe of that period, was 33ft (10m) long, too big to be merely a fishing boat, suggesting that the harbour was being used as a trading highway.

The Romans had a port at Hamworthy, to the west of the centre of Poole, but in Saxon times the major port was at Wareham, a little way up the River Frome (the river adding an extra defence, all coastal towns then being open to pirate attack).

As the Frome at Wareham began to silt, and with the arrival of larger ships, Wareham's fortunes declined: another port was needed in the harbour. Poole had begun life as a port under Lord Longspee of Canford (now Canford Magna), to the north. In 1248, coincident with Wareham's decline, Lord Longspee found himself in need of cash to finance his intention to join a Crusade. Longspee sold Poole a charter granting them independence from him for 70 marks and a nominal annual rent. He then left for the Holy Land and disappeared from history.

Free to develop, Poole expanded its trade rapidly, soon becoming prosperous, a prosperity aided by the adventures of Harry Paye, a privateer who is said to have brought more than 100 French and Spanish ships back to the harbour as booty. The French became so incensed with Paye's activities that, together with some Spaniards, they formed a raiding party and attacked Poole in 1405. There was a fierce battle with many killed, the raiders retreating after firing a few buildings.

Poole's prosperity continued to improve, Queen Elizabeth I granting it county status, the Charter noting the town to be 'distinct and separate from the County of Dorset'. The Civil War slowed the increase of wealth: Poole was staunchly Parliamentarian – Oliver Cromwell is reputed to have stayed at Byngley House – while most of Dorset was Royalist. Fear of a siege and then the Restoration inhibited Poole's growth, but in 1665 Charles II visited the town (staying in a house demolished in the 1960s: a plaque in the High Street marks the spot).

Two years later the king granted Poole a new charter and a period of phenomenal growth ensued. The basis this time was fishing near, and trade with, Newfoundland. Poole's ships took supplies to Newfoundland, collected salted fish, some of was taken to the Mediterranean where it was traded for wine and olives. The American War of Independence and the Napoleonic Wars stopped the trade, and the growth of Bournemouth inhibited Poole's attempt (a limited attempt it has to be said) to become a resort town. Today Poole is enormously popular with sailors and with day trippers from the local holiday resorts, as well as being a ferry and small trading port.

AN EXPLORATION OF POOLE

An exploration of Poole should start at the **Quay**, near the roundabout where cars are required to turn inland. At the far end of the pedestrianised section of the Quay is the Royal National Lifeboat Institution's **Boat House Museum**. The boat house dates from 1882 and now houses a lifeboat built in 1938 and which saw service at Dunkirk. Close to the roundabout is **Poole Pottery**. The pottery made the tiles for London Underground's stations and during the 1939–45 War was headquarters for the US Navy. Now a pottery again, visitors can watch a video exploring 2,000 years of pottery, or follow the various stages of manufacture. Children can have a go themselves, either as potters or plate painters. The site also has a shop, restaurant and bar.

Walk along the Quay (or use 'The Pirate' – a road train which runs a regular service) with the sea on your left, soon passing the **Aquarium Complex** which has not only aquaria with sharks and piranhas, as well as more local fish, but a reptile house with rattlesnakes among the snakes, and a collection of turtles; a pool with crocodiles and alligators; collections of insects, tarantulas, frogs and toads; and almost 1,000 yards of 'OO'–gauge model railway. There is also a coffee house, an art gallery with limited edition prints by major artists, and a gift shop.

The curious alleys to the right now are the old quays of medieval Poole, drained and converted to roads. Beyond the old quays is the town beam or Staple cross, standing outside the Customs House. As the plaque on the gallows-like beam notes, the original was erected to weigh goods being off-loaded at Poole so that import tax could be levied.

The **Customs House** is a replica of an earlier building (itself reputedly a replica of the Red Lion Coffee House). Opposite, on the Quay, the are Custom House Steps from where the Mayor of Poole (who is also the 'Admiral of the Port of Poole') sets out to 'beat the bounds' of the harbour, an ancient custom reinforcing the towns' rights over the harbour's fishing. The ceremony is enacted on an ad hoc basis. Close by is *Sea Music*, a 1991 sculpture which includes viewing platforms for the harbour and Quay activities.

From the town beam, head inland along Thames Street, passing the King Charles Inn, one of Poole's oldest. The name is disputed – is it a memorial to Charles II's 1665 visit, or to the landing, in 1830, of the exiled Charles X of France? To the left soon after, in St Clement's Alley, is the Watergate, another controversial piece of old Poole. Is this a section of the old town wall (evidence of the existence of which is sketchy), or just part of an old mansion?

Thankfully, no controversy surrounds **St James' Church**, an 1820 replacement for Poole's medieval church. The outside is quite simple, the inside rather more splendid: the pillars are of Newfoundland pine (once plastered to look like stone); there is an all-round gallery; and a fine collection of memorials to Poole's rich merchants, merchants who lived in houses such as Mansion House (now a hotel) and Poole House, the marvellous eighteenth-century brick houses in Thames Street. Beyond the church, West End House is equally impressive and from the same period. Follow St James' Close to its end passing the Old Rectory (or Golaffre House, named after a supporter of William the Conqueror: the Anglicised version of the name was Joliffe, the Joliffe's being one of Poole's wealthiest merchant families), and turn left into Market Street.

Soon, to the right, are **St George's Almshouses**, built by the Guild of St George in 1429, but altered and restored. The gables and chimneys are probably seventeenth century. At the far end of Levets Lane (the next left), in West Street, is Joliffe House, another fine merchant's house of the eighteenth century. Continue along Market Street, passing Byngley

• WATERFRONT MUSEUM •

To the right at the town beam is the **Waterfront Museum**, housed in an eighteenth-century warehouse and the adjacent Town Cellars, a fifteenth-century building cut in half when Thomas Street was extended to the Quay. The museum is a superb one, with exhibitions on smuggling, the Boy Scouts on Brownsea Island, Poole's history and archaeology. There are also frequent special exhibitions, tea rooms and a craft shop. Close to the museum is **Scaplen's Court**, a magnificent early sixteenth-century merchant's house which is now a museum of domestic life in old Poole.

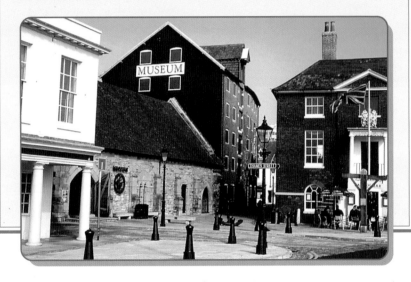

House, to the left, where Cromwell stayed, to reach the Angel Inn, an old coaching inn, and the Guild Hall, a gift to the town from its MPs in 1761. The symmetric stairways are clearly echoed in (or an echo of) the Customs House.

Turn right along New Orchard to reach the High Street. To the left, at the top of High Street, is Beech Hurst, another superb eighteenth-century merchant's house. Turn right along High Street: the plaque commemorating Charles II's visit to the town is on the right. The rear of

14 High Street (to view, turn right into New Street after viewing the memorial plaque, then first left along Cinnamon Lane) is the façade of a Tudor building, one of the few survivals of that period.

Next is **The Antelope**, a 'family and yachting hotel'. Originally built in the sixteenth century, but given a new façade in Georgian times, the Antelope was once the venue for ship and cargo sales 'at the candle'. A pin was stuck in a candle which was then lit. Bids were made, and the last man to bid before the pin fell 'won' the auction. Continue along High Street to return to the Quay.

This walk visits the best of Old Poole, but there are two other worthwhile sites: in West Quay Road, to the north-west of the town centre is the headquarters of the RNLI. Here there is the **Lifeboat Museum** illustrating the history and work of the Institute. Slightly further from the centre, to the east, is Poole Park, a pleasant area of parkland on the northern edge of an inlet of the harbour, now a shallow lake because of the railway embankment. The lake is a boating lake, and there are other attractions also aimed at younger visitors. **Gus Gorilla's Jungle Playground** is an indoor play area for younger children with slides, rope swings and a huge ball pool. There is also a restaurant. North (about 2 miles – 3km – from the centre, on the A3049) **Tower Park** is also aimed at younger visitors, but covering the age range from the very young to teenagers. The site has 10 cinemas, a Quasar laser-gun arena, ten-pin bowling, as well as Planet Kidz with slides and swings for younger children and Splashdown with a variety of water slides. Tower Park also has a leisure centre and a disco with three dance floors. There are several cafés and bars.

BROWNSEA ISLAND

Poole Harbour, once a home to BOAC flying boats and the Sunderlands of RAF Coastal Command, has several islands which, together with the marshy and heathland sections of the coast, form a Site of Special Scientific Interest. The sea life includes the European flat oyster while the bird life includes many waders and wildfowl, especially in winter. One of the newest breeding species is the little egret which first nested on Brownsea Island in the mid-1990s: the present population of the bird is now about 20.

Brownsea Island is the largest of the harbour's islands, and the most famous. There is no direct evidence of occupation of Brownsea before Saxon times, though the remains of a boat dating from the third century BC implies visits at least. In Saxon times Cerne Abbey had a chapel and hermitage on the island, though the chapel was sacked by Viking raiders in 1015. After the Norman conquest, Brownsea remained the possession of Cerne Abbey, the monks having sole right of habitation and to hunt its wildlife. After the Dissolution the island was seized by Henry VIII and in 1545 the king decided to build a fortress there to strengthen the defences of the south coast. The fortress, a blockhouse and walled courtyard surrounded by a moat crossed by a drawbridge, was defended by four cannons and a small permanent guard.

In the eighteenth century the island was owned by William Benson who planted the first trees and converted Henry VIII's blockhouse into an imitation 'proper' castle in which to live. The next significant place in the island's history was when Colonel Waugh bought Brownsea and opened a **pottery** making sewage and drainage pipes from the island's clay deposits. The pottery's success persuaded Waugh to build a worker's village for 200 employees, intending to produce fine porcelain. Sadly the island's clay was just not good enough and the project ended in failure and financial ruin.

Colonel Waugh's Bankruptcy

The immediate cause of Waugh's bankruptcy was an hilarious incident involving the colonel's nearly deaf wife Mary. During one of Waugh's absences a boat approached the island. It was full of Poole worthies intent upon asking the colonel to stand as the local MP. They called out to Mary but, being deaf, she misheard the request and, fearing that they were creditors, yelled back that they needed more time to pay. The worthies were staggered by the response and spread the word in Poole on their return. There was an immediate panic, bills were presented to Colonel Waugh and his bankruptcy rapidly followed.

The island was next bought by Cavendish Bentinck. He revived the pottery, but it soon closed for good, and renovated the church. The castle burnt down in 1896, but was rebuilt in 1901. It, together with a coast-guard house, the church and a small collection of houses from pottery days, are all that now exist on the island. Following its ownership by the reclusive Mrs Bonham-Christie from 1927 to 1961 the island, now uninhabited, was bought by the National Trust. It is run as a nature reserve. Visitors can explore the woods, which include areas of rhododendron, on the south side of the island, but the northern side is a reserve in which guided tours only are allowed. The woods are home to red squirrels and sika deer, while bird life includes a heronry,

Baden-Powell's Camp

In 1907, when the island was owned by Charles van Raalte, Major-General Robert Baden-Powell obtained permission to hold a camp for 20 boys on Brownsea. The boys were drawn from sources as different as Eton and Harrow, London's East End and the local villages. After a boat ride from Sandbanks, the boys – divided into four groups, or patrols as they were to become known: bulls, curlews, ravens and wolves – pitched their tents. The boys cooked their own meals, and spent the days learning the basics of tracking and craftwork. Baden-Powell was turning them into junior versions of the scouts he used in South Africa: they were boy scouts.

The camp was a success, inspiring Baden-Powell to commit his thoughts to paper, writing *Scouting for Boys*, and to form the Boy Scout movement in 1908. With his wife's assistance he formed the Girl Guide movement in 1910. A commemorative stone to the first scout camp can be seen towards the western end of the island, close to a camping ground still used by the Scout and Guide movement.

woodcock and nightjars, and many waders and wildfowl species, including bar-tailed and black-tailed godwits, spotted and common redshanks, pintail and shoveller ducks. In winter there are avocets. There is also a resident flock of peacocks. Brownsea is also excellent for butterflies and dragonflies and in spring has a spectacular show of daffodils.

UPTON AND THE LYTCHETTS

To the north-west of Poole is Holes Bay: a shallow, marshy inlet of the sea that served as a useful landward defence to medieval Poole. At its northern edge lies **Upton Country Park** centred on Upton House, a large, early nineteenth-century mansion. The park has good formal gardens and a fine collection of camellias and azaleas. There is a picnic area and hides from which to watch the birds in Holes Bay. There is also a reconstructed Romano-British settlement, an ambitious project that is a first in Britain. The stables of Upton House are a Heritage Centre exploring the history and natural history of the Poole area. The house itself is occasionally open: it is worth a visit for its elaborate decorations.

From Upton Park, follow the A35 past Upton, now a residential suburb of Poole, then turn right to reach **Lytchett Minster**, a pretty little village whose church (dedicated to St Peter ad Vincula) is known as St Peter's Finger! In the churchyard is the grave of Sir Francis Young husband, the adventurer/explorer who led several early expeditions to Everest after opening Tibet to the west. The gravestone has a carving of Lhasa's Potala Palace.

Close to the village, just a short distance westwards at **Organford**, Farmer Palmer's Farm Park has farm animals and play areas (one under cover and one including a straw mountain) designed for children up to eight years old.

From Lytchett Minster, head north towards **Lytchett Heath**, an equally attractive village also (and more commonly) known as Beacon Hill. Before reaching Beacon Hill, a turning to the left reaches the largest of the three Lytchett villages, **Lytchett Matravers**. The road to the village passes the Courtyard Centre, an arts and crafts centre. Here there is an art gallery and working craft centre, a licensed restaurant and a pets' corner for children. The addition to the village's name is from the Norman lords Maltravers, one of whom was involved in the murder of Edward II at Berkeley Castle, Gloucestershire. The village church was rebuilt in 1500, a brass plaque noting that the work was paid for by Margaret Clement. Margaret's will still exists: in it she gave 1d (one old penny) to each of the village's poor folk and $^3/_4$d (three-farthings) to the curate.

From the village, head east to the A350 and cross it to follow slower, but prettier, country lanes to **Corfe Mullen** where the old village still stands close to the River Stour, away from more recent development. The addition to the name is thought to be from *moulin*, French for mill, the river driving a water-wheel and mill in Norman times. In the church – a neat building, dedicated, unusually to St Hubert – the top of the font has the remains of its iron lid fasteners, the lid being to stop witches stealing Holy Water. To the south of the village there is a meadow nature reserve, famous for its green-winged orchids and other wild flowers. From Corfe Mullen it is a short distance only to Wimborne Minster.

WIMBORNE MINSTER

In 705 St Cuthburga, sister of King Ina of Wessex, founded a Benedictine nunnery on a site beside the River Allen, where excavations show it to have been formerly settled by the Romans. It is believed that the nunnery church stood where the minster now stands, though nothing survived a Viking raid in 1013. Wimborne had been an important site – King Alfred buried his brother, killed in battle, here in 871 – and in 1043, Edward the Confessor re-founded the religious house, but for secular canons under the leadership of a dean. The Deanery was dissolved in 1537, but its minster church became the parish church, maintaining one of the treasures of Dorset.

From the outside, the **minster** is impressive but hardly beautiful, the dark, mottled stone giving it a somewhat dour appearance, particularly on gloomy days, and the crossing tower being squat and curiously finished. The top is actually a later addition, replacing a spire which collapsed in 1600, and looks quite odd. Nevertheless, from an architectural point of view, the minster is a rare Norman survival and, as such, one of Dorset's most important churches. Inside, the minster is superb: but before entering, look out for the Quarter Jack on the west tower, a soldier who strikes the quarter-hours. Carved (for ten shillings) as a monk in 1612, the figure was repainted as a grenadier during the Napoleonic Wars. The figure is the subject of *Jack o'Clock*, one of Thomas Hardy's poems.

Entry to the minster is through the north porch: turn right to the base of the west tower to see one of the church's great treasures, an **astronomical clock** whose mechanism

Holy Trinity Chapel

Beside the chancel is **Holy Trinity Chapel** in which lies the tomb of Anthony Ettricke, a distinguished seventeenth-century barrister. Ettricke was magistrate of Poole from 1662 to 1682 and it was to him that the Duke of Monmouth was taken after his discovery at Horton. Ettricke committed the Duke to trial in London. In later life Ettricke became increasingly eccentric ('humorous, phlegmatic and credulous' in the words of a contemporary). He became convinced he would die in 1691 because of the symmetry of the date which read the same upside down, and insisted on it being inscribed on his tomb.

As he lived until 1703 the inscription had to be changed! Ettricke also fell out with the folk of Wimborne, and swore he would never be buried in their church, or outside it, or in their ground or above it. Later, wanting to be buried with his ancestors, he talked the church officials into allowing a burial in a wall niche so that part, at least, of his vow was upheld. From the chapel, stairs lead down to the fourteenth-century crypt and Lady Chapel with its beautiful arcading.

MODEL TOWN
EAST STREET
LEIGH ROAD
METHODIST CHURCH

Town Crier,
Wimborne Minster

and face date from about 1320. The 24-hour dial represents the pre-Copernican astronomical theory, the earth being at the centre with the sun, moon and stars revolving around it. The clock overlooks a fine font in Purbeck marble with a tall Victorian carved oak cover. Now walk the length of the church, with its lovely Purbeck marble columns, to **St George's Chapel**, to the left (north) of the chancel. Here is the monument of Sir Edmund Uvedale, carved in 1606 by an Italian sculptor. Sir Edmund lies on his side, apparently relaxed, perhaps even a little bored, waiting for resurrection day, his head supported by his right hand, his eyes open. You will note that as a result of a farcical restoration error, Sir Edmund has two left feet. St George's Chapel is the resting place of Daniel Defoe's two daughters, Hannah and Henrietta (the latter memorial tablet now lost), and also houses a rare Saxon oak chest carved from a single trunk. The chest, which has six locks, once contained relics.

Within the chancel is a memorial brass to King Alfred's brother, King Ethelred (not Ethelred the Unready) buried in Wimborne in 871. The brass, with an effigy of Ethelred in royal robes, was completed in 1440 and is the only brass memorial to an English king in existence. Also in the chancel is the tomb of John Beaufort, Duke of Somerset, and his wife Margaret. Beaufort was a grandson of John of Gaunt, and he and Margaret were the parents of Margaret, Countess of Richmond, the mother of Henry VII. The marvellous alabaster effigies are a fitting tribute to their pedigree.

Finally, follow the spiral staircase from the Choir Vestry to see the **Chained Library**, one of the minster's greatest treasures. The chains were made locally, but the design is that of Michelangelo for the Lorentian Library in Florence. The chains protect some priceless works, gathered together in 1616 and including books from the fourteenth century. The oldest is *Regimen Animarum* – Direction of Souls, a book of advice to priests – written on vellum by monks in 1343, but there are three Breeches Bibles from the late sixteenth century and a Polyglot Bible of about 1655. There are also some very rare secular books including one on the proceedings of the Royal Society in 1681 which has a description of the dodo and its eggs.

Although the Minster is Wimborne's main attraction, there is much else to see. To the west of the church (and close to the most convenient car park for visiting) is the **Model Town and Gardens**, a one-tenth scale model of Wimborne in the 1950s. This fascinating model can be explored by wandering the tiny streets. The site also include fine gardens and an exhibition centre with a model railway and old English fair.

Now walk along King Street towards the town, passing the Grammar School, (a Victorian building in Tudor style) on the right, to reach a crossroads. To the right along Deans Court Lane is **Deans Court**, a fine early Georgian house. The Court's gardens are occasionally open to the public. Turn left along High Street, going around an S-bend to reach Cook Row, on the left. This leads to Corn Market where the East Dorset Heritage Trust has an office from which audio tapes on Wimborne and Badbury Rings can be borrowed to

Priest's House Museum

A long High Street, on the right, is the **Priest's House Museum**. The house is sixteenth century, though the delightful bow-fronted façade is later. Inside there are reconstructions of an eighteenth-century parlour and Victorian kitchen, Victorian stationery and ironmonger's shops, a collection on rural life and another on 500 years of local schooling. The house's walled garden with its topiary, shrubs and colourful borders is exquisite.

help in exploration. The Corn Market also has some very fine buildings.

Continue along High Street to The Square, created when a medieval church was demolished in the nineteenth century. There are some fine eighteenth and nineteenth-century buildings here. Turn left across The Square, then right along West Borough, a superb road of mainly Georgian buildings. Beyond the thatched cottages is **Gulliver's House** where the smuggler Isaac Gulliver lived as a law-abiding citizen. Further along the road, close to Walford Bridge, a rebuilt medieval packhorse bridge, is the **Walford Mill Craft Centre**, where local craftsmen exhibit work for sale. There are two workshops on site (silk weaving and silver bead jewellery) and a good licensed restaurant.

Finally, those interested in unsolved mysteries may be interested to know that Montague John Druitt, many experts' first candidate as Jack the Ripper, is buried in Wimborne cemetery. He committed suicide in 1889.

AROUND WIMBORNE

From Wimborne, take the B3082 towards Blandford Forum, soon reaching a turn, to the left, to Pamphill, part of the Kingston Lacy estate. **Kingston Lacy** is one of the finest houses in Dorset. Built by Sir Roger Pratt in 1663 for Sir Ralph Banks, it was a replacement for the Banks' family home, Corfe Castle, which had been partially destroyed during the Civil War.

National Trust Walks

T he Kingston Lacy estate extended to over 16,000 acres, including Badbury Rings to the north and the villages of Pamphill and Cowgrove hamlet to the south. **Pamphill**, now owned by the National Trust, has been saved from development and is an outstanding example of how medieval Dorset probably looked. The Trust publishes a pamphlet with details of three short walks which explore the village, visiting the church, the dairy house, the old forge, the village school, even the village pond complete with ducks. The walks are both a delight and an education: but please respect the privacy of the villagers.

Originally brick, the house was remodelled by Sir Charles Barry (architect of the Houses of Parliament) in 1835. Barry encased the house in Chilmark stone, and added the corner chimney stacks, but did not alter Pratt's design concept. It therefore remains as the county's foremost seventeenth-century mansion, a masterpiece of elegance, its present state due to magnificent restoration by the National Trust who have owned the estate since 1981.

Inside there are art collections and furnishings to match. These were chiefly collected by William Bankes, a contemporary of Byron at Cambridge. Bankes added the Italian staircase and, with Barry's help, remodelled the rest to accommodate it and the furniture, furnishings and art which he sent back to England from Italy (where he lived to avoid prosecution as a homosexual). These furnishings alone make a visit worthwhile though the effect of some of Bankes' more outlandish ideas can be overwhelming – is the Spanish Room sumptuous or ostentatious? Either way it is quite fascinating, as are the collections of ancient Egyptian objects and the paintings. The parkland surrounding the house is worth a visit too,

having some beautiful trees and excellent lawns. The Egyptian obelisk is second century BC.

Continue along the B3082 to reach Lodge Farm on the right, a late fourteenth-century farmhouse, one of very few now in existence. The farm is also owned by the National Trust. After the farm, the road passes along a superb avenue of beech trees, planted by William Bankes of Kingston Lacy. Beyond, to the right, are **Badbury Rings**, another of Dorset's collection of excellent hill forts. The fort had two ditches and ramparts initially, a third being added at a later date (probably because of the advent of the sling.

After the Roman invasion, Badbury was close to the intersection of two roads and a small camp, *Vindocladia*, was set up beside it, the fort perhaps being used for horses. Later, in Saxon times, Badbury acquired its name and was used by Edward, son of Alfred the Great, as a camp for his army before his planned attack on his rival for the Wessex throne, Ethelwold, at Wimborne. The battle did not take place, Ethelwold fleeing to France.

New Forest Information Centre, Lyndhurst

The following resort guides, reached by moving from west to east along the Dorset coast, give a thumb-nail sketch of each resort's beach.

Lyme Regis

Pebble and sand. Safe for children, but care needed under the cliffs to the east of the town as they are loose and tide can cut base off. Restrictions on dogs. Lifesaving equipment.

Charmouth

Pebble and sand. Safe for children. Restrictions on dogs. Lifesaving equipment.

Seatown

Pebbles. Safe for children. Restrictions on dogs. Lifesaving equipment.

Eype

Pebbles. Care with children as beach is shelved. No restrictions on dogs. Lifesaving equipment.

West Bay

Pebbles and sand. Safe for children. Restrictions on dogs. Lifesaving equipment.

Chesil Beach

Pebbles. Care with children as beach is shelved (very sharply in places) and undertow is strong. In general, west end is safer than east, but this depends on weather and sea conditions. Restrictions on dogs at Burton Bradstock and West Bexington, but not at Cogden and Abbotsbury. Lifesaving equipment at all main areas.

Weymouth

Sand. Safe for children. Restrictions on dogs. Lifesaving equipment.

Ringstead

Pebbles and sand. Safe for children. No restrictions on dogs. Lifesaving equipment.

Lulworth Cove and Durdle Door

Shingle and sand. Safe for children. No restrictions on dogs. No lifesaving equipment.

Kimmeridge Bay

Grey shale. Safe for children. No restrictions on dogs. No lifesaving equipment.

Chapman's Pool

Shingle and sand. Safe for children. Can only be reached by walking. No restrictions on dogs. No lifesaving equipment.

Swanage

Sand. Safe for children. Restrictions on dogs. Lifesaving equipment.

Studland

Sand. Safe for children. Restrictions on dogs on Middle and Knoll sections, none on South and Shell sections. No lifesaving equipment.

Sandbanks

Sand. Safe for children. Restrictions on dogs. Lifesaving equipment.

Poole

Sand. Safe for children. Restrictions on dogs. Lifesaving equipment.

Bournemouth

Sand. Safe for children. Restrictions on dogs. Lifesaving equipment.

Christchurch

Sand. Safe for children. Restrictions on dogs on Highcliffe, Avon and Friars Cliff, no restrictions on Mudeford. Limited lifesaving equipment.

Then, in 1645, the Dorset Clubmen, a group of farmers and merchants looking for a negotiated end to the Civil War, gathered at Badbury. But most intriguing of all is the suggestion that Badbury was the site of the legendary battle between King Arthur and the Saxon, the *Mons Badonicus* of the Saxon Chronicles. Sadly, the name is the only link to this event.

To the south-east of Wimborne, close to **Hampreston**, are the Knoll Gardens and Nursery. The gardens are noted chiefly for their rhododendrons, azaleas and Australasian plants, but also have excellent flower borders and a very pretty water feature. The nursery sells plants that can be seen at the gardens, as well as a wide range of other plants and shrubs.

North of Hampreston, at **Stapehill** an early nineteenth-century Cistercian nunnery has been taken over as a craft centre and rural museum. The museum includes old farm machinery and tools, and a reconstructed pharmacy for both people and animals. The crafts are the old county crafts such as smithing. The old abbey gardens have also been laid out with excellent walks. One of the newest attractions is a delightful Japanese Garden. Close to Stapehill, at **West Moors**, the Aurelia Gardens use over 20,000 plants chosen for their foliage colour to create blocks of colour in an unusual, maze-like array. There is a natural pond and a collection of rare poultry breeds. Those interested in gardens will also want to go a short distance west of Wimborne where, at **Cowgrove**, the well-known artist and garden designer Lyd de Bray has opened Star Cottage, her garden and studio to visitors.

Finally, head east along the A31, then turn right at a roundabout beyond St Leonards to reach the **Avon Heath Country Park** where trails explore a good area of heathland. The Visitor Centre explains the importance of the remaining Dorset heath and the plan to increase the size of the Park's heath in the hope of re-establishing rare animals such as the smooth snake. There is a café by the centre. Alternatively, turn left in St Leonards, heading north to the **Moors Valley Country Park and Forest** where there is also a Visitor Centre, together with cycle hire for exploring the forest, a golf course and a miniature steam railway.

THE NEW FOREST

Few visitors to east Dorset will not take advantage of the proximity of the New Forest – just the other side of the River Avon. To cover all the visitor potential of the Forest would be too big an undertaking for this book, but a few sites within easy day-trip reach of Bournemouth should be mentioned.

The New Forest once covered the area from the Wiltshire border to the sea, from the Avon to the Solent. Although it was always forested, William the Conqueror ordered more trees to be planted (giving the Forest its name) and used it often for hunting. It was here on 2 August 1100 that William's son (William II, but usually known as William Rufus because of his reddish hair and ruddy complexion) was killed by an arrow during a hunt. The supposed place of death is now marked by the **Rufus Stone**. Historians still debate whether this death was an accident as claimed at the time, or a covert assassination by Rufus' brother Henry I.

Today's visitor will find the forest much depleted from its Norman size, by illegal cutting in medieval times and later by the need for oak for the British navy. Some visitors will also find it strange that the remaining forest sections are not completely wooded; but the New Forest was always a mix of woodland, heath and moorland. The forest is now studded with car parks, and from these beautiful walks explore the woodland and heaths. Most visitors will see New Forest ponies, which should be treated with caution, and deer – perhaps descended from those pursued by William I. Details of all the visitor sites in the forest can be obtained from the **New Forest Information Centre** at Lyndhurst.

Two of the best visitor sites to the west of the Avon lie on the edge of the forest. **Beaulieu** includes the remnants of a Norman abbey, a stately home and the **National Motor Museum**. The abbey was founded for the Cistercians in 1204 by King John, its church being consecrated in 1246 in the presence of Henry III. Today little remains, though the monks' refectory was converted into the Beaulieu parish church, and the abbey gatehouse was incorporated into Palace House in the eighteenth century.

The Palace House now forms one of Beaulieu's attractions, a stately home peopled by 'staff' from the 'Upstairs/Downstairs' period. Outside the house the extensive gardens are traversed by a monorail. At the far end of the garden is the National Motor Museum which explores the history of the motor car, but includes world land speed record breakers such as Bluebird, racing cars and cars used in famous films. There are also commercial vehicles and motor cycles.

Close to Beaulieu, and on the Beaulieu River, is **Buckler's Hard**. Here, the village where 50 ships of the British navy were built – with New Forest oak – has been reconstructed to portray life in an eighteenth-century village. The village's **Maritime Museum** includes models of ships built for Nelson, together with the tools of the shipwright's craft. There is a 2-mile (3km) walk along the river from Buckler's Hard to Beaulieu.

William the Conqueror

I t is said that William the Conqueror destroyed 22 Saxon villages to create his new forest, though the evidence for this is scant. Certainly, as a royal hunting preserve there were severe penalties for poachers: death if a deer was killed; amputation of the hands for a missed shot; blinding if deer were disturbed – these penalties were abolished by Richard I – and enclosing land was forbidden. But the locals did have right of pannage – being allowed to let their pigs feed on green acorns (which are poisonous to deer) from late September to November. The forest's laws were upheld by the Verderers and their assistants, called Agisters. The Verderers' Court in Lyndhurst can still be visited.

BOURNEMOUTH

Alice in Wonderland Family Park

Merritown Lane
Hurn
Open: Easter-mid-September, daily 10am-6pm, mid-September-mid-October, Saturday and Sunday 10am-6pm. Last admission 5pm.
℅ 01202 483444

Russell-Cotes Art Gallery and Museum

East Cliff Promenade
Open: At present open at weekends only 10am-5pm while refurbishment continues. It is hoped to fully open the site in Spring 2001
℅ 01202 451800

Shell House

137 Southbourne Overcliff Drive, Boscombe
Open: Can be viewed from the road at any reasonable time.

Shelley Rooms

Boscombe Manor, Shelley Park
Open: All year, Tuesday-Sunday 2-5pm
℅ 01202 303571

CHRISTCHURCH AND HIGHCLIFFE

Christchurch Motor Museum

Matchams Lane
Hurn
Open: All year, daily 10am-5pm (but open until much later in summer)
℅ 01202 488100
Bentley drives are available Monday-Thursday 10am-4pm, Friday 10am-3pm and Sunday 10am-1pm.
Booking is essential.

Christine's Secret Garden

Millhams Street
Open: All year, daily 10am-4pm
℅ 01202 471780 for information

Highcliffe Castle Park

Highcliffe
Recently Closed for major refurbishment. Expected opening times are daily 6am-10pm in summer, 6am-9pm in spring and autumn, and 6am-6pm in winter.
℅ 01425 270924/278807

Jet Heritage (Bournemouth Aviation Charitable Foundation Museum)

Hangar 600
Bournemouth International Airport
Hurn
℅ 01202 580858 or 581676

New Forest Perfumery

Castle Street
Open: All year, Monday-Saturday 9am-5pm. Also Sundays from May to September
℅ 01202 482893

Place Mill

Town Quay
Open: Easter, Spring Bank Holiday-mid-July and September, Saturday and Sunday 10am-5.30pm, mid-July-August, Daily 10am-5.30pm. Also open on Sundays in winter.
℅ 01202 487626

Red House Museum and Gardens

Quay Road
Open: All year, Tuesday-Saturday 10am-5pm, Sunday 2-5pm. Also open on Bank Holiday Mondays.
℅ 01202 482860

St Michael's Loft Museum

Christchurch Priory
Open: May-September, daily
10.30am-12.30pm, 2.30-4.30pm
☎ 01202 485804
The priory is open throughout the year

Museum of Electricity

Bargates
Open: Easter-September Monday-Friday 12noon-4.30pm. Open for longer in July and August: please ring for details.
☎ 01202 480467

POOLE, POOLE HARBOUR AND THE SURROUNDING AREA

Aquarium Complex

Poole Quay
Open: July and August, daily 9am-9pm, September-June, daily 10am-5.30pm
☎ 01202 686712

Brownsea Island (National Trust)

Open: April-September, daily from 10am. Ferries depart Poole Quay approximately every 30 minutes (the trip taking 20 minutes), the last boat from the island leaving in the early evening, the exact timing depending on tide and weather. Check for last sailing time before departing Poole. A shorter crossing is available from Sandbanks. There are also occasional sailings from Bournemouth and Swanage, but these take much longer.
☎ 01202 631828 for ferry information from Poole Quay
☎ 01202 666226 or 01929 462383 for ferry information from Sandbanks
☎ 01202 707744 (National Trust Office) for information on the island

and opening times.
For information on guided tours of the Dorset Wildlife Trust Reserve on the north of the island, ☎ 01202 709445

Compton Acres

Canford Cliffs
Open: March-October, daily 10am-6pm or dusk.
☎ 01202 700110

Courtyard Centre

Cottage Farm, Huntick Road
Lytchett Minster
Open: All year except Christmas week, daily 10am-5pm.
☎ 01202 623432

Farmer Palmer's Farm Park

Organford
Open: mid-February-December. In term times Saturday and Sunday 10am-4pm. Out of term times daily 10am-5.30pm (4pm in winter). Closed Christmas Day and Boxing Day.
☎ 01202 622022

Gus Gorilla's Jungle Playground and Diner

Swan Lake Building
Poole Park
Open: All year, Monday-Friday 10am-6pm, Saturday and Sunday 9.30am-6pm
☎ 01202 717197

Poole Pottery/Museum

Poole Quay
Open: All year, Monday-Thursday 10am-4pm, Friday 10am-12noon. Shop, restaurant etc are open during lunch hour and close later. The museum is open 10am-3pm.
☎ 01202 667556

RNLI Boat House Museum

Poole Quay East
Open: Easter-September, daily
10.15am-12.30pm, 2.15-5pm (but
manned by volunteers so occasionally closed)
℅ 01202 663000 for information

RNLI HQ Museum

West Quay Road
Poole
Open: All year, Monday-Friday
9.30am-4.30pm. Closed on Bank
Holidays
℅ 01202 663000

Scaplen's Court Museum

High Street
Poole
Open: August Monday-Saturday
10am-5pm, Sunday 12noon-5pm.
℅ 01202 262600

Tower Park

On the A3049, 3km north-east of the
centre of Poole
Open: All year, daily 10am-12mid-
night (but individual facilities have
individual times: in general the
children-based facilities are open
10am-7pm)
℅ 01202 723671

Upton Country Park

Upton
Open: Park: All year, daily, any
reasonable time
Heritage Centre: All year, daily
except Monday 10am-5pm
House: Certain Sundays - telephone
for details
℅ 01202 672625

Waterfront Museum

4 High Street
Poole
Open: Easter-October Monday-
Saturday 10am-5pm, Sunday
12noon-5pm; November-Easter
Monday-Saturday 10am-3pm,
Sunday 12noon-3pm.
℅ 01202 262600

NEW FOREST

Beaulieu (National Motor Museum/Palace House/ Abbey Ruins)

Open: All year, daily 10am-5pm
(6pm from Easter to September)
Closed Christmas Day
℅ 01590 612123 or 612345

Buckler's Hard

Nr Beaulieu
Open: March-Spring Bank Holiday
Monday, daily 10am-6pm, Spring
Bank Holiday-September, daily
10am-9pm, October-February, daily
10am-4.30pm. Closed Christmas
Day
℅ 01590 616203

New Forest Visitor Information Centre

High Street
Lyndhurst
Open: All year, daily 10am-6pm
℅ 01703 282269

WIMBORNE MINSTER AND SUR- ROUNDING AREA

Aurelia Gardens

Newmans Lane, West Moors
Open: February-November daily
10am-6pm

Avon Heath Country Park

St Leonards
Open: All year, daily 11am-4pm,
October-June: ring for details
☎ 01425 478470

Kingston Lacy House (National Trust)

Pamphill
Open: House: April-October, Saturday-Wednesday 12noon-5.30pm
Parkland: Easter-October, daily 11am-6pm, November-mid-December, Friday-Sunday 11am-4pm or dusk. Also open on 'Snowdrop Days' in January: please ring for details.
☎ 01202 883402

Knoll Gardens and Nursery

Hampreston
Open: April-September, daily 10am-5pm, March, October and November Wednesday-Sunday 10am-4.30pm.
☎ 01202 873931

Lodge Farm (National Trust)

Nr Kingston Lacy House
Open: By appointment only. Applications in writing to Kingston Lacy Estate Office, Hillbutts, Wimborne, Dorset BH21 4DS

Moors Valley Country Park and Forest

Nr St Leonards
Open: All year, daily 7am-8pm or dusk, though some attractions have different times.
☎ 01425 470721

Minster Church

Wimborne Minster
Open: Church: All year, daily 9.30am-5.30pm

Chained Library: Easter-October, daily 10am-4pm
☎ 01202 884753

Model Town and Gardens

King Street
Wimborne Minster
Open: Easter-last Sunday in September, daily 10am-5pm.
☎ 01202 881924

Priest's House Museum and Garden

23-27 High Street
Wimborne Minster
Open: April-October Monday-Saturday 10.30am-5pm. Also open on Sundays from June-September and Bank Holiday weekends 2-5pm.
☎ 01202 882533

Stapehill Abbey/Gardens/Museum

Stapehill
Open: Easter-September, daily 10am-5pm, October- Easter Wednesday-Sunday 10am-4pm, but closed from Christmas to the end of January
☎ 01202 861686

Star Cottage

8 Roman Way, Cowgrove
Open: Easter-October Saturday, Sunday and Bank Holidays 2-5pm; November-Easter Saturday and Sunday 2-4pm.
☎ 01202 885130

Walford Mill Craft Centre

Stone Lane
Wimborne Minster
Open: Easter-Christmas Eve, daily 10am-5pm. January-Easter, Tuesday-Sunday 10am-5pm
☎ 01202 841400

I n this chapter we explore the north-eastern corner of Dorset, the towns of Blandford Forum and Shaftesbury and the villages of Cranborne Chase, another of Dorset's distinctive geographical features. Finally, we slip over the border into Wiltshire to visit Salisbury.

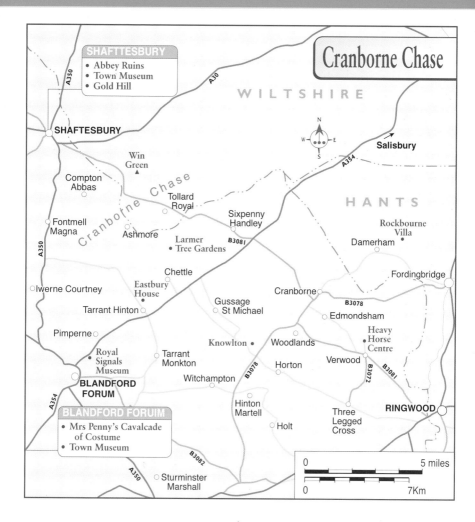

Cranborne Chase

W I L T S H I R E

SHAFTESBURY

Salisbury

Win Green ▲

Compton Abbas

Fontmell Magna

Ashmore

Tollard Royal

Sixpenny Handley

Larmer Tree Gardens

B3081

HANTS

Rockbourne Villa

Damerham

Chettle

Eastbury House

Iwerne Courtney

Tarrant Hinton

Gussage St Michael

Cranborne

B3078

Edmondsham

Fordingbridge

Pimperne

Knowlton

Woodlands

Heavy Horse Centre

Royal Signals Museum

Tarrant Monkton

Horton

Verwood

B3078

B3072

B3081

BLANDFORD FORUM

Witchampton

BLANDFORD FORUIM
- Mrs Penny's Cavalcade of Costume
- Town Museum

Hinton Martell

Holt

Three Legged Cross

RINGWOOD

B3082

Sturminster Marshall

0 ——— 5 miles

0 ——— 7Km

BLANDFORD FORUM

Blandford grew up by a ford of the River Stour, its name a corruption of the Celtic name for its position, implying a settlement much earlier than archaeology confirms. The addition to the name is medieval: at that time the town was Chipping Blandford, from *ceping*, Old English for a market. It seems that an educated local, translating the name into Latin for one reason or another created Blandford Forum, a title that has confused those visitors looking for Roman remains ever since, as there are none.

Unusually for such a well established town, little is known of Blandford's medieval history, but it was granted a Charter in 1605 and became prosperous as the market town for the fertile Stour Valley and the uplands of western Cranborne Chase.

In a celebrated and much quoted passage, Daniel Defoe described the town as 'handsome' and 'well-built' during his travels in 1724. He noted its position on the local road from London to Exeter and that 'no town hereabouts has so large a number of gentlemen's seats round about it as this'. Defoe wondered whether this accumulation of gentleman was due to the 'pleasant downs adjoining which can hardly be equalled in the world'. That may well have been a factor, but Defoe also noted that Blandford was 'chiefly famous for making the finest bone-lace in England'. Lace and button-making were Blandford's specialities, these industries, together with the market, making it wealthy and attracting the gentlemen Defoe enthused over.

On 6 June 1731, disaster struck when a fire in a tallow chandler's thatched cottage (close to the present King's Arms) got out of control and destroyed over 90 per cent of the town. Though appalling for the inhabitants, this disaster, and another that followed within a century when machines replaced the town's button makers, mean that Blandford is of major interest to visitors, particularly students of architecture.

Following the fire the town was rapidly rebuilt and the lack of development after the wane in prosperity means that it remains almost time-capsuled, the finest Georgian town in England.

EXPLORATION OF BLANDFORD

The rebuilding of the town was undertaken by a local firm of architects and builders, the unfortunately named William and John Bastard (who actually traded as Bastards of Blandford!), work being completed by 1760 and including a **memorial** to the great fire. That memorial is a convenient starting point for an exploration of the town. It was erected in 1760 to mark completion of the rebuilding and originally had a pump, both to provide water for dousing future fires, and also to

Blandford Church

B ehind the memorial to the Great Fire is the town church, built of greensand and curiously shaped due to the need to use only the original space. The Bastards wanted a spire on top of the tower, but the cupola was probably built instead to save money. Inside the church is inspiring, its Portland columns giving it a lofty, airy feel. The organ is by George Pike England, one of few of his works to have survived. It is said that George III presented it to Blandford when it proved too large for the Savoy Chapel in London. There are also some interesting memorials, one to George Vince, a lesser-known member of Scott's last polar expedition who died in Antarctica. In the churchyard is the Bastard family tomb: a memorial tablet in the church lists the brothers' buildings.

quench the thirst of farmers and animals on market days, this being the Market Square. The monument, with its Doric columns and Hellenic pediment, is in Portland stone and has an inscription that notes 'Gods Dreadful visitation by fire' and 'the DIVINE MERCY, that has raised this Town, like the PHAENIX from it's Ashes, to it's present beautiful and flourishing state'. Hardly poetic (or even correctly spelt or punctuated), but very heart-felt.

Opposite the fire monument is the Bastards' house, a model of elegance. Through the archway is **Blandford Museum** which explores the town's history. From the monument, walk through Market Place (with the church on your right), soon reaching the **Town Hall**, also on your right. As with the monument, the hall is classical, with a triangular pediment. The hall's fine lines, with its triple arches and wrought iron gates, speak of the confidence of reborn Blandford. Opposite the hall is the Old Red Lion Inn and, further along, the old Greyhound Inn, once the town's most famous coaching inn.

Turn right along Salisbury Street, soon passing the King's Arms, on the left, the reputed starting point for the 1731 fire. Go past The Plocks, on the right, to reach No 38, birthplace of Alfred Stevens, one of the foremost artists of his day whose most famous work is the monument to Wellington in St Paul's Cathedral. Further on, also on the right, are the **Ryves Almshouses**, built in 1682 and one of the few buildings to have escaped the fire. The single- storey houses, built by George Ryves for ten poor folk (who wore a distinctive grey gown: today there are only five elderly folk

living here, and they do not have to wear grey gowns), is most notable for its inscription which refers to it as a 'Gerontocomium'.

Reverse the route and turn left along The Plocks to reach Lime Tree House (on the right) now the home of **Mrs Penny's Cavalcade of Costume**, a superb collection, gathered by Mrs Betty Penny, which illustrates 250 years of fashion history.

Continue past Church Lane, then bear right into Sheep Market Hill. To the left, along The Close (on the right, and unmissable) is the large **Old House**, another survivor of the fire. Built in 1625 for Protestant refugees from Bohemia, the house has a typically Bohemian roof and chimneys. Continue down Sheep Market Hill, passing Almshouse or Church Walk on the right, named after an eighteenth-century almshouse. This narrow alley, with its delightful houses, is extremely attractive. At the bottom of the Sheep Market Hill (reputedly haunted by a headless sheep which runs up and down at midnight) is the Market Place.

Slightly further away from the Market Place are two other sites of historical interest. To the east (about 400 yards along East Street and the Wimborne Road) is **St Leonard's Chapel**, the only surviving building from medieval Blandford. Despite the name, and the ecclesiastical windows, it is believed that the building was part of a thirteenth-century leper hospital. The key to the chapel can be obtained from Blandford Museum, but there is little to see.

Slightly further away to the north is **Milldown**, now a recreation ground but with some fine wild land, well known for its butterflies and birds, which includes a long

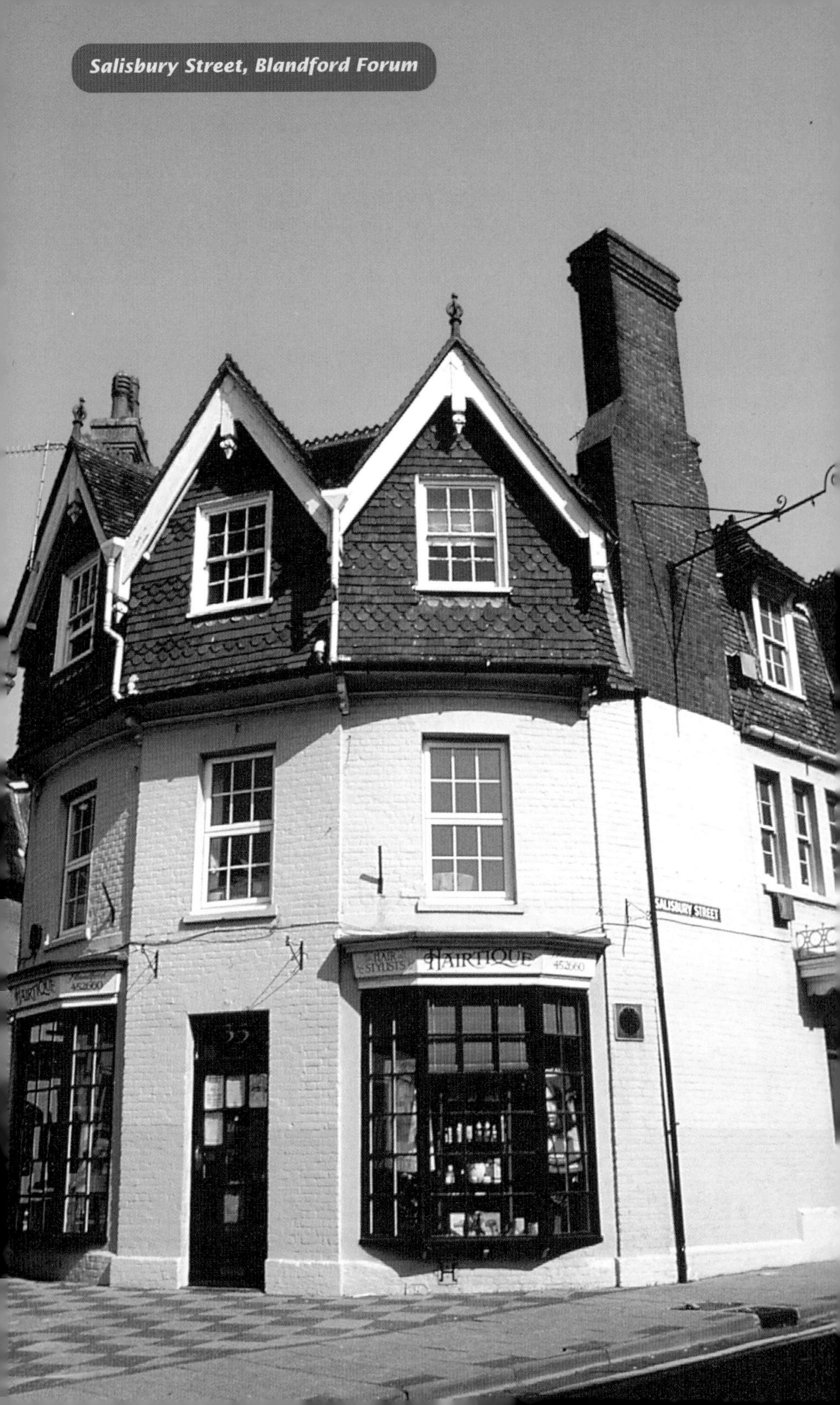

Salisbury Street, Blandford Forum

stretch of the old trackbed of the Somerset and Dorset railway. The 'S and D' linked Bournemouth with Bridgwater, Wells and Bath and was known as the 'Serene and Delightful' or the 'Slow and Dirty' depending upon the individual passenger's point of view.

CRANBORNE CHASE

To the east of the A350 which runs almost due north-south between Blandford Forum and Shaftesbury, lies a raised plateau, a chalk downland, its eastern and southern edges well-defined, its northern and western margins less clear cut, drifting away towards Wiltshire. The plateau is Cranborne Chase, an ancient royal hunting reserve.

William the Conqueror gave it to his wife who gave it to their son, William Rufus. The Chase remained in royal hands until the Civil War. After the Restoration it remained in private hands, most notably with the Pitt-Rivers family (one of whom – Augustus Henry Pitt-Rivers – founded the famous museum in Oxford). The family acquired the Chase in 1714 and exercised an almost feudal hold over their tenant farmers and villagers. Chase Law not only prevented any modernisation by the residents of the Chase, but also fostered lawlessness by preventing the proper policing of the area.

Smugglers used the Chase as a thoroughfare and frequently hid their contraband on it, a fact that often led other criminals to visit the area. In one famous incident at Hook Wood, a company of soldiers finally sent to halt the smugglers' activities were overpowered, robbed of their horses and weapons, and were lucky to escape alive. Finally, after over a century of conflict with the Pitt-Rivers family, the Chase dwellers forced Parliament to repeal the Chase Law in exchange for an annual rent. Today, despite new farming techniques, the Chase still feels closer to an older world than the modern one, its sense of isolation heightened by the relatively few villages and the woodland that still cloaks much of the downland.

To explore the Chase, head north-eastwards from Bland-ford Forum, taking the A354 towards Salisbury. The road bypasses **Pimperne**, a large village which Henry VIII gave to Catherine Howard and then, when she lost her head, to Catherine Parr. Henry's arms can be seen on the old vicarage beside the church. The other side of the main road from Pimperne is **Blandford Camp**, originally set up in the eighteenth century to house the 7th Hussars who were active against local smugglers. During the Napoleonic Wars there was a semaphore signal station here. The camp was used for training during the 1914-18 War, and as an American hospital after the Normandy landings in 1944. In 1964 the Royal Corps of Signals moved here, and visitors can explore the history of military signalling in the camp museum.

THE TARRANT VALLEY

Continuing along the A354, the next village is Tarrant Hinton, the first reached of several fine villages of the Tarrant stream. In all, there are eight villages and hamlets strung out along the beautiful water-buttercup dappled stream, the highest being **Tarrant Gunville**, reached by turning left at Tarrant Hinton.

Doggett's Ghost

The churchyard at Tarrant Gunville holds the body of William Doggett, a steward at Eastbury House. Doggett was embezzling money from Lord Temple, and killed himself when he was discovered. Some say Doggett blew his brains out, the bloodstains causing a still visible stain beside the drive. It is also said that a coach drawn by four headless horses and driven by a headless coachman stops in the driveway to pick up Doggett's ghost before driving on over the cattle-grid at the house entrance, the wheels rattling the grid bars. Doggett's ghost is easily recognised by the yellow silk ribbons that tie in his knee breeches. Unusually for a suicide, Doggett was buried in the churchyard, and when the church was rebuilt in the mid-nineteenth century his grave was disturbed and the coffin removed for reburial. The coffin was opened and to the horror of the exhumers Doggett was found to be rosy cheeked, his body totally whole, with no sign of decomposition. And, around his knees, there were yellow silk ribbons. The locals were convinced that Doggett was a vampire, but it is not recorded that they drove a stake through his heart.

Close to the village is all that now remains of **Eastbury House**, a massive building by Sir John Vanbrugh, the architect of Blenheim Palace. It was built for George Dodington, a founding Governor of the Bank of England, but inherited by his nephew George Bubb when Dodington died in 1720 before its completion. The house cost £140,000, a vast amount for the day. When Bubb died, the inheritor, Lord Temple, tried to sell it. No buyer could be found and apart from the stable blocks the house was demolished (by gunpowder) in 1775. What remains is impressive, leading the visitor to wonder what the house must have been like. The stables, converted to a house, were once home to Josiah Wedgwood's widow and son Thomas. Thomas Wedgwood was almost the inventor of photography, having worked out how to produce an image on a sensitised plate (but not how to fix it) before he died in 1835. His memorial can be seen in the church.

Tarrant Hinton has nothing to compare to Eastbury, though the church is lovely. Inside there is a fine Art Nouveau iron lectern. Those following the delightful road along the Tarrant stream now pass through Tarrant Launceston, Tarrant Monkton, with some attractive cottages and Tarrant Rowston to reach **Tarrant Rushton**. From the airfield to the east, the gliders for D-Day were towed into the air.

Next is **Tarrant Keyneston**, whose churchyard has the table tomb of Thomas Bastard, brother of the Bastards who rebuilt Blandford, and his son, both of whom were also architects and builders. To the north-west of the village, the road to Blandford cuts through Buzbury Rings, another hill fort with a series of ditches and ramparts.

The last village, little more than a hamlet and at the end of a track, is also the most historically interesting. **Tarrant Crawford** was the site of the largest and one of the richest nunneries in England, founded in the early thirteenth century by Bishop Poore for Cistercian nuns. The brothers Herbert and Richard Poore, successive Bishops of Salisbury and responsible for the building of Salisbury Cathedral, were born in Tarrant Crawford. It was Richard Poore who founded the nunnery and he was buried here, as was Queen Joan of Scotland, the daughter of King John. Of the nunnery nothing now remains, though it is conjectured that parts of Tarrant Abbey House are old monastic buildings. The hamlet's little church is a contemporary of the abbey and has some rare fourteenth-century wall paintings.

Those who have followed the Tarrant Valley reach the River Stour close to the stream's confluence. To the left, staying close to the Stour and heading for Wimborne, are Shapwick and Sturminster Marshall. **Shapwick's church** is so close to the river that it often flooded, one village story telling of a funeral when a sudden rise in river level carried away the coffin which was never seen again. The church has some good brasses, including one, to Mary Oke, from the mid-fifteenth century. Look, too, for the gravestone, in the floor of Anne Butler who was, a rhyming couplet reminds us, a 'prudent modest maid'.

Sturminster Marshall is a larger village with two greens, one with the old village stocks, the other with a (restored) maypole of impressive size and complexity. To drive between the two villages, the visitor must cross the medieval eight-arched White Mill Bridge, beside which is White Mill. The mill is mentioned in the Domesday Book, though what is now seen dates from a rebuild in 1776. In the care of the National Trust, the mill's fabric and machinery have been renovated and it is open to the public.

Head west to the A350 and turn right to return to Blandford, soon reaching **Spetisbury**, a pleasant but straggling village close to which is the hill fort of Spetisbury Rings (also known as Crawford Castle). The Somerset and Dorset railway cut through the hill fort revealing the skeletons of almost 100 men and objects, including a Roman shield. It seems that here, too, the Romans faced opposition to their advance.

THE GUSSAGE VALLEY

To continue the exploration of Cranborne Chase, follow the A354 from Tarrant Hinton, taking the next turning left to reach **Chettle**, a lovely little village most notable for **Chettle House**, one of the finest English Baroque houses in the country.

The house was designed by Thomas Archer, an associate of Vanbrugh, and built by the Bastards of Blandford, completion being about 1720. The house was built for George Chafin, the Head Ranger of Cranborne Chase whose son, the Rev. William Chafin, wrote *Anecdotes of Cranborne Chase*, a book of odd and hair-raising stories about smugglers, poachers, wardens and their battles on the Chase. Memorials of those battles – helmets, cudgels and so on – can be seen at the house. Chettle House was eventually bought by Edward Castleman, a Wimborne solicitor, who restored it. His tasteful work on the interior of the house equals the quality of the external appearance. Some of the carvings are the work of Alfred Stevens. Outside, the gardens are peaceful and include a croquet lawn which visitors can use (booking necessary).

The next right turn leads to the villages of the Gussage Valley. The first village, **Gussage St Andrew**, actually lies to the left of the main road, a hamlet comprising a twelfth-century flint church, once the chapel of a nunnery, and a large farmhouse. Within the church there are scraps of medieval wall paintings including what is claimed to be the only representation of the suicide, by hanging, of Judas. To the right from the main road, **Gussage St Michael** is larger, but not much, and is beautifully positioned. Further along the valley, **Gussage All Saints** is the biggest of the valley villages with a fine collection of cottages and a church which is medieval despite its Victorian appearance.

From the Gussage valley the visitor will find interest to the north, south and east. Southwards is **Moor Crichel**, like Milton Abbas a new village built when Humphrey Sturt, the local MP and builder of Horton Tower, decided to 'improve' the position of his house. The house had been built in 1742, but was enlarged by Sturt some 30 years later. The interior is said to be among the finest in England – the house was said by Sacheverell Sitwell to be the loveliest in Europe – but is sadly not open to the public.

South again, past New Town, where Moor Crichel's inhabitants were moved by Sturt, is **Witchampton**,

claimed by many to be one of Dorset's finest. With its two 'big' houses, an array of timber-framed brick and thatch cottages (the brick being an unusual Dorset feature) and a neat church, it is extremely attractive, a lovely little place. But do not be entirely deceived by the prettiness; there are a couple of dark homilies hereabouts: the pretty bridge over the River Allen has a notice threatening deportation to anyone who damages it, and a memorial tablet in the church notes that 'there is no rest like that within the urn'. To the east there is a remnant of ancient Dorset heathland ringed by attractive villages.

HORTON COMMON AND HOLT HEATH

To the east (more correctly southeast) of the Gussage Valley is a wild piece of country, a section of old Dorset heathland ringed by pretty villages. **Holt Heath** especially is a fine section of heath, now a National Nature Reserve set up to protect its mix of dry and boggy ground. It can be explored, but it is advisable to keep to the tracks so as to avoid the bogs. Horton Common is a higher, and therefore drier, section of heathland studded with ancient burial mounds. It is named after the village reached by heading southeastwards from Gussage All Saints.

Horton was the site of a monastery built in the last half of the tenth century by Ordgar, the Saxon Earl of Devon. Leland maintains that the building was 'sumtyme a hedde monastery, svns a cell to Shirburn', though Tavistock Abbey seems to have been most interested in the monastery. When Ordgar died his son, Ordulph, finished the building.

• HORTON TOWER •

Close to the village, **Horton Tower** was built in 1762 by Humphrey Sturt as an observatory tower for deer. It is a strange site, for despite its antiquity it looks like a Russian Vostok rocket ready on its launch pad. On closer inspection the illusion is shattered, for the tower is a dangerous, crumbling ruin. It was topped by a cupola, but that collapsed earlier this century. Also close to the village, Horton Hollow is haunted by a cloaked woman. The ghost, perhaps of a nun, is shy, appearing to be as afraid of the living as they are of her. She is seen infrequently, usually reappearing just as the panic created by her last manifestation is dying away.

Horton Village

It had been Ordgar's wish that he should be buried here, but the Abbot of Tavistock came and took his body by force for burial at Tavistock. This 'Christian' act seems to have been to ensure that any pilgrims who might like to visit Ordgar's tomb should take themselves, and their indulgence money, to Tavistock. Later a nunnery was added to the monastery, an unusual but possibly popular addition, but then the whole was plundered by a Danish raiding party. The buildings were repaired, only to be razed by the Abbot of Tavistock for unspecified reasons. The parish church, dedicated to St Wolfreda who added the nunnery, incorporates some of the monastery church. It has a sundial with a strange Latin inscription. Translated it assures the reader that opportunity is bald at the back. This is a reference to Old Father Time having a single forelock of hair, and the necessity to grasp it firmly as he approaches you. If you do not you will discover that opportunity, like Time, is bald at the back!

Circling the great heaths anticlockwise, a lovely road past Horton Tower soon reaches a turn, to the right, to **Hinton Martell**, a pleasant village whose church may have been part- designed by Thomas Hardy. The road then soon reaches **Holt**, little more than a hamlet: go east now, following the road across Holt Heath – there is a car park by the forestry plantation at the heath's western edge – to reach Three Legged Cross at the edge of Horton Common. To the left from here is **Monmouth's Ash**, traditionally the site of the capture of the Duke of Monmouth.

Now head north to **Verwood**, an attractive village close to one of Dorset's most unusual visitor sites. To the north of the village is the **Dorset Heavy Horse and Pony Centre** with a collection of shire horses, of several breeds, together with a miniature pony centre. There is also a collection of wildfowl. The Centre has a café and picnic area. Those interested in riding as well as viewing horses, can also trek on Icelandic ponies. The Icelandic is unique in having five gaits, the fifth – the *tolt* – being claimed to be the most comfortable for riders. The treks cover a section of fine forest. Also close to Verwood, to the northeast and almost on the Hampshire border, is **Cranborne Common**, a large area of wet heathland, designated a nature rserve for its plant and birdlife.

From Verwood, head west along the B3081. A turn to the right leads to **Edmondsham**, an attractive village with a delightful village pump. Edmondsham House is a superb Tudor manor house to which Georgian wings were added in very good style. The house has been in the hands of the same family for over 400 years, the family offering a guided tour. Outside there are six acres of organically maintained gardens, especially beautiful in spring when the bulbs flower. There are also a dairy and stable block added in Victorian times, and a medieval cockfighting pit.

To return to the Gussage Valley, continue west along the B3081, reaching a gnarled old oak (at Grid Reference 051100) with a plaque commemorating a day in 1552 when the young Edward VI sat below the tree (or its predecessor) and touched local folk for the King's Evil. The tradition that the king could cure the disease (a skin problem, probably

Monmouth is, of course, the Duke of Monmouth. After the Battle of Sedgemoor on 6 July 1685, the Duke fled to Dorset with three of his most trusted lieutenants. A reward of £5,000 was offered locally for his capture when two of these companions were taken near Holt Lodge on the morning of 7 July. Tempted by the money, an old woman, Amy Farrant, reported that she had seen two men among the fields of rye, peas and oats that bordered Horton and Holt heaths, and the search moved that way. On the morning of 8 July the duke's last companion was found. Since this man was not executed, but pardoned, it is likely that he told of the duke's position, and within two hours Henry Parkin found Monmouth huddled in a ditch beneath an ash tree. It was said that a mob calling for his death had to be restrained as Monmouth was taken to Anthony Ettricke, the local magistrate, at Holt Lodge. But it is also told that Henry Parkin wept when he realised that it was the duke he had discovered, and that Amy Farrant, who received only £50 of the reward money, was shunned by her neighbours until she died. The locals shivered at the mention of her name and her house was cursed.

At Holt Lodge the duke was searched. His pockets contained a watch, a purse, a pocket book and some raw peas. He was hungry and exhausted as he was taken to Ringwood en route for London. When he arrived there on 13 July he immediately started bargaining hard for his life. He asked the king for forgiveness, offered to change religion, swore that he had not read the declaration accusing James of poisoning Charles II before he had signed it. Finally he complained of a cold in the head. The reaction to the latter was swift: he was assured that a good cure for that was coming shortly.

As a strong believer in astrology, Monmouth next remembered that an Italian astrologer had once told him that if he could outlive St Swithin's Day, 15 July, he would survive the year. But the king ordered his immediate execution and set the date for 15 July itself. Despairingly Monmouth tried to have the date put back, but to no avail, and he mounted the scaffold knowing that he would now not outlive St Swithin's Day. On the scaffold Monmouth was calm, much calmer than Jack Ketch, the executioner, who had often bungled beheadings, being more at home with a rope and a common man, as we have seen at Dorchester. Ketch bungled again, missing completely with his first swing of the axe and being totally unnerved by Monmouth's reproachful look. Such a mess did Ketch make that the crowd tried to lynch him.

Before he placed his head on the block Monmouth gave Ketch six guineas, telling him, 'Pray do your business well'. The duke also gave money to another, asking him to give that to Ketch as well if he did a good job. One can only hope that this latter purse-holder took the first six guineas off of the axeman, and gave the whole lot to charity. The present Monmouth's Ash replaced the original about a century ago.

Above: Early Morning on Cranborne Chase

Left: Knowlton Church

Below: Cranborne

scrofula) arose in Edward the Confessor's reign and held firm until the early eighteenth century. Whether the boy king cured any of his subjects here at Remedy Gate is not recorded, but he could not help himself: the following year Edward died.

KNOWLTON AND CRANBORNE

Close to Gussage All Saints lies **Knowlton**, a strange but fascinating place. In Neolithic and Bronze Age times this part of Dorset was clearly important, the remains of a large number of intricate – though not very visible – sites littering the landscape. At Knowlton there are several henge sites, circular or near-circular banks and ditches. Britain's most spectacular henge is Stonehenge, a few miles north in Wiltshire, but not all such sites had stones. At Knowlton the largest henge is D-shaped, but there are smaller circles. These were not fortresses, nor do they mark the sites of villages. They were clearly for ritual purposes, but exactly what is a mystery. Close by there are a number of burial mounds.

A more curious feature lies to the north. The **Dorset Cursus** runs for 6 miles (10kms), Britain's largest prehistoric site, though it has been ploughed in places and is sometimes difficult to see. It consists of a parallel pair of banks about 300 ft (90m) apart running north-east/south-west, but not perfectly straight. The name is an eighteenth-century fancy, early historians believing it to be a racecourse. It certainly was not, but its exact purpose is unknown.

The fascination of Knowlton is that at the centre of the largest henge lie the ruins of a Norman church. The Venerable Bede states that in 601 the Pope issued instructions that ancient pagan sites should not be destroyed, but purified with holy water and altars. The Christian calendar is known to incorporate more ancient festivals, and here at Knowlton the Pope's edict was carried out exactly. In medieval times the villagers of Knowlton were killed by Black Death. The village was never re-populated and the church roof collapsed. Now only a ruin remains within the ancient bank.

North of Knowlton is **Wimborne St Giles**, a very pretty village by the side of the River Allen, its old stocks preserved behind railings. To the south of the village the river feeds a large, sinuous lake at the head of which stands St Giles House, home of the Earls of Shaftesbury (the Ashley Cooper family). Built in the 1650s but refurbished later, the house was home to the Chase Court when the Earls owned the Chase. The house is not open to the public. The centre of the village is the green, overlooked by low alms-houses built by Sir Anthony Ashley in 1624. They are attached to the church or, rather, it is the other way round as the church is later. After a fire in 1908, the church was renovated by Sir Ninian Comper, one of the twentieth century's most individual church architects.

St Giles' Church is Comper at his best (or worst, depending on your point of view). The stained glass (by Comper himself) is excellent and the memorials, some restored after the fire, are worth the visit on their own. The best is the elaborate painted tomb of Sir Anthony Ashley and his wife, complete with twin effigies, a kneeling daughter and canopy. The 7th Earl of Shaftesbury also lies here, despite attempts to have him buried in Westminster Abbey in recognition of his charitable works. The statue of Eros in London's Piccadilly Circus is actually a memorial to the Earl, the bow pointing towards Wimborne St Giles.

Now head north-east to visit **Cranborne**, the village after which the Chase is named. Though larger than most of the local villages, Cranborne's present size belies its former importance: medieval Cranborne was one of Dorset's most important towns. A Benedictine Abbey was founded here in 980, but after Abbot Giraldus founded another at Tewkesbury in 1091, he moved Cranborne's monks there, leaving only a small priory, a daughter house to his new, grand Abbey. At the time of the Dissolution there were just two monks. But despite its small size, Cranborne's monastery (as always) was a source of wealth and influence, the town becoming the local market and the local lord building his manor house here. When the turnpike and then the railway bypassed the town, it declined to the pleasantly-sited village we see today.

The village is set on the River Crane which flows amiably beside Water Street before disappearing beneath The Square. A short step away is the church, its size betraying the former size and importance of Cranborne. Inside there are some early, but faded, wall paintings. From the church an avenue of beech trees leads to the manor house, a wonderful house sadly not open to the public – though its splendid gardens are. It began in the thirteenth

century as a royal hunting lodge but was extended several times, most notably by Robert Cecil, Earl of Salisbury. It is, therefore, one of the oldest domestic houses in England. The old Chase Court dungeons are near the kitchen. The gardens, claimed by aficionados to be among Dorset's best, are divided into many separate sections – herb garden, water garden and so on.

ACROSS THE CHASE

From Cranborne, head west, then turn right along the B3081. As this road nears the A354 it crosses the Cursus and, soon after, Ackling Dyke, the Roman road that linked Badbury Rings to Old Sarum. Apart from a short section where the A352 follows the Dyke, the old road can be followed along its entire length: the short section to the south of the B3081 is a marvellous way of exploring the local Chase. At the main road, a right turn soon leads to the Hampshire border, marked by Bokerley Ditch, dug in the fourth century AD by the Romano-British to try keep the Saxons out.

Cross the main road and continue along the B3081. This is the finest route across the Chase, reaching the best viewpoint of it. The road goes through **Sixpenny Handley** – look for the old signs writing this as 6d Handley (though the name is actually from the Saxon Saxpena) – a 'new' village, the old one having been destroyed by fire in 1892. An old village story maintains that deer poached on the Chase were once hidden in a hollow tomb in the churchyard. The road now makes a fleeting visit to Hampshire, passing through Tollard Royal (close to which are the Larmer Tree Victoria Pleasure Gardens, laid out by General Pitt-Rivers in the 1880s for the enjoyment and education of his estate workers. There are peacocks and free-flying macaws, a children's play area and various building curios) to regain Dorset near the top of Zig-Zag Hill which descends to Shaftesbury. Close to the top of the hill is **Ashmore**, with its splendid pond, while a road northwards leads to **Win Green** (in Wiltshire), one of the finest viewpoints of the Chase. Win Green (owned by the National Trust) is the highest point of the Chase – at 921 ft (278m). It is topped by a clump of beech trees but still offers breathtaking views over Dorset, Wiltshire, Hampshire and Somerset.

SHAFTESBURY

Shaftesbury lies at the base of Zig-Zag Hill, but can also be reached by following Cranborne Chase's western edge. From the centre of Blandford Forum a road heads north, close to the River Stour. On the far side is Bryanston Park, the grounds around the huge house built in the 1890s for Viscount Portman. The house is now a public school.

Turn left along the A350, then bear right with it, ignoring the A357 to Sturminster Newton. Beyond **Stourpaine**, whose centre, off the main road to the left, is very pretty with thatched cottages and an attractive church, the left side of the Iwerne Valley is dominated by **Hod Hill** and **Hambledon Hill**.

After Maiden Castle, Hambledon and Hod are the most impressive hill forts in Dorset and both are believed to have been among the 20 towns taken by the Roman general

Road Diversion

Between Hod and Hambledon Hills, the main road performs a strange meander around Stepleton House, the so of detour that would hardly be countenanced today. The story is that William Beckford, uncle of the owner, dined the county commissioner when the road was proposed, and at the height of a convivial evening, when the commissioner was having difficulty in focusing his eyes and following logical arguments, Beckford got him to sign a paper agreeing to the horseshoe bend.

Vespasian. To Hambledon, the northernmost hill, one and a half millennia later came another army – Cromwell's – in search of the Clubmen who had revolted against both king and Parliament in an effort to obtain peace. They wanted none of this civil war and unfurled a banner that stated: *If you offer to plunder our cattle, Rest assured we will give you battle.* The outcome, as with Roman against Briton, was inevitable: the ill-equipped, ill-trained Clubmen were smashed, 300 being herded into Iwerne Courtney church as prisoners, and 60 left dead on the hill. Cromwell lost 12 men, and his temper.

As well as being an exceptional hill fort site, Hambledon Hill is a National Nature Reserve, famous for its flowers and butterflies, flourishing on one of the last sections of uncultivated chalk downlands in Dorset. In April early gentian and meadow saxifrage thrive, while

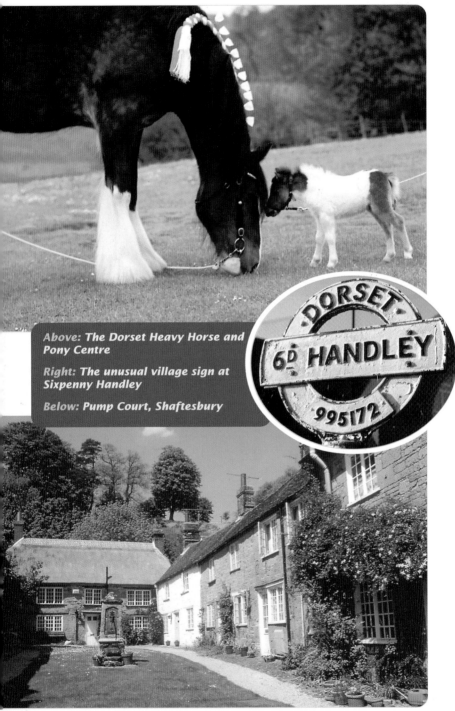

Above: The Dorset Heavy Horse and
Pony Centre

Right: The unusual village sign at
Sixpenny Handley

Below: Pump Court, Shaftesbury

Golden Hill, Shaftesbury

orchid lovers will find early purple and, later, bee and pyramidal orchids. The butterflies include several skippers and the very rare chalkhill and Adonis blues. It is also a marvellous viewpoint: it is sometimes possible to see the Needles on the Isle of Wight, but usually the view is more local, of the Stour valley and the chalk ridge beyond.

Iwerne Courtney, also called – and more usually, if less romantically, by the locals –**Shroton**, sits beside the Iwerne. It is a pretty place with a fine Gothic church. To the northwest of the village, Shroton Lines recalls a large military camp set up in 1754. Legend has it that Lt-Col James Wolfe, an officer at the camp, used the slopes of Hambledon Hill to train his men for their subsequent attack on Quebec. Further north, beyond **Iwerne Minster** – whose church has one of only three surviving medieval spires in Dorset – there is another excellent section of chalk downland. **Fontmell Down**, owned by the National Trust, is also excellent for flowers and butterflies, with similar species to those found on Hambledon Hill.

The Down is named after **Fontmell Magna** which lies below it. The village, set on a stream that springs from the Down, is the oldest for which a record exists, being mentioned in a Saxon charter. A local legend maintains that the church bells originally hung in Shaftesbury Abbey, having been buried to defeat Henry VIII's bailiffs, forgotten and then rediscovered by a ploughman in about 1800. On the Downs side of the village, Springhead is an attractive group of cottages beside a lovely pond. Continue northwards through pretty Compton Abbas, then around Melbury Hill to reach Shaftesbury.

The defensive qualities of the isolated hill on which **Shaftesbury** sits were almost certainly obvious from earliest times. Geoffrey of Monmouth maintains that King Lear founded the town in 950 BC, and some historians claim it is the site of a Celtic settlement, *Caer Pallashore*, but its true origins have been obscured by later building. These later works began in the ninth century when King Alfred founded a Benedictine nunnery of which his daughter Aethelgure was the first Abbess. In 979 the body of the boy king, Edward the Martyr, murdered at Corfe Castle, was buried in the nunnery, his remains making Shaftesbury one of the most important pilgrimage centres in England. King Cnut died at Shaftesbury in November 1035, possibly during a visit to the abbey to pray at Edward's relics. One legend has it that Cnut died of a heart attack whilst praying, but it is generally agreed to have been following a stroke while playing chess.

Later Saxon kings authorised the opening of mints at the town which helped its prosperity, and by the mid-fourteenth century Shaftesbury was one of the richest towns in southern England, its nunnery the richest in the entire country. It was said at the time (though only in a whisper or a private place) that if Shaftesbury's Abbess married Glastonbury's Abbot they would have held more land than the king. At that time there were twelve churches in the town. Sadly, the very richness of the nunnery ensured that at the Dissolution it was demolished: only in 1861 were its foundations discovered and excavated. These are now open to the public, a small museum displaying the best of the excavated stonework and tiles.

A WALK ROUND SHAFTESBURY

From the abbey ruins, Shaftesbury should be explored at leisure. It is a wonderful place, Dorset's only hill town, with lovely views from surprising places. It is best to wander at will, but the following route takes in most of the town's best features. From the abbey, follow Park Walk to reach the top of Gold Hill, on the right, Shaftesbury's most picturesque (and photographed) road. Ahead and left, the High Street has lovely buildings and leads to Salisbury Street (ahead and right) and Bell Street (left and then right), both of which are very pretty.

At the top of Gold Hill is the Town Hall, built in 1826 and, beside it, St Peter's Church with features from the fourteenth to the seventeenth centuries. Also at the top of the hill is the **Town Museum** with good collections on Shaftesbury's history and its old industries. One curiosity is the Byzant, a gilded palm tree (of sorts) that was carried in procession from Shaftesbury to Enmore Green, at the base of the hill, to the north-west, each year to symbolise the town's right to use Enmore's water. The procession was discontinued in the 1830s when the town's own supply was installed.

Gold Hill is steep and cobbled, some of its cottages raw stone, some white-washed, some roofs red-tiled, some thatched, wonderfully picturesque with the lovely Dorset countryside beyond. Down one side run steps and a hand-rail, useful if the view causes you to forget your step. At the bottom, turn right along St James' Street. St James was once,

like Enmore Green, a separate entity, but is now part of the town. Its main street is a delight, particularly the set-back Pump Court where the houses are grouped around the old water pump. Turn first right, then go ahead to return to Park Walk and the abbey.

SALISBURY

Few visitors to north-eastern Dorset will deny themselves the opportunity of visiting Salisbury, one of England's finest small cities, its magnificent Cathedral the centre of a Close that is a haven of calm. Salisbury almost requires a book of its own and a few paragraphs hardly does it justice, but here we shall content ourselves with visiting its major sites.

The starting point for any tour must be the **Cathedral**. Begun in 1220 by Bishop Richard Poore, it was completed in 1258, a soaring building in Early English style, a masterpiece of the stonemason's art. Inside, be sure to look at the Purbeck marble pillars which carry the spire. The spire is 404ft (123m) high, the tallest in England and is set on a magnificent tower. The original design was for a small lantern tower for which the pillars were installed. Standing below them, the distinct bow caused by the massive weight they are carrying can easily be seen.

At the west end of the church, the medieval clock is among the oldest in the world. At the other end is a superb revolving glass prism engraved by Lawrence Whistler. Between the two, are a number of excellent tombs. The cathedral also has wonderful cloisters (though it was never part of a monastery) planted (in 1837, to commemorate

Queen Victoria's accession) with cedars of Lebanon. The Chapter House displays one of only four (and the best preserved) surviving copies of Magna Carta.

The Cathedral stands in **Cathedral Close**, arguably the most beautiful Close in England. Originally a cemetery, the graves were moved in the eighteenth century and the ground was levelled and lawned. At the north-west corner is the late medieval North Gate. Close by is Mompesson House, built for a rich merchant (whose tomb lies with the cathedral) in the early eighteenth century. Next south is the **Regimental Museum of the Royal Gloucestershire, Berkshire and Wiltshire Regiment**, housed in 'The Wardrobe', so called because it was the Bishop's storeroom.

South again is the **King's House**, originally built at the same time as the cathedral, but rebuilt in the fifteenth century. This wonderful building now houses the Salisbury and South Wiltshire Museum with exhibits on Stonehenge, Old Sarum and the history of Salisbury. There are also collections of costume, lace and embroidery, ceramics and paintings. Between the King's House and The Wardrobe is the thirteenth-century **Medieval Hall** where visitors can enjoy a 40 minute show on the history of the town.

Now walk past the Cathedral (with it on your right) to reach the fourteenth-century St Anne's Gate. To the right are the Deanery and, beyond, Bishop Wordsworth's School. Go through the gate: the wall to the right, enclosing the Close, is contemporary with the gate, the latter giving access through it. Turn left along St John's Street, then left again along New Street. At its end a left turn will return you to North Gate.

For a short tour of the centre of Salisbury, go ahead along Crane Road, then turn right by the Compleat Angler (Isaak Walton's son – also Isaak – was a canon of the Cathedral) to walk beside the River Avon. On reaching a road (Bridge Street), turn right. A left turn now reaches St Thomas' Church, an impressive fifteenth-century church with a marvellous contemporary Doom (Day of Judgement) painting.

Continue along Silver Street, bearing left with it to reach the **Poultry Cross** which, like many of the nearby houses, is fifteenth century. This old market area is fascinating: at one time the demand for market space was such that produce was segregated. As well as the Poultry Cross there was also a Cheese Cross, and the nearby inn names offer other clues about the goods on sale. The Market Place is also the site of Salisbury's other museums, the library housing the Edwin Young Collection of nineteenth and twentieth-century paintings of Salisbury and the local area, and the John Creasey Museum with books and memorabilia of the famous crime writer.

CLOSE TO SALISBURY

Old Sarum has one of the most fascinating of all British historical sites. There have been Neolithic and Bronze Age finds locally and the site was certainly an Iron Age hill fort. It was then occupied by the Romans and the Saxons. The Normans built a castle at its centre, and a cathedral at its edge, and later a medieval town was crowded within its Iron Age ramparts. And then everything was moved to New Sarum – Salisbury – and the site was abandoned.

Equally close, a short distance to the west at **Wilton**, Wilton House is a superb stately house, the home of the Earl of Pembroke. It is lavishly furnished (including early Wilton carpets and Chippendale furniture) and has a reconstructed Tudor kitchen and Victorian laundry. There is a collection of teddy bears and a phenomenal dolls house. Outside there are superb formal gardens and a large landscaped park, together with a children's play area. Close by, visitors can watch modern Wilton carpets being made at the famous carpet factory.

The Spire at Salisbury Cathedral

Cathedral Close Salisbury

BLANDFORD FORUM

Mrs Penny's Cavalcade of Costume

Lime Tree House, The Plocks
Open: All year, Monday and Thursday-Sunday 11am-5pm (4pm from October-March). Closed Christmas Day.
℅ 01258 453006

Town Museum

Bere's Yard
Open: Easter-September, Monday-Saturday 10am-4pm
℅ 01258 450388

Cranborne Chase

Chettle House
Chettle
Open: Late April-September, daily except Tuesday and Saturday 11am-5pm.
℅ 01258 830209

Cranborne Manor House Gardens

Cranborne
Open: March-September, Wednesday 9am-5pm. Also occasionally open at other times: ask at the Tourist Office in Blandford for details.
Please note that the house is not open.
℅ 01725 517248

Dorset Heavy Horse and Pony Centre

Verwood
Open: Easter-October, daily 10am-5pm
℅ 01202 824040

Edmondsham House

Edmondsham
Open: House: April-October, Wednesday 2-5pm
Gardens: April-October, Wednesday and Sunday 2-5pm
Both the house and gardens are also open on Easter Sunday and Bank Holiday Mondays
℅ 01725 517207

Larmer Tree Gardens

Nr Tollard Royal, Wiltshire
Open: Late April-September, Thursday, Sunday and Bank Holidays 11am-6pm. Also open Monday-Wednesday from mid-July-August
℅ 01725 516453/516228

Royal Signals Museum

Blandford Camp
Open: All year Monday-Friday 10am-5pm. Also open on Saturday and Sunday 10am-4pm from mid-February-October.
℅ 01258 482248

White Mill (National Trust)

Sturminster Marshall
Open: Easter-October, Saturday, Sunday and Bank Holidays 12noon-5pm
℅ 01258 858051

SHAFTESBURY

Abbey Ruins and Museum

Park Walk
Open: April-October, daily 10am-5pm
℅ 01747 852910

Town Museum

Gold Hill
Open: Easter-September, daily 11am-5pm
℅ 01747 852157

Salisbury

Cathedral
Open: Cathedral all year, daily 7.15am-6.15pm (8.15pm in July and August)
Chapter House all year daily 9.30am-5.30pm (7.45pm in July and August)
℅ 01722 555120

Edwin Young Collection

Public Library
Market Place
Open: Under review at time of writing. Please telephone for details
℅ 01722 410614

John Creasey Museum

Public Library
Market Place
Open: All year, Monday and Tuesday 10am-5pm, Wednesday and Friday 10am-7pm, Saturday 10am-4pm
℅ 01722 330606

Mompesson House (National Trust)

Cathedral Close
Open: Easter-October, Saturday-Wednesday 12noon-5.30pm
℅ 01722 335659

Old Sarum (English Heritage)

Open: Easter-October, daily 10am-6pm
November-Easter, daily 10am-4pm
℅ 01722 335398

The Royal Gloucestershire, Berkshire and Wiltshire Regiment Museum

Cathedral Close
Open: March-November, daily 10am-5pm
℅ 01722 414536

Salisbury and South Wiltshire Museum

The King's House
Cathedral Close
Open: All year, Monday-Saturday 10am-5pm. Also open on Sunday 2-5pm during July and August
℅ 01722 332151

Salisbury in Light and Sound

Medieval Hall
Cathedral Close
Open: April-September daily shows at 11am, 1pm, 2pm, 3pm, 4pm amd 5pm
℅ 01722 412472

Wilton Carpet Factory

Wilton
Open: All year, Monday-Saturday 9.30am-5.30pm, Sunday 11am-5pm
℅ 01722 744919/742733

Wilton House

Wilton
Open: Easter-October, daily 10.30am-5.30pm
℅ 01722 746729

To the west, the Somerset border pushing south, and the sea pushing northwards forming Lyme Bay, compress Dorset: at Golden Cap it is barely 8 miles (13km) from the shore to Somerset. In this chapter we explore this area of Dorset, heading east towards Dorchester, firstly inland, then along one of Britain's most interesting sections of coastline.

BEAMINSTER AND THE MARSHWOOD VALE

Occupying a lovely position in a hollow of Dorset's western downs, **Beaminster** (pronounced Beminster, sometimes even Bem'ster by the locals) is one of the best of all the county's small towns. Originally a market town, Beaminster became a leading town for the making of woollen cloth and, later, for making sailcloth and ropes. Like many other local towns and villages, Beaminster was at the mercy of fire. In 1644 it was deliberately set ablaze by an occupying Royalist force and there was another bad fire in 1684. Then, in 1781, a major fire devastated the centre of the town which, as a consequence, is now occupied by a harmonious group of buildings dating from the late eighteenth and early nineteenth centuries. Here, too, the centre was spared further development at the expense of the townsfolk: the railway missed the town and its prosperity declined.

As elsewhere, this tragedy for the townsfolk is a bonus for the visitor: lovers of Hardy's novels will be especially pleased as Beaminster is the age of the Wessex of the novels, an exact copy of the physical backdrop of the stories. Those Hardy pilgrims who follow Hogshill Street to Clay Lane will be rewarded by a view of Beaminster's Old Rectory. In *Tess of the d'Urbervilles* this is Emminster Vicarage where Angel Clare's parents lived.

Hogshill Street is ahead and right if you stand in The Square with the church on your left. The Square, once the centre of Beaminster's market, is now dominated by 'Julia' as the market house/memorial at its centre is known. Julia, more correctly the Robinson Memorial, was raised in 1906 by Vincent Robinson of Parnham House as a memorial to his sister. On the corner of Hogshill Street is the Pickwick Inn, formerly the King's Arms, the town's most important inn. The inn was severely damaged in the 1781 fire which is said to have started in a tinsmith's workshop in its rear courtyard.

Head down Church Street – the Eight Bells was the Five Bells until more bells were added to the church's peal – to visit **St Mary's Church**, with the most spectacular tower of any of Dorset's churches, a 100-ft (33m) tower beautifully close-buttressed and decorated, and topped by pinnacles. As with most of the town, the church and tower is built of lovely yellow limestone which enhances its attractiveness. Rather less attractive is a local story that, during the Bloody Assizes, several local men were hanged from the tower. At the end of Church Street, beyond the church, the little building was the town almshouse until the middle of this century – as the inscription notes – and was restored to celebrate Queen Elizabeth's Silver Jubilee in 1977.

Turn right along Shadrack Street. At the top, on the left, **Daniels House** was the home of James Daniel, who is buried near Stoke Abbot. Turn right (the Old Rectory is to the left) to return to The Square. Elsewhere in the town, the

James Daniel – saved by the straw

One of the men who fought with the Duke of Monmouth at Sedgemoor was James Daniel, a Beaminster lawyer. After the battle, Daniel fled back to his house in the town's Shadrack Street. There he learned that soldiers were on their way to arrest him. Knowing the likely outcome of capture, Daniel fled again, this time to Knowle Farm on the road towards Stoke Abbott. But the soldiers had been tipped off about his escape and were close behind him. Daniel hid beneath straw in a barn. When the soldiers searched the barn they plunged their bayonets (in best Hollywood tradition) into the straw, and (in equally good tradition) missed him every time.

After his escape, Daniel stayed in hiding for several years, but was eventually able to return home and to practise law again. Convinced that his life had been spared by God he decided he must be buried at the site of his escape: he bought the barn, demolished it and turned the site into a cemetery for himself and his descendants. It can be visited with the farm owner's permission.

museum, housed in an old chapel, explores Beaminster's history.

Close to Beaminster are several sites which will be of great interest to visitors. To the north, off the A3066, are **Horn Park Gardens**, several beautiful gardens separated by trees and shrubs, surrounding a house designed by a pupil of Sir Edwin Lutyens. The Bluebell Wood and Wildflower Meadow are particularly good (the latter with over 160 different species, including orchids). Many of the unusual plants seen in the Gardens are also for sale.

About the same distance to the south, just off the A3066, is **Parnham House**, a really lovely mansion surrounded by woodland but with formal gardens to its front. The house is an Elizabethan manor enlarged later and then refurbished by John Nash in about 1810. With its warm stone, Parnham is breathtaking. Inside it is equally attractive: part of the house is used to display furniture made by the owner John Makepeace and his students. Visitors can watch the furniture being made and buy pieces at the studio shop. The house also has a café. Equally good are the gardens which include an interesting tree trail, on which the craft uses of each identified species is explained.

Just south of Parnham is **Netherbury** whose church contains the weathered effigy of Sir Thomas More, not the famous one, though a relative. This Sir Thomas was Sheriff of Dorset and a renowned eccentric who one day released all the prisoners in Dorchester jail on a whim. The horrified locals complained, and Sir Thomas only retained his position at the cost of his house, Melplash Court, which stands to the south-east of the village.

Now head east, taking the B3163, then turning right, to reach **Mapperton Gardens**. The gardens surround a fine Jacobean manor house with its own church. Close to the house are a large croquet lawn and an orangery. Below these are the formal part of the gardens, which includes topiary, grottoes and ponds laid out in the 1920s. There are two fish ponds and, beyond, a wild garden planted in the 1960s, and woodland and spring gardens.

WEST OF BEAMINSTER

To the west of Beaminster are a handful of villages on the last of Dorset downland. Take the B3163 to **Broadwindsor**, a terraced village with a fine church. Thomas Fuller was the vicar here just before the Civil War. He was a poet and writer (writing histories of the Crusades and 'the worthies of England') and was well loved for his ability to preach sermons which mixed profound messages and humour. His congregations are said to have fallen about laughing at times. When the Civil War began, Fuller, a staunch Royalist, became chaplain to King Charles. He was replaced by John Pinney who, legend has it, was challenged to (and won) a preaching competition in a local field by an Anabaptist traveller. Fuller, we can assume, would have beaten both of them.

It may have been Fuller's influence that brought Charles II to Broadwindsor in 1651. He did not sleep in the house which carries the plaque, but in an inn which stood on the same site before it was destroyed by fire.

Broadwindsor's **Craft and Design Centre** is a collection of local craftsmen and artists on a site with shop outlets and a good restaurant. To the south of the village, Lewesdon Hill, a National Trust property, is a

marvellous viewpoint, but quite a steep climb. To the south-east the view is over **Stoke Abbott**, a pretty village with a fine oak tree at its heart, from close to which two springs emerge, one feeding an animal trough, the other the village's water supply until this century. One village inhabitant, James Searle, has the unenviable record of being the last man to have been publicly hanged.

To the south of Pilsdon Pen is **Bettiscombe**, where the Manor is reputedly the home of a screaming skull, the screaming heard each time someone attempts to remove the skull from its niche in the house. Close by, **Marshwood** is the village which gives its name to the Vale but is set on the wooded surround rather than on the barren floor. To the south-west are two further hill forts, **Lambert's Castle** and **Coney's Castle**, each now partially wooded, but with fine views to the Vale and the sea.

North of Pilsdon, at the base of the downland scarp is the village of **Thorncombe**. In the church here are the best brasses in the county (or even in the country), to Sir Thomas Brook (died 1419) and his wife Joan, who died in 1437. The two figures are over 5ft (1.5m) high.

Beyond Thorncombe is **Forde Abbey**, set right on the Somerset border. Forde was founded in 1141 by twelve Cistercian monks after they had failed in an attempt to found an abbey in Devon. The abbey grew in wealth and influence, but had declined to the same number of monks at the Dissolution though building work continued almost to the day Henry VIII's men arrived. Forde was partially demolished, what was left being

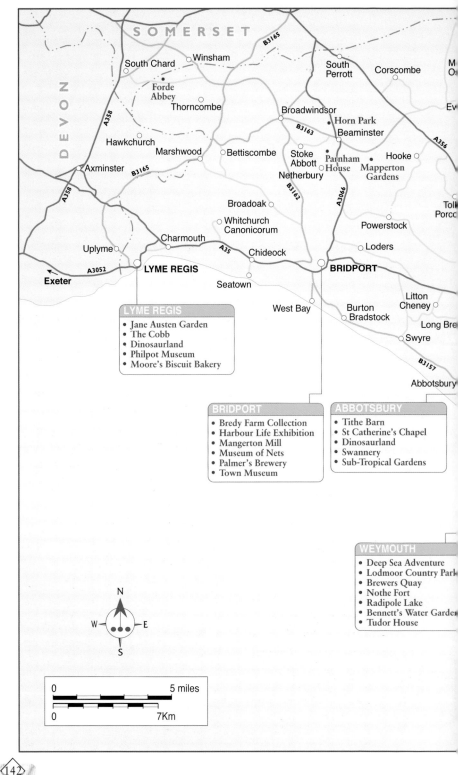

SOMERSET

DEVON

South Chard
Winsham
B3165
South Perrott
Corscombe
M
Os

Forde Abbey
Thorncombe
Broadwindsor
B3163
Horn Park
Beaminster
Ev

A358

Hawkchurch
Marshwood
Bettiscombe
Stoke Abbott
Netherbury
Parnham House
Mapperton Gardens
Hooke
A356

Axminster
B3165
A358

Broadoak
Whitchurch Canonicorum
Powerstock
Loders
Toll Porco

Uplyme
Charmouth
A35
Chideock
BRIDPORT

A3052
Exeter
LYME REGIS
Seatown
West Bay
Burton Bradstock
Litton Cheney
Long Bre
Swyre
B3157
Abbotsbury

LYME REGIS
- Jane Austen Garden
- The Cobb
- Dinosaurland
- Philpot Museum
- Moore's Biscuit Bakery

BRIDPORT
- Bredy Farm Collection
- Harbour Life Exhibition
- Mangerton Mill
- Museum of Nets
- Palmer's Brewery
- Town Museum

ABBOTSBURY
- Tithe Barn
- St Catherine's Chapel
- Dinosaurland
- Swannery
- Sub-Tropical Gardens

WEYMOUTH
- Deep Sea Adventure
- Lodmoor Country Park
- Brewers Quay
- Nothe Fort
- Radipole Lake
- Bennett's Water Garden
- Tudor House

N
W — E
S

0 — 5 miles
0 — 7Km

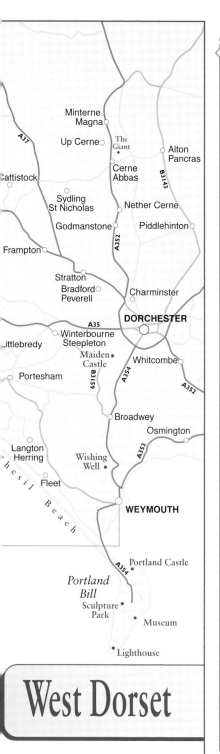

Minterne
Magna

A37

Up Cerne

The
Giant

Alton
Pancras

Cerne
Abbas

B3143

Cattistock

Sydling
St Nicholas

Nether Cerne

Godmanstone

Piddlehinton

A352

Frampton

Stratton
Bradford
Peverell

Charminster

DORCHESTER

A35

Winterbourne
Steepleton

Littlebredy

Maiden
Castle

Whitcombe

B3159

A354

A352

Portesham

Broadwey

Osmington

Langton
Herring

Wishing
Well

A353

Fleet

WEYMOUTH

Chesil Beach

Portland Castle

A354

*Portland
Bill*

Sculpture
Park

Museum

Lighthouse

West Dorset

To the west of Broadwindsor, follow the B3164 to reach **Pilsdon Pen**, the highest hill of Dorset, standing 907 ft (279m) above the sea, 93 ft (28m) short of being a mountain. Its south-eastern tip shows the remains of a hill fort, and from the ramparts there is a view that is unrivalled in west Dorset. Below is the Marshwood Vale – famous for its oaks, but with a poor clay soil – while beyond a gap in the Vale's encircling hills is the sea.

View to the coast from the Pilsdon Pen path

In 1795, Racedown, the house on the western edge of the Pen was offered for rent, with 'two parlours... four excellent bed-chambers ... and two necessaries' and was taken by one William Wordsworth, poet. Here he wrote The Borderers and often he climbed to the Pen to survey Marshwood Vale. It was, he maintained, the finest view in all England, while his sister Dorothy claimed that Broadwindsor was 'the place dearest to my recollection upon the whole surface of the Island'.

eventually sold, in 1649, to Edmund Prideaux, Attorney-General to Oliver Cromwell. Edmund's son entertained the Duke of Monmouth at Forde in 1680. Though this visit was legal, Prideaux was seen (probably rightly) as a Monmouth sympathiser and was imprisoned after Sedgemoor. He was released, but fined a sum that ruined him. Later, the house was rented by the philosopher Jeremy Bentham.

The house in which Bentham stayed was the work of the first Edmund Prideaux, who incorporated what remained of the Abbey into his private house. As the abbey church had been demolished, Prideaux turned the old Chapter House into a private chapel. The house itself incorporates the Great Hall (unfinished at the Dissolution), the monks' refectory and dormitory. The result is splendid – many experts claim Forde to be among the best mid-seventeenth century houses in Britain – but slightly formal. Of the furnishings, the greatest treasures are the Mortlake Tapestries, based on Raphael's works for Pope Leo X, a present from Queen Anne to Sir Francis Gwyn, the owner in 1702.

The abbey's gardens are as attractive as the building, with trees and shrubs surrounding a large lake and excellent flower beds. In spring the crocuses and daffodils are beautiful.

BEAMINSTER TO DORCHESTER

From Beaminster, take the B3163 which heads east, then north, passing the turn to Mapperton Gardens to reach the A356. To the left from here there is another excellent viewpoint, at Wynyard's Gap, and

South Perrott, a picturesque village somewhat marred by the main road.

Also left (and then right, down a steep hill) is Corscombe, another attractive village. It was once the home of Thomas Hollis, the eighteenth- century free thinker who endowed several universities (including Harvard in the USA) and published ideas on diet that were centuries ahead of their time. He believed among other things, that it was best to limit consumption of sugar, butter and alcohol. Hollis was a republican who called one of his coppices Stuart because he enjoyed beheading it! Court Farm at the northern edge of the village was once a Grange of Sherborne Abbey.

But we are turning right, towards Dorchester. Almost immediately a left turn – Benville Lane – can be followed down into a shallow valley, then up again to reach Evershot and the Melbury villages. Evershot is one of Dorset's highest villages and is Evershead in *Tess of the d'Urbervilles*. Hardy changed the inn's name to the Sow and Acorn. At the east end of the village, Melbury Gate leads to Melbury Sampford, a vast, early sixteenth-century house built for Sir Giles Strangeways. The house is rarely open to the public. If it is, take the opportunity to see the central hexagonal tower and the lovely church beside the house. The house can also be seen by following the public footpath through its park.

To the north of the house is Melbury Osmond where Thomas Hardy's mother was born, and where his parents were married in 1839. Not surprisingly, Hardy had an affection for the area and it is used in *The Woodlanders*, the village being called King's Hintock. The church has been 'restored' since then, but one curio which survived this work is the Saxon carving on the north church wall. It is said to be 'Abraham's ram caught in a thicket', but that interpretation requires imagination.

Melbury Bubb, on the eastern side of the A37, is a pleasant village with a rare Saxon font. It is believed that the font was once a cross shaft, but was hollowed and re-used as a font. The carved animals – primitive but energetic – are upside down. This must be deliberate as it can hardly have be an accident – but why? Just north of the village is the smallest church in Dorset (and the second smallest in England) measuring only 29 ft by 13 ft (9m by 3.9m). It is dedicated to St Edwold, a Saxon prince who was buried at Cerne Abbas, and is now disused.

Visitors who have explored the Melbury villages can now follow the A37 to Dorchester. It follows the course of a Roman road and descends Break Heart Hill. From the plateau-like summit ridge of the hill a left turn reaches (at Grid Reference 631038) the Cross and Hand, a site of legends. At Batcombe, below the stone, another legend has the local squire, a 'conjuror' (warlock), leaping his horse over the church, breaking off one of the tower's pinnacles as he did. The legend is probably based on the real fall of a pinnacle as one has certainly been repaired.

Further along the top of Break Heart Hill another left turn leads to **Sydling St Nicholas**, sitting, wonderfully picturesque, in a little valley. Sir Francis Walsingham, Elizabeth I's Secretary of State, was once the lord of the manor here and it may have been he who built the huge tithe

The Cross and Hand Stone

This stone pillar, whose origins are uncertain (it may be a Saxon boundary post), is associated with several local legends. The hand of the name is said to be engraved on it, but it is no longer visible, while the cross refers to a legend that the pillar is the shaft of an ancient cross.

One legend relating to the stone is that a priest from Cerne Abbas, called to minister to a dying man, lost the sacrament during his journey through a wild night. Returning to find it, the priest discovers it lit by a ray of light from heaven and surrounded by a protective circle of animals. Hardy used this legend as the basis of a poem, and another legend for a section in *Tess of the d'Urbervilles*. In that tale a local criminal is nailed by the hands to the pillar, then hanged and buried beneath it. Hardy has Tess swear never to tempt Alec again at the pillar, in the mistaken belief that it is the shaft of a cross.

barn. In the church there is a memorial to Lady Elizabeth Smith – somewhat macabre, her husband rising from a tomb at the base – who, legend has it, lost nine children before any of them could be christened. At the base of Break Heart Hill the A37 reaches the A356.

Back on the A356, a right turn descends to **Hooke**, a pretty village close to which is Hooke Park, a large area of woodland in which deer

The Julia or Robinson memorial at Beaminster

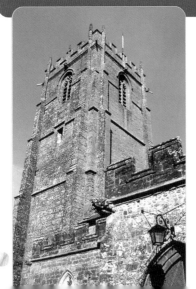

Below left: Whitchurch Canonicorum Church
Below right: Carving of St Wite, Whitchurch Canonicorum Church

roam. In spring the bluebells are a joy. South again is **Powerstock**, one of Dorset's prettiest villages. In the churchyard (to the right of the path as you approach the main door) is a thirteenth-century dole table, a rare survival. From these tables, charitable doles of bread were distributed to the local poor. Such donations have given us the expression, to 'dole-out', and the word dollar. To the south-east of the village are the remains of a castle, originally a motte and bailey, but later converted into a hunting lodge by King John. Of this lodge nothing now remains.

Further south-east is **Eggardon Hill**, topped by a hill fort, several ramparts and ditches. From it there are magnificent views, south to Golden Cap and the sea, north-west to Pilsdon Pen, and, closer, over the lovely local country.

Continuing eastwards along the A356, the next village, to the right, is **Toller Porcorum**, a village whose lovely name loses a little of its shine when it is realised it derives from the pigs that once made the local area famous. Though larger than its neighbouring Toller village, the smaller village has greater treasures than the pig village.

To reach **Toller Fratrum**, return to the main road, turn right then soon, right again. The addition to this village's name is a reference to its ownership by the Knights Hospitalers (the Brethren of the Order of St John of Jerusalem, '*Fratrum*' from 'brethren'). The great treasures lie in the church (dedicated unusually to St Basil). One is a Norman font carved with curiously doll-like figures. The other is a small carving of Mary Magdalene wiping Christ's feet with her hair. Some experts claim this to be Saxon, but most believe it to be Norman. Elsewhere in the village, Little Toller Farm is the early sixteenth-century manor house of John Samways and has some curious carvings of its own, including a monkey holding a mirror.

The tragedy behind Lassie

On New Year's Eve 1915, the battleship HMS *Formidable* was torpedoed by a German submarine as she made her way up the Channel. The storm which had been brewing when the torpedo struck, hit with ferocity as the crew was abandoning ship, causing many of its lifeboats to capsize and hastening the sinking of the ship. Many of the crew were lost, their bodies washed up along the length of Lyme Bay.

In Lyme Regis a local inn was turned into a makeshift mortuary. The landlord's dog, a crossbreed, but mostly collie, kept approaching one of the bodies, eventually licking its face and hands. Appalled at the dog's morbid interest, the officials tried to shoo the dog away, but without success. When someone decided to see what the dog found so interesting, he discovered that sailor John Cowan was still alive.

It is believed that this incident was the basis of the *Lassie* films, the story of Lyme's 'sheepdog' being assisted by the fact that the *Formidable's* captain had his own dog on the bridge when the torpedo struck and the dog was believed to have stayed with is master.

Continue along the A356 to **Maiden Newton**, a large, pleasant village with some good old houses. The door in the north wall of the church is thought to be the original Norman door and to be hanging on its original hinges, making it one of the oldest in Britain. To the north is **Cattistock**, rightly called 'elbow streeted' by William Barnes. The church is acknowledged as the finest mid/late-nineteenth century church in the county. The tall, elegant tower is its finest asset. South of Maiden Newton is **Wynford Eagle**, named after William d'Aquila, William the Eagle, who was given it after the Conquest: look for the eagle perched on the porch gable of the manor house. The tympanum of the church, a Norman survival of later restoration, also has two bird-like carvings. Are these wyverns or eagles?

Now continue along the main road into Dorchester. The road by-passes **Stratton**, where Thomas Hardy saved the windows and doors of the church from destruction by restorers in 1891, having them re-set in the new church, and **Bradford Peverell**, where the New Barn Field Centre recreates an Iron Age settlement: there is also a display of old craft tools, a working potter and a nature trail, each of which is worth a little time before the county town is reached.

LYME REGIS

In 774 King Cynewulf of the West Saxons granted land at the point in Lyme Bay where the River Lym meets the sea for the boiling of sea water to extract the salt. That is the first mention of the settlement that was to grow into Lyme Regis. Early Lyme – after the salt extractors had long gone – was probably a fishing port, but it seems likely that an early form of **The Cobb** was here by the time Edward I made the town a borough (a royal decree that added 'Regis' to the name) in 1279. The Cobb would have helped Lyme's fishing fleet, but also aided its development as a trading port.

Certainly by the sixteenth century Lyme Regis was one of the south coast's most important ports, a combination of legitimate trade and the riskier, but better rewarded, smuggling making the town very wealthy. In 1588 Sir Francis Drake's fleet – which included several local ships – had a minor skirmish with the Spanish Armada in the bay, but in 1685 the town saw a much more significant event when the Duke of Monmouth landed on the beach to the west of The Cobb. The Duke is claimed to have spent his first night in England in what is now Monmouth House, Monmouth Street. After the failure of his rebellion, a dozen Lyme men were hanged at the exact spot where the Duke had landed.

By the time of Monmouth's landing, Lyme Regis was already in decline, its position, in a steep valley with limited chance of development, leading to trade moving elsewhere. The town was saved from ruin by the new fashion for sea-bathing. This began at Lyme in about 1760 (though it did not become really fashionable until George III bathed at Weymouth in 1789), leading to a new rush of building: many of Lyme's best houses date from the late eighteenth and early nineteenth centuries.

Monmouth's Rebellion

James, Duke of Monmouth, was the eldest son of Charles II by his Welsh mistress, Lucy Walter. The Duke was in Holland, as a guest of William, Prince of Orange, when his father died and his uncle became king as James II. Since James II was William's father-in-law, and hated the Duke, William ordered Monmouth out of Holland. This action appears to have been the spur to Monmouth's ambition and he decided on a rebellion, sparked from the largely Protestant West Country where, he believed, he would be supported against Catholic James.

The Dutch supported, if quietly, this plan, and on 11 June 1685 Monmouth landed at Lyme Regis. With him he had just 82 men, but his hopes for an army were raised when the cry 'Monmouth and a Protestant religion' went up around his dark green standard. The duke, encouraged by his reception, signed a declaration that he was rightful king and that James had poisoned Charles II to obtain the throne. In four days Monmouth's army had increased to 1,000 men and 150 horse, and with these he set out for Taunton.

By 24 June he had reached Pensford, south of Bristol, and on the 26 June a skirmish at Norton St Philip left 80 royal troops dead and Monmouth a temporary victor. By now his army numbered 3,500 men, with 500 horse, but it became nervous after summer rain left the men cold and sodden. On 6 July on Sedgemoor, Monmouth met the royal army and was utterly defeated. It is estimated that 2,000 of his men died, such a devastation that the rebellion was finished: all Monmouth could do was flee to the Dorset heathland, to his capture near Horton and execution.

Jane Austen stayed at the town, writing part of *Persuasion* here (and setting a section of the novel in the town – Louisa Musgrove has her fall at The Cobb: traditionally the scene of the fall was 'Granny's Teeth', the protruding stone steps near the Aquarium, but some historians claim they post-date Jane's visit to the town). The **Jane Austen Garden** on Marine Parade by Front Beach is a memorial to her stay. It is on the site of a now demolished house in which it was claimed she stayed – until it was discovered to have been built several years after her visit.

There were other literary visits too. Henry Fielding is said to have based the character of Sophie in *Tom Jones* on a local girl, Sarah Andrews. It is also said that Fielding attempted to elope with Sarah but was thwarted by her guardian. Fielding's view on Sarah's guardian, a downright insulting one, can be seen at the Philpot Museum. More recently, John Fowles has added to Lyme's literary history, living here and setting a famous part of *The French Lieutenant's Woman* on The Cobb. The film of the book was also made, in part, in the town, The Cobb featuring in the dramatic advertising shot for it.

On The Cobb stands the **Marine Aquarium and Cobb History**, with tanks holding local fish and sea life and a display on the town's history.

At the landward end of The Cobb, the Victorian-built, aptly-named Ozone Terrace, stands to the left. Walk along Marine Parade, passing Jane's Garden to reach Bridge Street, with the Guildhall and the excellent **Philpot Museum** which has a tremendous collection of local fossils, and displays of local geology, history and natural history.

In Coombe Street, to the north, is **Dinosaurland**, housed in an eighteenth-century chapel, with models of dinosaurs and a collection of local fossils. The steep, tight streets of Lyme at this eastern end are worth exploring, though the heart of the town will always be close to the sea.

LYME REGIS TO BRIDPORT

Beyond the fossil-rich cliffs lies Charmouth, reached by the Coastal Path which heads inland over Timber Hill to avoid the crumbling cliffs, or by a road which is even more fearful of the cliff, going around Timber Hill to reach the village. The piece of coast that walkers and drivers avoid is now a nature reserve covering The Spittles and Black Ven, areas of landslip where rare salt-resistant plants cling to the unstable soil. After heavy rain the cliffs become even more unstable: the whole area is gradually slipping into the sea.

Charmouth, perched between Black Ven and the River Char, but set back from the sea, just in case, is a pleasant seaside town. Here Jane Austen sat in 'unwearied contemplation', and today's visitors can do much the same. The whole village still has a Georgian air, but interestingly, the Queen's Arms, for all its appearance, is not Georgian, having

been formed by the linking of two sixteenth century cottages. One of these has the initials of Thomas Chard, the last Abbot of Forde Abbey, carved on a door frame: presumably the village was owned by the abbey and, perhaps, the monks, too, came here to rest and watch the sea.

Walking Around Charmouth

East of Charmouth the coast is free of roads, except where easy country allowed a dead-end road to be laid to the shore. This is land for the walker, the Coastal Path making the most of the cliffs and the views they offer. Beyond Charmouth there is another area of landslips, Cain's Folly, before Golden Cap is reached. At 626ft (191m) this is the highest cliff on Britain's Channel coast, the flat-topped sphinx-like headland seen from Lyme Regis. The name is from the exposed sandstone rock of which the headland is formed, called greensand despite its colour being a yellow-orange. **The Golden Cap Estate**, a National Trust property covering the cliffs from Cain's Folly to Seatown, is another nature reserve, conserving plants such as southern marsh orchid and other fine meadow flowers on the eastward side. But here the threat to the rare habitats protected by the reserve is not from man, as parts of the cliff are eroding inland by as much as a metre each year.

• MARY ANNING, THE LYME REGIS FOSSIL HUNTER •

Mary Anning was born in 1799, the daughter of a carpenter. From an early age Mary, her brother Joseph and their father searched for fossils in the local cliffs, selling them as curios to supplement Mr Anning's earnings. The best fossils they kept, and Mary soon became well known among England's gentlemen fossil-hunters and collectors. Mr Anning died in 1810 and, in the following year, Mary and Joseph made their most famous discovery, the fossilised skeleton of an **ichthyosaur**, a fish-eating, sea-living reptile. It took several years to free the skeleton from the cliff, Mary selling it to the British Museum for the princely sum of £23. In 1824 Mary discovered a **plesiosaur** (some people's favourite candidate for the Loch Ness Monster) and four years later the first ever intact **pterosaur** (a winged reptile).

The finds made Mary famous and comparatively wealthy, but she was a difficult woman to deal with, often bad-tempered and rude, and spent most of her days alone digging in the cliffs. It is now conjectured that her bad moods were the result of pain from cancer and the increasing amounts of laudanum she took in an effort to control the pain. She died in 1847.

Lyme Bay's blue lias cliffs are still packed with fossils, but before grabbing a hammer and heading that way, please remember that the cliffs are very unstable: indiscriminate hammering is not only vandalism but potentially lethal. It is better to explore the beach where, even now, glorious ammonites can be found.

Fossil Cliffs at Lyme Regis

The village church, a pretty building, overlooks a churchyard in which lies a man killed in a duel in 1792. Inside the church there is a memorial to a vicar, Edward Bragge, who, legend has it, was so fond of his food that he asked to be buried in a coffin made from his dining table, a request apparently carried out by his dining friends.

The town's **Heritage Coast Centre** explores the natural history of the local coast and the fossils to be found in nearby cliffs.

The main road from Charmouth heads inland to **Morcombelake** where Moore's Biscuit Bakery is open to visitors who can watch the making of Dorset knobs and other local specialities. There is also a small art gallery and museum.

In Morcombelake a left turn leads to **Whitchurch Canonicorum**. Standing at the edge of the Marshwood Vale, this lovely village has a church often known as the 'Cathedral of the Vale'. The church is dedicated to St Wite (also known as St Candida), a ninth or tenth century Saxon martyr killed by raiding Vikings. Her relics became the object of pilgrimages and acquired a reputation for miraculous cures, particularly for those with crippling diseases, and a shrine was created around them. This shrine can still be seen in the church, a very rare survival from Saxon times and the best in the country. The shrine is pierced by three holes: crippled pilgrims would place a limb through one of these holes to touch the reliquary inside,

Charles II's lucky escape

In September 1651 Charles was in Dorset after escaping from Worcester, waiting while Colonel Francis Wyndham organised his escape to France. Colonel Wyndham gave Captain Stephen Limbry, a Bridport ship owner, £50 to smuggle two businessmen to France so as to 'avoid creditors', and a Charmouth rendezvous was agreed. The King was taken to Charmouth, but Limbry's ship did not arrive. Wyndham took the King to Bridport and put him in the George Inn while he investigated Limbry's non-appearance. He found that Mrs Limbry, fearful of her husband's mission (as there was an automatic sentence of death on anyone helping the fugitive King who was rumoured to be in the area), had locked him in their bedroom after removing all his clothes. Wyndham rushed back to the George and ushered the King out of Bridport. And only just in time as a Charmouth blacksmith had noticed that Wyndham's horses had been shod in Worcester and had alerted the authorities. It is said that as the King left Bridport eastwards, the search party under Captain Macey arrived at the town's western end.

At the entrance to Lee Lane a monument marks the spot where Wyndham and the King turned north along the lane: less than five minutes later Macey's troops rode past, heading for Dorchester. The monument, raised on 23 September 1901, 350 years to the day after the King's lucky escape, records an event that changed British history.

or place a piece of cloth in the hole and then wrap it around their limb. Inside the shrine is a lead casket containing bones which are indeed very ancient and those of a woman of about forty. The shrine is an extraordinary link with our ancient ancestors and well worth visiting. St Wite clearly gave the village its first name, the second coming from its co-ownership by the canons of Salisbury and Wells. The church in which the shrine rests is itself worth seeing, an impressive building in a fine setting. Besides the shrine it has a memorial brass to Sir George Somers, the Elizabethan sailor usually credited with the discovery of Bermuda, though it had actually been discovered several years before he was unfortunately shipwrecked on it. From the top of nearby Hardown Hill there are marvellous views of both the coast and Marshwood Vale.

Next along the main road is **Chideock**, pronounced Chiddick. The church houses a mother-of-pearl cross which, tradition has it, was brought from Palestine, and a superb black marble effigy of a knight. Again by tradition this is Sir John Chideock who built a castle on the hill spur to the north of the village. Due to a somewhat unfortunate misplacement of a 'D' and a 'G', one of the church's bells is inscribed LOVE DOG. Nothing but mounds and ditches now remain of Sir John's castle, but there is a large wooden cross commemorating five Catholic priests martyred here for refusing to conform to Protestantism after the Civil War. They held services in a barn in the grounds of Chideock Manor, on the site of which there is now a Roman Catholic church built in the 1850s by Charles Weld. Weld also built the family mausoleum in the churchyard. This takes the form of a Greek cross: the fine Crucifix was the work of Charles Weld himself.

From Chideock a road heads south to the beach and inn at **Seatown**, while the main road heads east to Bridport, passing a turn to **Symondsbury**, famous as the home of Dorset's best thatchers.

BRIDPORT

The country around the old town of Bridport grew the finest hemp in Britain – the hemp used to make ropes – perhaps since the time of the Romans, as it is known that hemp grew here during their occupation. Certainly by early medieval times Bridport's rope-works were famous, making ropes for shipping and also making fishing nets. So important were the town's ropes for the navy that Henry VII actually decreed that all hemp grown within 5 miles (8 kms) of the town was for the exclusive use of naval rope-makers.

Rope made Bridport wealthy, a prosperity jeopardised when the navy decided to build its own ropeworks at Portsmouth and Woolwich. But the decline in ropemaking was accompanied by an increase in net productions as British trawler fleets began to exploit the Newfoundland fishing grounds. Today net and rope production is still carried on in Bridport, though on a smaller scale and using nylon and other man-made fibres: the hemp fields have long since disappeared. One happy note is that Bridport makes the nets for Wimbledon's tennis courts. A less happy note was struck not so many years ago by the phrase 'stabbed by a Bridport dagger'. This macabre

Above and below: **Lyme Regis**
Opposite page: **Golden Cap from Seatown**

expression meant to be hanged, as it was Bridport that supplied the executioner's hemp nooses.

Bridport's ropemaking past is evident in the layout of the town, the long straight alleys leading away from the main streets being the old rope walks. The town's ropemaking history is also explored in the town museum in South Street, while at **Loders**, a village to the east of Bridport, an extension of the museum covers the history of netmaking, with occasional demonstrations of the art: ask at the Bridport museum for details. At the top of South Street, which widens to form the old market place, is the Town Hall, a late eighteenth-century building with a fine clock tower and cupola. Opposite is the site of the George Inn where Charles II stayed.

Bridport's three main streets, which join at the Town Hall, have an array of fine eighteenth- and nineteenth-century houses. The town church, in South Street is of similar age (the Quaker's Meeting House and Almshouses opposite are older), but further along South Street, towards the sea, is **The Chantry**, a strange building probably dating from Bridport's medieval era. On its southern face there is a curious iron stand which, legend maintains, once held a fire basket, the house being an early lighthouse. But could a fire have been built so close to the wall?

One final site near Bridport that is worth visiting is **Mangerton Mill**, a working seventeenth ventury water mill and bygones museum to the north of the town, just off the A3066 (Beaminster) road.

BRIDPORT TO WEYMOUTH ALONG THE COAST ROAD

Head south in Bridport taking the road for West Bay, passing Palmer's Brewery which can be visited on guided tours. **West Bay** was built as a port for Bridport, but was never able to accommodate large ships. Later, attempts to turn it into a seaside resort were no more successful. But despite these failures, it is a charming little place with a neat little harbour. The Harbour Life Exhibition explores West Bay's history.

From West Bay the coast road soon reaches **Burton Bradstock**. This very pretty village, set back from the sea, once competed with Bridport as a ropemaking centre. When it lost that battle it began to spin flax to make cords and shoelaces. Grove Mill, at the eastern end of the village, was built in 1803, the first flax-swingling (beating) mill in England. To the north, **Shipton Gorge**, a pleasant village is named not from any geological feature, but for the Norman de Gorge family, while to the east, at Bredy Farm, there is a collection of old farming tools and machinery.

East again is **Swyre**, the home of John Russell who went to Wolfeton House to act as interpreter to the Austrian archduke and went on to greatness. In 1822 Richard Bishop, a young fisherman from Swyre, was imprisoned for 'unlawfully making a light on the sea coast', which suggests an attempt, at least, at wrecking. Such was the reputation of this section of the coast for sea-based lawlessness that in 1752 it was said that 'all the people of Abbotsbury, including the vicar, are thieves, smugglers and plunderers of wrecks'.

Close to Swyre is **Puncknowle**, pronounced Punnel, once home to Henry Shrapnel who invented a fragmentation bomb used in the Crimean War, and whose name has entered the language. On the coast is West Bexington which most experts agree marks the western end of Chesil Beach, the extraordinary pebble beach that runs from here to Portland.

ABBOTSBURY AND THE FLEET

The road avoids the beach, soon reaching **Abbotsbury**, dominated by the chapel of St Catherine on the summit of Chapel Hill to the south. The chapel was built in the fifteenth century with walls of immense thickness that make it tiny inside despite its sturdy appearance. This strength may have been to withstand the buffeting of sea storms, the knoll being very exposed. The exposure works in both directions, for the chapel is readily visible from the sea and was used as a landmark, a function which, together with the masses said here for the souls of dead sailors, may have given rise to the alternative name of Seamen's Chapel.

The chapel is only one of the village's architectural treasures. Indeed, for so small a place so remotely set, Abbotsbury is a wonder, an immaculate collection of delightful cottages set in streets that were certainly not built for cars. There is said to have been a church here before the founding of the abbey, and the name Abbotsbury is also said to have preceded the abbey. This seems strange, but may imply that the area, already sacred, was owned by the Abbot of Glastonbury.

Abbotsbury's first abbey was endowed by Orc, or Urc, a house carle (lord) at the time of Cnut, whose wife, Thola, gave her name to a village on the Piddle stream – Thola's Piddle, Tolpuddle. All that is left of the abbey are small sections of the church and gatehouse.

Dedication

The chapel's dedication is to the patron saint of spinsters, and local girls getting uncomfortably close to the back of the shelf came here to ask the saint's help in finding a husband:

*St Catherine, St Catherine,
lend me thine aid
And grant that I never may
die an old maid
A husband, St Catherine
A good one, St Catherine
But arn-a-one better than
narn-a-one, St Catherine.*

The village's fine **tithe barn**, reached by going towards the Swannery, probably formed part of the abbey estate, but as it was also useful to the laity it has survived. Originally 270ft (83m) in length, it is one of the largest in England and with its position next to the beautifully restored village pond, it is a delight. The barn houses the **Tithe Barn Children's Farm** where children can meet farm animals and pets, and help with feeding, milk a wooden cow, drive junior tractors or play in the bale mountain. The barn presently houses the only display of the Chinese terracotta warriors outside China.

Above: St Cathrine's Church, Abbotsbury

Right: Transport to the Swannery at Abbotsbury

Swannery, Abbotsbury

North of the barn is the church. Inside, the canopy of the pulpit has two bullet holes, a memory of the Civil War when it was defended by 13 Royalists, all of whom were captured. The same skirmish, the result of Abbotsbury being held for the Crown by Sir John Strangways against the Parliamentarians of Sir Anthony Ashley Cooper, saw the destruction of Strangways' house – Abbey House. The record of the battle notes that 'the business was extreme hot for six hours'. The Parliamentarians had not realised that there was gunpowder stored in the house and when it exploded after they had fired it, many of them were killed. The present Abbey House replaced the original shortly after the end of the war.

Beyond the tithe barn is the **Swannery**, an artificial, or largely artificial, pond created originally by the monks from the abbey. The Swannery is at least 600 years old: in the early sixteenth century a traveller noted that 'here from all time whereof the memory of man is not to the contrary there was, and as yet is, a certain flight of wild Swans and Cygnets called "a game of wild swannes". The monks probably ate the swans even though they were, and are, a royal bird. On average there are 400–800 birds, all mute swans, feeding, as with the wilder fowl of the Fleet, on eelgrass.

The mute swan is a fine sight in the air, an elegant bird on the water, and an amazingly comical performer during the transition between the two. It is a heavy bird, up to 30lb (14kg) in weight, and flight is achieved only after much noisy wing beating and wild running across the water. Visitors to the site can watch the swans being fed, watch an audio-visual show on the history of the Swannery in the old swanherd's house, or visit the old duck decoy pipes where wild ducks were decoyed into traps. The traps are still used, but now the ducks are released after ringing. Cygnet hatching (end May-end June) and swan ringing (biennially, on a day in late July) offer the chance to see birds at very close quarters.

Swan ringing is a continuation of the ancient custom of 'swan-upping'. Another of Abbotsbury's ancient customs is still flourishing: in early May, on Garland Day, flowers are thrown in the sea, a custom with pagan origins, the flowers being to placate the sea gods.

At the western end of the village, close to Chesil Beach are the **Sub-Tropical Gardens**, with 20 acres of superb gardens. The gardens are surrounded by evergreen oaks and this, together with the sea being so close, means they are virtually frost free, allowing some very unusual plants to flourish, including citronella. The camellias and rhododendrons are superb, as are the daffodils in spring and the roses in summer. There is an excellent restaurant at the site.

Beyond Abbotsbury is **Portesham**, where Thomas Masterman Hardy spent his boyhood in the lovely Manor House. Here, as at Wimborne Minster, a man requested to be buried neither inside or outside the church. As a result, William Weare has a tomb which penetrates the church wall, the main part being on the outside of the south wall. The tomb's inscription refers to the Civil War during which Weare, a staunch Royalist, had all his property confiscated.

On **Blackdown**, above the village, there is a monument to Hardy and

Dorset's other Thomas Hardy

Thomas Masterson Hardy was born on 5 April 1769 at Kingston Russell House, the second son of the landed Joseph Hardy. After spending his boyhood at Portesham, at the edge of Joseph's Blackdown estate, Thomas joined the navy at the age of 12 as servant boy to the captain of HMS Helena. His rise through the ranks was slow, but steady: he was lieutenant on HMS Meleager in 1793 when he first met Captain, later Admiral, Nelson. In 1803 Hardy was given the command of HMS Victory, and was in command of Nelson's flagship at the Battle of Trafalgar. It was in Hardy's arms that Nelson died, his last words being 'kiss me (or 'kismet'), Hardy'.

Hardy brought the dead Admiral home and was prominent at his funeral. He was made a baronet soon after and became First Sea Lord. He retired to the governorship of Greenwich Hospital and died there in 1839. The monument to him on Blackdown (looking suspiciously like an upturned Olympic flame holder) was erected in 1870. It is 70ft (21m) high and has outstanding views from the top.

a collection of excellent prehistoric remains. This area must have been very important to Bronze Age folk, but in one way they were very well served, the Valley of Stones (west of, but close to the crossroads to the west of the Hardy Monument) being littered with the sarsens need for their memorials. To the east of the valley, the **Grey Mare and Her Colts** are the romantically named remains of a chambered long barrow, while further north-west is the **Kingston Russell stone circle**, originally about 80 ft (24m) feet in diameter and consisting of about twenty stones. Closer to the Hardy Monument is the **Hell Stone**, a badly restored long-barrow chamber whose name is more interesting than the site. Is this, as with Heel Stone at Stonehenge, a mispronunciation and then mis-spelling of Hele Stone – Sun Stone?

From Portesham, take the B3157 south-eastwards where a right turn leads to **Langton Herring**, a village

with an unspoilt centre. The village inn has a beam made from a ship's mast, kept as a reminder to locals as a fisherman had been hanged from it for some long-forgotten crime. The next right turn leads to Fleet.

Stretching for over 8 miles (12km) behind Chesil Beach, **The Fleet** is a nature reserve, set up to protect its collection of fine plants, vast beds of reeds and eelgrass, the latter being food for the waterfowl and swans.

The Fleet is a very long piece of water, but narrow – only about 900 yards at the widest point and merely 70 yards at the narrowest. It is remarkably shallow, probably never deeper than 5 yards and frequently only half that. This ribbon of water is connected to the sea, at the aptly named Small Mouth, by a channel less than 100 yards wide. This bottleneck for the sea restricts the Fleet tides and the salinity of its waters. Everywhere the Fleet is brackish, but fresh water running in along its length means that the salt content progressively diminishes as Abbotsbury is approached. This variation in salinity has meant that the Fleet's margins are a unique grading of fresh and salt-water marshes with a fascinating ecology.

To date, over a hundred species of plants have been identified in the Fleet-Chesil area. The Fleet waters themselves support a normal range of sea creatures, including over 20 species of fish, and about 150 species of bird have been seen in t he area. The chief interest lies in wildfowl and waders, the ducks and geese feeding on the eelgrass, the waders on the invertebrate water animals. The below-water life of the Fleet can be observed by taking a trip in the glass-bottomed boats which sail from 'Abbotsbury Oysters' near the Ferrybridge Inn, close to where the Fleet and sea meet.

The village of **Fleet** will be well known to those who have read *Moonfleet*, the classic smuggling adventure story written by John Meade Falkner, a Weymouth man. The historical side of the book is supported by the remains of old Fleet church – destroyed when the great storm broke through Chesil Beach – with its brasses to the last Mohunes. Beneath the old chancel is the tomb of the Mohunes where John Trenchard was trapped with the skeleton of Blackbeard Mohune and the spirit kegs. The new village church was built in a safer position.

The nearby Moonfleet Hotel has a 'Why Not?' bar (of course) from the inn of that name in the book, the name deriving from the crosspall, a broad Y, on the Mohune coat of arms. The hotel has had a varied history: it was once a manor house and served time in the 1939–45 war as an American anti-aircraft gun emplacement. The gunners presumably had a grandstand seat of runs the Dambuster squadron made across the Fleet to try Barnes Wallis's bouncing bomb.

BRIDPORT TO WEYMOUTH ALONG THE INLAND ROAD

The A35 from Bridport to Dorchester is a fine road with lovely views of the folded hills around Askerswell and **Litton Cheney**, a pretty village nestling among the folds. To the south of **Long Bredy**, the next village, is Kingston Russell House where Captain Thomas Hardy was born. The house, a fine seventeenth-century mansion, can be seen from the church which stands at the top end of the village. **Littlebredy** – the single word rather than two as in the 'Long' village is correct – is off limits to visitors' cars, but is worth the walk. Though its cottages are nineteenth-century copies of the medieval style, the village is wonderfully picturesque.

Back on the main road the visitor is crossing country dotted with Bronze Age burial mounds and standing stones, as well as earlier long barrows. Soon the first of the Winterbourne villages is reached. **Winterbourne Abbas** is badly affected by the A37, but the church with its gargoyled tower is worth a look. To the west of the village and close to the main road, Nine Stones is a small stone circle (about 26ft – 8m) in diameter. Bear right in Abbas, taking the B3159 to **Winterbourne Steepleton**, a prettier village. The church has a Saxon core, and a rare tenth-century sculpture of an angel. The final Winterbourne village,

Winterbourne St Martin is now known as **Martinstown**, a straggling place close to Maiden Castle.

Continue along the B3159, passing Maiden Castle to reach **Upwey** which has, it claims, the only true wishing-well in southern England. The well is actually a spring and George III famously drank its waters from a gold cup, the cup becoming the original Gold Cup at the Ascot races. Visitors can also try the waters and make a wish. Upwey Mill was used by Thomas Hardy as the model for Overcombe Mill in *The Trumpet Major*.

The B3159 now reaches the A354. Turn right, but before continuing to Weymouth, one last detour is worthwhile, taking a right turn to **Nottington** to see a curious octagonal house built in 1830 as a spa house for a spring claimed to have miraculous healing powers. The spring was famous for over 200 years – George III drank its waters in 1791 – but has, as with all other spas, declined. The house (supposedly built with eight sides because its owner had seven sons and each wanted his own room) is now in private hands.

WEYMOUTH

To the east of Weymouth beyond the Lodmoor Country Park, on a hill above Dorset's River Jordan, there are the remains of a Roman temple, implying an early settlement in this area. But Weymouth as we know it began life as a pair of towns on opposite sides of the River Wey, that on the southern bank called Weymouth and that on the north Melcombe Regis. Ironically Melcombe was the bigger town, and is still the centre of the town, but it was the smaller town's name that was adopted when the two amalgamated.

The two ports were wool trading ports, and were clearly wealthy as they supplied as many ships for Edward II's siege of Calais as Bristol. But in 1348 the Black Death arrived in England, the first infected rats coming ashore at Melcombe Regis. The plague halved the population in two years, and raids by the French further impoverished the towns. Trade gradually improved, an added importance accompanying Henry VIII's decision to build Sandsfoot Castle here as part of his south coast defences. The Nothe (the name is a corruption of 'nose') was also provided with guns. In 1597 the first bridge linked the two ports, so making the ferry that shuttled between the two redundant.

With the development of Britain's American colonies, Weymouth's fortunes rose again, though the Civil War brought a sudden halt. Nothe Fort was occupied by Royalists who attacked Parliamentarian Melcombe Regis. A cannonball lodged high in the wall of a house in Maiden Street is a reminder of the conflict. The Parliamentarians repulsed the attack and laid siege to Nothe: in only three weeks the fort surrendered.

Weymouth's trade with America resumed, the carrying of convicts to Australia adding further ships to the town's port. But trade was in decline. The outlook for Weymouth seemed bleak by the mid-eighteenth century, but was saved by the rise in popularity of seaside resorts. In 1790 Dr Crane, a local doctor wrote, *Cursory Observations on Sea Bathing* in which he extolled the virtues not only of bathing, but of drinking sea water (a pint per day!).

Weymouth Harbour

In 1789 George III visited the town, staying ten weeks as he recovered from an illness. During his time he bathed – naked, from a hut hauled into the water. The King came every year until 1805, his bathing being accompanied by a band (on shore) playing the National Anthem, and the town's fortunes rose again as British high society were towed, in horse-drawn bathing machines, into the water of Weymouth Bay.

Today Weymouth makes the precarious, uneasy living of many British seaside resorts. Cheap Spanish holidays, with their guarantee of sun and warm seas killed the postwar prosperity, causing the town to rethink its amenities. The resort will always be at the mercy of the weather: when the sun shines, Weymouth's long beach of level sand is a fine place to be, but now when it does not the visitor facilities are very much better.

A TOUR ROUND WEYMOUTH

To start an exploration of Weymouth, where better than the harbour, still a busy place, especially in May when the annual trawler regatta is held. At the harbour, visitors can take a boat to the Channel Islands or France or enjoy the shows at the Pavilion Theatre. **The Deep Sea Adventure**, housed in a large brick warehouse on the quay, details the history of diving and has displays on some of the area's famous shipwrecks. There is also an exhibition about the *Titanic*. Sharky's, one of the newer areas, is an adventure play area for children.

Now follow the seafront promenade northwards, admiring the beach on your right and the Georgian buildings on your left. The statue of George III was erected by a grateful town in 1809, four years after his last visit. From the statue the other memorial to George III can be seen – the horse and rider cut in the chalk hills above **Osmington** (a pretty village a short distance east of Weymouth). Those wanting a closer look can follow a footpath on the hillside, above and below the carving.

At nearby **Sutton Poyntz**, the **Wessex Water Museum** has a collection of old pumping machinery in the buildings erected in 1856 to supply Weymouth with clean drinking water.

The statue of the king is best seen with a backdrop of the houses paid for by the prosperity his visits brought. Behind that delightful backdrop lies the centre of modern Weymouth. To the north of the statue are some of Weymouth's best Georgian houses, in Gloucester Terrace – the Gloucester Hotel is the house the Duke of Gloucester, George III's brother, built for himself – and Crescent Street (planned as a Crescent – Royal Crescent – but built as a terrace). The cast iron clock commemorates Queen Victoria's 1887 Jubilee: there is also a bronze statue of the Queen Victoria.

Going inland from the Jubilee Clock, the visitor passes the railway station to reach **Radipole Lake**, an RSPB bird reserve which is good for waders and warblers in summer, and wildfowl in winter. There are good paths and information boards, and a visitor centre.

To the south of the river, just across the bridge, is Holy Trinity, the parish church of old Weymouth (the southern port). The look of the old town is best captured in **Trinity Street**, close to the church. Here, Tudor House is late sixteenth- century, built of Portland stone with stone mullions and twin gables. The house (originally two cottages) was saved from demolition, restored and furnished in period style by Walmsley Lewis, and can be visited.

Close to Trinity Street, in Hope Square near the Old Harbour, is **Brewer's Quay**, the Victorian Devenish brewery now converted into shops, craft workshops and visitor attractions. The attractions include the Timewalk Journey on which you can see, hear and smell six centuries of Weymouth history as you walk through displays on the Black Death, the Civil War, Smuggling and other themes of local interest. Discovery is a multimedia interaction science exhibition aimed at children. Brewer's Quay also has a café and a bar, and there are regular art and craft exhibitions.

East from the Old Harbour, beyond Nothe Gardens, is **Nothe Fort**. The Nothe had defensive guns from the sixteenth century, but the fort is much later, dating from 1860 when it was built as a defence against a seaborne invasion that never came (for which reason all the forts built at the same time were known as Palmerston Follies, after Lord Palmerston, the Prime Minister). Nothe had 12 gun batteries and over 70 rooms on three levels. Today it has many displays and lifesize dummies illustrating life in the fort and Weymouth's part in the 1939-45 War. There is also a collection of weapons – from huge coastal guns to side arms – and another of military vehicles. The views from the fort are worth the visit in themselves. Of the Sandsfoot Castle built by Henry VIII, little remains: it lies to the south of the Nothe, towards Portland.

We also head for Portland, but take one detour en route, to visit **Bennett's Water Gardens**, about 2 miles (3km) west of the town centre, just off the B3157 to Bridport. The gardens are flooded clay pits in which grow over 100 species of water lily. The ponds also attract dragonflies, herons and kingfishers. There is also a tropical house, and a family nature trail and a tearoom.

PORTLAND

Portland is a huge lump of limestone, $4\frac{1}{2}$ by $1\frac{1}{2}$ miles (7km by 2.5km) joined to the mainland by the pebble bank of Chesil Beach. At the landward side it rises to 500 ft

(150m), but at its tip – Portland Bill – it is a mere 20 ft (6m) above the sea. It is a curious place, virtually treeless, chiselled by quarries, crowded with fortresses and prisons, and with a surprisingly large number of inhabitants, spread among four 'villages'.

The difficulties of traversing Chesil Beach meant that from earliest times a ferry transported folk to the mainland. In 1824 a storm killed the ferrymen and it was decided to build a bridge. Ferry Bridge, opened in 1839, still takes visitors to the 'island'. At its mainland side, close to the Ferrybridge Inn, is **Abbotsbury Oysters**, an oyster farm where visitors can watch the process of producing oysters for the table, as well as sampling the shellfish. From the site run the glass-bottomed boats which explore the Fleet's sub-surface life.

The early inhabitants of the island kept sheep (the Portland sheep, now only seen in Rare Breeds Trust Centres), but in the seventeenth century there was a sudden boom in stone quarrying following Inigo Jones' decision to use Portland stone for the Banqueting Hall in Whitehall. St Paul's Cathedral was faced in Portland stone and it became much sought after. More recently Portland stone was used for the United Nations building in New York.

Portland Castle is the best preserved of Henry VIII's chain of defensive fortresses along England's southern coast, constructed against a feared invasion from Catholic Europe in the wake of Henry's break with the Pope. The castle saw action only during the Civil War when it changed hands several times. The castle was on three floors, the guns in the middle one, with the gunmen below and the governor above.

Beyond the castle are **Portland Heights**. From the car park there are tremendous views of the naval and helicopter base, Chesil Beach and the harbour. Close by is **The Verne**, built as a fortress in 1860, but now the prison. Interestingly, the fortress was built by convicts who were housed in the original prison to the south-east, now the Young Offenders' Institution. The convicts also built the breakwater which creates Portland Harbour, one of the world's largest harbours.

The Heights are in Fortuneswell, the largest of Portland's villages. To the south is **Easton** where the Tout Quarry has been turned into a wildlife refuge and outdoor museum of quarrying techniques. It is also a sculpture park with works formed directly from the rock. Close by, St George's is the best of the island's churches. Set on a barren and weatherswept site, it was built on a grand scale, but with some eccentricities – the half dome over the central crossing and the elaborate tower.

On the other side of Easton from St George's is a very interesting complex of buildings. From the museum car park, **Portland Museum** is the first to be reached. It is housed in a pair of thatched cottages, one of which was the home of Avice, the heroine of Thomas Hardy's *The Well-Beloved*. The museum was founded in 1930 by Dr Marie Stopes, the famous birth control pioneer. It houses displays on the geology, history and natural history of Portland. Marie Stopes Cottage has displays of shipwrecks and smuggling.

Walk past the museum and the café towards Church Ope Cove, **Continued on Page 169**

ABBOTSBURY

Sub-Tropical Gardens

Open: March-October, daily 10am-6pm (last admission 5pm). November-February, daily 10am-4pm (last admission 3pm). Closed Christmas Day, Boxing Day and New Year's Day.
☎ 01305 871387 or 871153

Swannery

Open: Mid-March-late October, daily 10am-6pm (last admission 5pm).
☎ 01305 871858

Tithe Barn Children's Farm

Open: February Half Term-October, daily 10am-6pm. November-mid-February, Saturday and Sunday 10am-6pm
☎ 01305 871817

BEAMINSTER AND THE SURROUNDING AREA

Beaminster Museum

Whitcombe Street
Beaminster
Open: Easter-September Tuesday, Thursday, Saturday and Bank Holiday Mondays 10.30am-12.30pm, 2.30-4.30pm.
☎ 01308 863623 or 862773

Craft and Design Centre

Broadwindsor
Open: February-23 December daily 10am-7pm.
☎ 01308 868362

Forde Abbey

Nr. Thorncombe
Open: House: April-October, Wednesday, Thursday, Sunday and Bank Holidays 1-4.30pm
Garden: All year, daily 10am-4.30pm
☎ 01460 221290

Hooke Park

Hooke
Open: Easter or April-October, Wednesday, Sunday and Bank Holidays 2-5pm
☎ 01308 862204

Horn Park Gardens

North of Beaminster, off the A3066
Open: April-October, Sunday-Thursday (including Bank Holidays) 2-6pm
☎ 01308 862212

Mapperton Gardens

East of Beaminster, off the B3163
Open: March-October, daily 2-6pm
% 01308 862645

New Barn Field Centre

Bradford Peverell
Open: Easter-September, daily 10am-5pm
☎ 01305 267463

Parnham House

South of Beaminster, off the A3066
Open: Easter or April-October, Tuesday-Thursday, Sunday and Bank Holidays 2-5pm
☎ 01308 862204

BRIDPORT AND THE SURROUNDING AREA

Bredy Farm Old Farming Collection

Nr Burton Bradstock
Open: Late May-September, Monday-Friday 10.30am-5.30pm
☎ 01308 897229

Harbour Life Exhibition

West Bay
Open: April-September, daily 10am-5pm (closed on Sundays November-May)
☎ 01308 420997

Mangerton Mill

Mangerton
Open: Easter-September Tuesday-Sunday 11am-5.30pm. October Tuesday-Sunday

2-5.30pm. Also open on Bank Holiday
Mondays.
☎ 01308 485224

Museum of Net Manufacture

Loders, Nr Bridport
Open: by arrangement only. Ask at the
Bridport Town Museum
☎ 01308 422116

Palmer's Brewery

West Bay Road
Bridport
Open: Tours at Easter, April, May and
September, Wednesday at 11am, June-
August, Tuesday-Thursday at 11am.
Booking can be made through the Wine
Shop, ☎ 01308 427500

Town Museum

South Street
Bridport
Open: April-October, Monday-Saturday
10am-5pm.
☎ 01308 422116

Lyme Regis and the surrounding area

Charmouth Coastal Heritage Centre
Sea Front, Charmouth
Open: Fortnight at Easter, then
Whitsun-September daily 10.30am-
5pm
☎ 01297 560772

Dinosaurland

Coombe Street
Lyme Regis
Open: All year, daily 10am-5pm (open
9am-8pm in August)
☎ 01297 443541

Marine Aquarium and Cobb History

The Cobb
Lyme Regis
Open: Easter-October, daily 10am-5pm,
(closes later in July and August)
☎ 01297 443678

Moore's Biscuit Bakery

Morcombelake
Open: Bakery: All year, Monday-Friday
9am-5pm
Art Gallery/Museum: January-May and
October-December, Monday-Friday
9am-5pm. June-September, Monday-
Friday 9am-5pm, Saturday 9am-1pm.
Closed on Bank Holidays and for two
weeks at Christmas/New Year.
☎ 01297 489253

Philpot Museum

Bridge Street
Lyme Regis
Open: Easter-October, Monday-Saturday
10am-5pm, Sunday 10am-12noon and
2.30-5pm
☎ 01297 443370

Portland

Lighthouse
Portland Bill
Open: Easter-October, daily 11am-
4.30pm unless fog horn is sounding or
maintenance is being carried out
☎ 01305 820495

Portland Castle (English Heritage)

Open: Easter or April-October, daily
10am-5pm
☎ 01305 820539

Portland Museum

217 Wakeham
Open: Easter-October, Friday-Tuesday
10.30am-1pm, 1.30-5pm. Open daily
during school summer holidays
☎ 01305 821804

Tout Quarry Sculpture Park

Open: At any reasonable time
☎ 01305 821638

Continued overpage

WEYMOUTH AND THE SURROUNDING AREA

Abbotsbury Oysters

Ferrybridge
Open: All year, daily, but times dependent upon tides. Please ring beforehand. The site's 'Oyster Bar' is open Easter-September, daily 10am-6pm.
☎ 01305 7888867

Bennett's Water Gardens

Putton Lane
Chickerell
Open: April-August, Tuesday-Sunday 10am-5pm, September, Tuesday-Saturday 10am-5pm. Also open on Bank Holidays
☎ 01305 785150

Brewer's Quay

Hope Square, Old Harbour
Weymouth
Open: shops etc, Museum and Timewalk: All year except for 25-27 December and last fortnight in January, daily 10am-5.30pm (open until 9.30pm during summer school holidays, and 6.30 at Easter).
☎ 01305 777622
Open: Discovery: March-December, daily 10am-5.30pm (9.30am-9pm during summer school holidays). January and February, Wednesday-Sunday 10am-5.30pm (but open daily during school holidays)
☎ 01305 789007

Deep Sea Adventure and Sharky's

9 Custom House Quay
Weymouth
Open: All year, daily 9.30am-7pm (open until 8pm in July and August)
☎ 01305 760690

Fleet Observer (Glass-bottomed boat)

Ferrybridge
Open: June-September, daily sailings (90 minute duration) at 10am, 11.45am, 1.45pm and 3.30pm. Evening trips by arrangement. May and October - trips by arrangement
☎ 01305 773396

Model World

Lodmoor Country Park
Weymouth
Open: May-September, daily 10am-6pm
☎ 01305 781797

Nothe Fort

The Nothe
Weymouth
Open: mid-May-mid-September, daily 10.30am-5.30pm. Mid-September-mid-May, Sundays and Bank Holidays 2-5.30pm
☎ 01305 787243

Sea Life Park

Lodmoor Country Park
Weymouth
Open: March-October, daily 10am-5pm (open until 9pm in July and August). November, December and February, daily 11am-3pm
☎ 01305 788255

Tudor House

3 Trinity Street
Weymouth
Open: June-September, Tuesday-Friday 11am-4.30pm. October-May, first Sunday of the month, 2-4pm
☎ 01305 812341/788168

Upwey Wishing Well

Upwey
Open: Easter-September, daily 10.30-6pm
☎ 01305 814470

Wessex Water Museum

Sutton Poyntz
Open: By appointment only
☎ 0117 929 0611

passing under the arch of **Rufus (or Bow and Arrow) Castle**, perhaps built by William Rufus and certainly built during his reign. It was rebuilt in the fifteenth century but is now in ruins and not open to tourists. Turn right along the coastal path, descending the steps and then turning right, uphill, to pass the ruins of St Andrew's Church, a medieval building. Continue uphill passing Pennsylvania Castle, built for John Penn, the island's governor, who was the grandson of William Penn, the founder of Pennsylvania. The path now leads back to the museum car park.

At the extreme tip of Portland, **Portland Bill**, there are two lighthouses. On the left is the lower, older light, built in 1788 and originally fired by coal. It is now a bird observatory and field centre, a good spot for watching migrating birds. The newer lighthouse can be climbed for an enhanced view, the cliffs here being quite low. The main attraction of the headland is Pulpit Rock, an isolated lump of rock offshore. A fast current known as Portland Race, a danger to shipping, rips across the Bill.

Chesil Beach

West Bexington to Portland is 21kms (14 miles) – it is 29kms (18 miles) if Cogden and Burton Beaches are considered to be part of Chesil. At its highest the pebble ridge is 14m (45ft) above mean sea level: at the Fleet the beach is 200m wide. Chesil's pebbles must weigh at least 50 million tons.

The size and colour of the pebbles change along the beach length from small, cream pebbles to the west to large, grey pebbles near Portland. The grading of size allowed the smugglers who landed their cargoes at night to tell their position on the beach from handling the pebbles.

In the age of sail, Chesil Beach was the most feared of all the local stretches of coast. Ships going up-channel were in serious difficulties if they were blown into West Bay: they had little chance of rounding Portland and the sharp, sickle-shaped edge of Chesil Beach tore out their bottoms. Shipwrecked sailors who managed to get close to the beach were not assured of safety: the beach is severely sloped, the undertow awesome, and many drowned almost within touching distance of rescuers on the shore.

On the nights of fierce storms the sucking noise of the undertow is audible in Dorchester. It was probably heard in 1824 during a great gale known locally as 'The Outrage', when the sloop Ebenezer was hurled by the waves onto the crest of the shingle ridge. When the storm abated the ship was hauled down into the Fleet where it floated well enough to be towed to Portland for a refit. The gale pushed waves half a mile inland, wrecked Fleet church and village, and left a hundred bodies on Chesil Beach.

Chesil Beach Centre

Beside the A354 (Weymouth-Portland road) at the eastern end of the Beach
Open: April-September 11am-6pm; October-March 11am-4pm
☎ 01305 760579

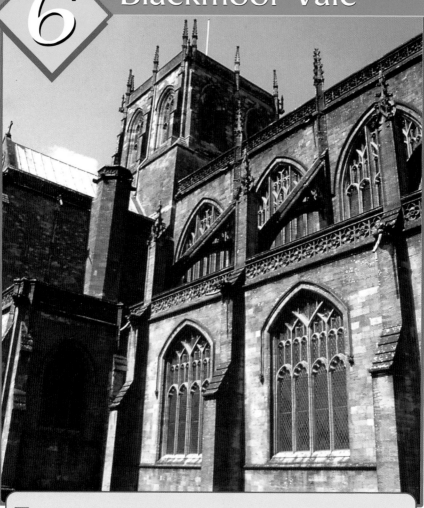

I n the north of the country, right on the Somerset border,
lies Sherborne, the most beautiful of all Dorset's towns. To
the south and east of Sherborne lies the Blackmoor Vale, a
gently rolling and lush area which Thomas Hardy called the
Vale of Little Dairies. In this chapter we explore Sherborne in
detail, then explore the Vale, making a foray over the borders
of Wiltshire to visit Stourhead and Longleat, two of southern
England's most entertaining stately homes.

SHERBORNE – THE ABBEY CHURCH

The heart of Sherborne, in all senses of the word, is the **Abbey Church** of St Mary the Virgin. It is a wonderful building with a brilliance in its architectural parts and yet a simplicity and dignity in its whole, and a history which, in length and splendour, is the envy of many of England's better known cathedrals.

The history of the town precedes that of the abbey. The Saxons called the emerging town *Seir Burna*, clear stream, but the original document refers to the Celtic name *Lanprobi*. The 'lan' of the name is from the British word *llan*, still preserved in many Welsh names, and refers to the settlements built by the early Celtic monks, settlements consisting of the hermit cell of a monk and the dwellings of a few followers.

When King Ine of Wessex decided, in 706, that his western boundary had moved too far from the cathedral city of Winchester, he

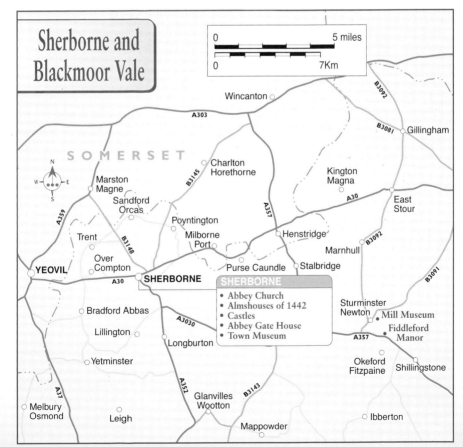

Sherborne and Blackmoor Vale

0   5 miles
0   7Km

Wincanton

A303

B3092

B3081   Gillingham

SOMERSET

Charlton Horethorne

Kington Magna

Marston Magne

Sandford Orcas

Poyntington

East Stour

A30

A357

Trent

Milborne Port

Henstridge

B3092

Marnhull

Over Compton

YEOVIL

A30

Purse Caundle   Stalbridge

SHERBORNE

B3091

SHERBORNE
- Abbey Church
- Almshouses of 1442
- Castles
- Abbey Gate House
- Town Museum

Bradford Abbas

A3030

Lillington

Longburton

Sturminster Newton   Mill Museum

Fiddleford Manor

A357

Yetminster

Okeford Fitzpaine   Shillingstone

A352

Glanvilles Wootton

B3143

A37

Melbury Osmond

Leigh

Mappowder

Ibberton

Sherborne's Miracles

At the end of the tenth century, miracles were reported at Sherborne, associated with the tomb of Wulfsin, a former bishop. The bishop's coffin was opened and a 'sweet smell came forth'. This miracle was final proof of Wulfsin's sainthood and Sherborne became a place of pilgrimage, its position further enhanced when the relics of St Juthware were brought here. Juthware, the daughter of a local lord, was beheaded by her step-brother who had been urged on by his mother, the girl's step-mother. The girl lifted up her severed head and walked to the village church where she laid it on the altar before collapsing. The church, at Halstock, about 7 miles (12km) south-west of Sherborne, held the saintly relics until they were moved, in about 1050, to the new cathedral at Sherborne.

divided the see, asking Aldhelm, Abbot of Malmesbury, to choose a site for a new cathedral. St Aldhelm seems to have been not only a great Christian, but a great scholar. He was a linguist, the first Englishman to speak Latin and Hebrew, a superb lute player and singer. He was also a man with an eye for the countryside, for it was to Sherborne that he came to build his cathedral. With the expansion of the western boundary of Wessex, or Selwoodshire as this part of west Wessex was then called, the see of the new cathedral expanded, eventually stretching all the way to the borders of Cornwall and Gloucestershire. Only with the creation of the sees of Crediton and Wells was Sherborne reduced to more manageable size.

St Aldhelm did not live to see the diocese at its peak, or its division, for he died four years after being made bishop. Of his cathedral nothing visible remains, though Saxon work of about three centuries later can still be recognised. The intervening three centuries were eventful, confirming the great Saxon bishops

as soldiers of their God. Bishop Ealstan of the mid-ninth century accompanied King Egbert into battle. Ealstan outlived Egbert and officiated at the burials of the next two Wessex kings, both of whom lie in the abbey. In the end, he too was buried there. Ealstan's successor, Heamund, continued the warrior tradition, assisting in warding off the invading Danes. He was killed in battle in 871.

Bishop Alfwold's new cathedral did not involve the demolition of the old one, but soon after it was constructed the Normans came. After the Conquest, Sherborne lost its position as a cathedral town, as the see was transferred to Old Sarum. However, Sherborne continued as an important religious centre. At the close of the tenth century a Benedictine monastery had been founded beside the church and this was enthusiastically supported by the Norman conquerors.

At the Dissolution the monastic buildings were sold off, the townsfolk buying the abbey as their parish church for £66-13s-4d, but with an extra £250 for the roof lead. Allhallows, the original parish church, was demolished soon after. There were no additions to the Abbey until 1921 when the east bay of the Lady Chapel was added, so what we see is a perfect medieval church: after John Constable had visited Sherborne he wrote to his wife that he had been to a 'fine old Town with a magnificent church, finer than Salisbury Cathedral'.

The outside of the abbey is of great interest, so pause before going inside. The western end shows the remains of the north wall of Allhallows Church, and the frontage includes work from all the phases of major building. The lower wall is Saxon: the recess in the wall centre is the remains of the Saxon tower and the little building at the northern end of the front protects a complete, excellently preserved,

Dispute between the townsfolk and monks of Sherborne

Although the monastery pleased Sherborne's Norman overlords, it was less enthusiastically supported by the townsfolk of Sherborne. Though the abbey was the monks' church, the townsfolk were allowed to hold services in the nave, where a font was placed for baptisms. Aggravation seems to have flared early and led to the town building its own church, **Allhallows**, probably on the site of St Aldhelm's original church at the abbey's west end.

There followed a series of bad-tempered incidents. The font in the nave was still the 'official' font and the monks moved it and narrowed the doorway leading from Allhallows to the nave, which was used by the townsfolk during baptisms. The Allhallows vicar countered by setting up his own font and ringing the church bells at times guaranteed to cause maximum disturbance to the monks who, of course, had limited periods of sleep as they followed their daily canonical round of prayers and services.

In 1437 an official inquiry found for the monks, the new font was destroyed, the bells silenced. The townsfolk were not appeased and another font was erected. This was too much and the monks persuaded 'one Walter Gallor, a stoute Bocher [butcher] dwelling yn Sherborne' to enter Allhallows where 'he defacid clene the Fontstone'. (The language and erratic spelling of Leland, the sixteenth-century traveller, is perfect for this story.) Next 'a Preste of Alhalowes shot a shaft with fier into the Toppe of that part of S. Marye Church (the abbey), that divided the Est Part that the Monks used from that the Townes-men used; and this Partition chauncing at that Tyme to be thakked (thatched) yn the Role was sette a fier and consequently al the hole Chirch, the Lede and Belles meltid, was defacid.'

Leland's description is poetic but does not hide the fact that the vicar of Allhallows used a flaming arrow to burn down the abbey. The stone of the abbey choir was reddened by the heat and the incident is commemorated in a boss in the choir vault which shows the flaming arrow.

Saxon doorway. This protective shed commemorates the survival from damage of the abbey during the only heavy air raid that the town suffered in the 1939-45 War. At the south end of the front is the Norman doorway that sparked the conflict that led to the abbey fire (see panel). The central doorway is from the major rebuilding (the reason why the roof was thatched at the time of the fire) carried out in the fifteenth century in Perpendicular style. Entrance to the abbey is not through any of the west-front doorways, but through the magnificent Norman porchway in the south front.

Inside, there is much to admire – the Saxon doorway, the Early English doorway to the Lady Chapel, the memorials and from a much later time the marvellous engraved glass reredos in the Lady Chapel, the work of Lawrence Whistler in 1968. But of all the abbey's treasures, the greatest is the roof vaulting, among the finest to be found anywhere. The vaulted roof of the Lady Chapel is the earliest, being thirteenth century. While this roof is excellent, it does not have the beautiful symmetry of form or intricacy of the later, fifteenth-century vaults.

The earliest fan vaults are from the West Country, the first complete example being the cloisters of Gloucester Cathedral, from 1412. The Sherborne roof is much bigger,

• THE CONSTRUCTION OF STONE VAULTS •

Fully to appreciate the Sherborne roof vaulting, it is best to know a little about its construction. A vault is produced by ribs rising from the tops of columns and meeting at a central rib that runs parallel to the rows of columns. The space between ribs is filled with flat stone slabs called spandrels. To add stiffness to the structure, and also for decorative effect, further ribs called liernes run between the main structural ribs. There are several vault types, the differences between them depending on several constructional points, including the

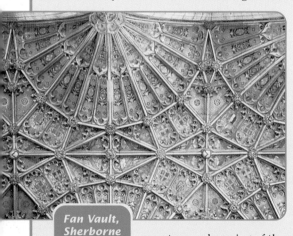

Fan Vault, Sherborne Abbey

curvature and spacing of the main ribs. At Sherborne the biggest roofs are fan vaults, in which several structural ribs rise from the same column and have the same spacing and curvature. At the head of the column the rising ribs really are fan-like.

Sherborne

however, the choir vault dating from around 1450 and being the earliest major fan vault in existence. The reddening of some columns of the vault is from the fire of 1437, the thatching presumably having been a temporary roof while the vault was being constructed. The immense weight of stone caused the vault to sag, the main ridge dropping about seven inches in the four centuries to 1856. At that time the whole vault and its support were rebuilt, an apparently colossal undertaking that was completed for just £425. The Victorians also restored the vault, painting and gilding the bosses which cover rib joints, and the spandrels.

The nave vault was built 60 years after that of the choir. It is very similar, but lierne ribwork and its associated tracery replaces the painted spandrels of the earlier work. The last fan vault is that in north transept. It has perhaps the most intricate stonework, though this is partially obscured by the organ. This vault also started to collapse and is now supported by a marvellous piece of modern, hidden engineering. Steel beams cross above the vault and steel rods drop from these to vault ribs into which they are screwed.

The height of the vaults adds wonderfully to their great beauty, giving the whole a majestic appearance. The roof bosses also form an interesting collection of medieval sculpture. In the earliest – choir – vault they are of foliage, but there is an owl being mobbed by crows, dogs with a bone, dragons, lions and some human figures. One of these is Green Man, thought to be based on a surviving folk memory of Celtic tree worship.

SHERBORNE – THE TOWN

Close to the abbey are the **Almshouses** of St John the Baptist and St John the Evangelist, built in 1442 for 'twelve pore feeble and ympotent old men and four old women', to be cared for by a housewife. The accommodation was on two floors, men below and women above. The building was extended in good style in 1858 to cater for sixteen men and eight women, and at the same time the laws governing the inmates were changed. Clearly there had been problems, for it was decided that expulsion could result from 'profane cursing and swearing... drunkenness... [and] promoting strife and debate'.

There is a fine view of the abbey from Abbey Close to the west of the Almshouses, while in Half Moon Street, linked to the Close, there is a row of shops, originally built in the sixteenth century and with one continuous room on the first floor, a room once used as the Church House.

Now walk up Cheap Street, with the abbey on your left. Cheap Street is the old market area, the name deriving from *ceping*, Saxon for a market. **The Conduit** was the monks' washroom, built in the early sixteenth century as a single-entrance building. The name derives from this usage, the water being piped into the trench inside. To celebrate the Restoration the plumbing was altered subtly, and for two days the Conduit ran with 'claret besides many Hogsheads of March beer'. Next is the **Abbey Gate House**, dating from the fifteenth century. It now houses the town museum with displays on the history of the town and abbey, and the local natural history.

Further on, at the junction with Abbey Road, is Abbeylands, a timber-framed house with an overhanging upper storey. At the top of Cheap Street there is interest to both left and right. To the left is **The Julian**, built in the sixteenth century although considerably restored, on the site of an inn of the same name. The name is from St Julian, a saintly East Anglian contemporary of Chaucer. Despite the name, the saint was a lady, though this does explain the dedication of an inn to her.

Raleigh

It was at the new castle that Raleigh was doused with ale by a servant who thought he was on fire as he smoked a pipe of his newest import from the American colonies – tobacco. Or so it is said. Raleigh was 'exiled' to Sherborne by Elizabeth in her fury over his marriage to Bess, her lady-in-waiting, but lost the estate when James I decided to have him removed permanently. Brave to the end, Raleigh tested the executioner's axe, deciding that it was sharp medicine, but a cure for all ills. When the axeman, as was customary, held up the head to the watching mob, there was none of the usual cheering. The crowd remained silent, except for one man who shouted that England did not have another such head to cut off.

Beside the house is a triangular stone set at an angle in the corner. This is a splashback: in the days before there were public conveniences, dark corners were much favoured by late-night travellers. Such stones discouraged such behaviour in a fairly straightforward manner.

From the Julian, bear left into Hospital Lane to reach Abbey Grange, once part of the abbey's tithe barn. Beside it is **Sherborne School**, which incorporates some of the old monastery buildings, noticeably the fourteenth century cloisters. By then the school was old: a case can be made for foundation at the same time as the first cathedral, that is in 705, and one story has Alfred the Great educated here. Certainly a school existed in the eleventh century, though the present one was founded by a royal charter of Edward VI in 1550.

To the east of the town centre are Sherborne's two castles. The **old castle** is a picturesque ruin. It dates from the early twelfth century, having been constructed by Roger of Salisbury, an early Norman bishop: it is more likely that the building was a fortified palace rather than a true castle. It must have been a reasonably formidable place even so, for its present state is largely due to its being 'slighted' (rendered useless as a fortress by demolition, in this case by cannon fire and the undermining of the walls) by Parliamentarians after it had been held for the king in the Civil War. The destruction of the castle was actually only completed by the Roundheads, as a previous owner had given up an attempted restoration late in the sixteenth century. That owner was Sir Walter Raleigh who acquired the castle estate from Elizabeth I, who persuaded the Church to part with it so that she could give it to her favourite.

Above left: The Conduit, Sherborne   Above right: Sherborne Old
Castle   Below: Sherborne New Castle

After his failure to restore the old building, Raleigh built the **new castle**, Sherborne Lodge as it was originally called. Since that time it has been extended twice: initially soon after Raleigh died, and again in the eighteenth century when the surrounding parkland was also landscaped by Capability Brown. The extensions were by the Digby family who have owned the castle since Raleigh's death.

The new castle is beautifully furnished and has an excellent collection of paintings. The castle stands in 20 acres of Brown's landscaped parkland where there are fine lakeside walks. The park is different now from the one walked by Raleigh and his beloved Bess, but it is easy to see why they loved Sherborne. As he was being driven past the town and estate on his way to London and death, Raleigh noted that it had all been his, but had been taken away from him.

TO THE SOMERSET BORDER

From Sherborne, take the B3145 northwards, soon reaching a crossroads with a turn to **Poyntington** to the right. Poyntington is a pretty village with a medieval courthouse beside the church, in which Judge Jeffreys is said to have held an assize, but our route is left to **Sandford Orcas**. This attractive stone-cottaged village was part of Somerset until 1896, but sits well in its new county, the Tudor manor house being very much Dorset. It was built in the early sixteenth century by Edward Knoyle and is reached via a gatehouse with separate archways for pedestrians and carriages. Inside the house there is

a fine array of Jacobean woodwork. The house is well worth a visit, as is the village church which has memorials to members of the Knoyle family.

South-west from Sandford Orcas is **Trent**, which also has a manor house (not open to the public). It was here that King Charles II stayed for several weeks during his flight from Worcester to the Dorset coast and a boat to France. During his stay at the house he attended church as a servant so as to avoid rumours of a secret guest. The church, one of few in Dorset with a spire, is a delight, though the king would not have seen the notice requiring pattens and clogs to be removed before entry as it was not positioned until the nineteenth century. Inside the church are some fine memorials, including one to Colonel Francis Wyndham, who harboured the king and organised his escape. Lord Fisher, Archbishop of Canterbury in the 1960s, retired to Trent Rectory and died here in 1972. He is buried in the churchyard. Close to the church are some beautiful old buildings, perhaps the best being the chantry or priest's house, probably dating from about 1500.

Southwards are the two Compton villages, Over Compton, on the hill and Nether Compton in the valley. At Compton House in **Over Compton** is **Worldlife Butterflies**, with live butterflies and displays on conservation, and the Lullingstone Silk Farm with displays on silk production. The nearby church was rebuilt by Robert Goodden whose spectacular statue dominates the interior.

Southwards our tour crosses the A30 and reaches **Bradford Abbas** with its beautiful church, almost like a cathedral in miniature, with a superb 90ft (27m) tower. Inside there are beautifully carved bench ends.

South again, a left turn leads to Thornford, but we continue south to **Yetminster** where the village school was founded by the scientist Sir Robert Boyle, formulator of Boyle's Law. The school, at the western end of the village, was built in 1697 and is one of a fine collection of seventeenth-century buildings that make up the centre of the village. The yellow stone of the old cottages makes them very attractive, the fact that they stand beside the delightfully name River Wriggle even more so. To the west of Yetminster is the hamlet of **Ryme Intrinseca** with a claim to the most curious name in Dorset. It means the 'inner part of the border', probably referring to an ancient estate.

Head south towards Chetnole, then turn left to **Leigh** where, to the south of the village, at the top of a shallow hill there is a hexagonal earthwork about 25 yards across. This was the Miz Maze, a turf maze maintained annually by the village youths until about 1770 when the custom ended. Mazes were anciently believed to be an alleyway of man's tortuous path to heaven, and this may have been the reason this maze was created.

Now head north-eastwards, crossing the western tip of the Blackmoor Vale to reach the A352 near **Longburton**, a village strung out along the main road. In the church there are a series of fine effigies.

Now follow the main road northwards back to Sherborne, perhaps detouring one more time, taking a left turn to **Lillington**, a small, isolated village where, on 1 November 1593, Walter, the son of Sir Walter Raleigh and Elizabeth Throckmorton – his beloved Bess – was baptised. Walter was the couple's second child, their first son, born the year before, dying as an infant. The baptism took place here, rather than in Sherborne, because Raleigh was still keeping his marriage secret from Queen Elizabeth. Young Walter was killed in 1617 during a skirmish in the West Indies.

BLACKMOOR VALE: SHERBORNE TO STURMINSTER NEWTON

To explore the southern edge of the Vale, leave Sherborne southwards along the A352, soon turning left along the A3030. This road rises across the southern flank of Holt Hill to reach **Bishop's Caundle** where there are several good thatched cottages. The southern edge of the Vale can be explored from here, taking narrow roads that lead to Glenville's Wootton, then around Dungeon Hill, topped by a hill fort, to reach the Area of Natural Beauty (AONB). Climbing over the ridge at Buckland Newton takes the visitor into the Piddle Valley.

From Bishop's Caundle the main road descends into the valley of the Caundle Brook before reaching the deer park, on the left, around Stock Gaylard House, built in the eighteenth century. Here a right turn along the B3143 is a more direct route into the Piddle Valley, passing through **King's Stag**, reputedly named after a white deer that Henry III found while out hunting. It was so beautiful the king did not have the heart to kill it, and on hearing that Sir Thomas de la Lynde, the Sheriff of Blackmoor, had killed it, he imprisoned him, only releasing him on payment of a huge fine. The king is also said to have levied the 'White Hart Tax' on the locals.

Just off the main road to the east of Stock Gaylard is **Lydlinch**, the subject of a poem by William Barnes. Ahead now is **Sturminster Newton**. The town is reached by crossing a medieval bridge over the River Stour. The town, known locally as 'Stur' and the undisputed capital of the Blackmoor Vale, is a pretty place (despite Leland's description of it as 'no great thing, and the building of it mene'). Thomas Hardy lived here for two years, writing *The Return of the Native* at 'Riverside', and William Barnes was born at nearby Bagber and christened in Stur's church.

The centre of the town is delight-ful, and many of the side streets have lovely old timber-framed houses. To the north of the centre, in Bath Road, the chapel beside the ruins of the old town workhouse now houses the town museum which explores its history and that of Blackmoor Vale. Newton Mill, on the main road side of the old Stour bridge, dates from the seventeenth and eighteenth centuries. After falling into disrepair it was restored in the 1980s and can be visited.

To the east of Stur, **Girdlers Cop-pice** and **Piddes Wood**, on either side of the A357, are nature reserves, the Coppice now being re-coppiced for charcoal and hurdle making. Paths explore the beautiful woodland and meadows of the reserves. Just be-yond, to the left, is **Fiddleford Manor**, a mid-fourteenth-century manor house (one of Dorset's old-est). The manor has been carefully restored and is worth visiting for the roof alone, a magnificent structure. The house is in the hands of English

Heritage. Nearby is a mill with an inscription, dated 1566, which exhorts the miller to do his best.

A left turn now leads to Child Okeford and Hambledon Hill, while ahead is **Shillingstone**. The village had the tallest maypole in England – 110 ft (34m) – until 1890 when it was blown down in a gale, never to be replaced. At that time the village was called Shilling Okeford, more in keeping with the other Okeford villages. To the east of the village, at **Gain's Cross**, there was once a curious haunting, with the ghost of a man most foully murdered sitting in vigil on a gate. The gate, a wooden one, collapsed in time, either from age or the ghostly weight and was replaced by a metal one. This apparently stopped the haunt-ing – perhaps the new gate earthed the spirit, or there is an other-world version of piles brought on by sit-ting on cold metal.

From Okeford Fitzpaine a lovely lane leads below the steep side of Bell Hill to **Ibberton**, a spring line village with a church named after St Eustace (Eustachius, a Roman general martyred for his faith), a very rare dedication. A spring by the side of the church is known as Stachy's Well, also from St Eustace, though quite why the well bears the saint's name is unknown.

Turn right just before Woolland, leaving the escarpment to reach **Hazelbury Bryan**, where the village church and school – its heart if you like – are in a small hamlet with the odd name of Droop. A right turn in the main village leads back to Sturminster Newton, but first go left to **Mappowder** where the church has some interesting details. The tiny effigy of a knight holding a heart is believed to cover the heart burial of a member of the Coker family killed on a Crusade.

The Cokers lived at Mappowder Court for many years, but sold it in 1745 to a John Spencer. Spencer's son, also John, was created Earl Spencer in 1765: one of his direct descendants was Diana, Princess of Wales. The church also has a Green Man, a man with leaves or vines growing from his mouth, as seen in Sherborne Abbey. The face is on the east side of the nave. The novelist Theodore Francis Powys was a resident of Mappowder and is buried in the churchyard.

STURMINSTER NEWTON TO GILLINGHAM AND SHERBORNE

From Stur, two roads head north. The B3092 to Gillingham is the more interesting, though the B3091 which heads north-east to Shaftesbury crosses fine country. On the B3092 the first village is **Hinton St Mary** where a large fourth-century Roman mosaic pavement was found in 1963. The pavement is now in the British Museum. North again is

Marnhull, Thomas Hardy's Marlott, the home village of Tess. The Pure Drop Inn of the book is likely to have been modelled on the village inn, though attempts to discover the Durbeyfield cottage have led to the annoyance of private residents. Marnhull is a scattered village, something of a disappointment to lovers of the book who expect (and want) a smaller, prettier place.

Continuing along the B3092, the visitor bypasses Todber and passes through pretty Stour Provost to reach the A30 crossing at **East Stour**. Here eighteenth-century author Henry Fielding spent the first three years of his married life in the manor house which passed to him from his mother (he had also spent his boyhood here). At the end of this idyllic time he had managed to spend his inherited fortune and was forced to work, moving to Lowden and becoming a successful author. His most famous work, *Tom Jones*, may not have originated here, but some of the ideas behind it surely did.

Cross the A30 and continue along the B3092 to **Gillingham**. The somewhat disjointed town was once the centre of a royal hunting forest of which nothing now remains. Later it was an important silk milling and brick-making town. Sadly the best of the old silk mills burnt down a few years ago. These aspects of the town's history are explored in the town museum in Chantry Fields, a new area of the town, to the southwest of the centre. The town church is also worth visiting. It has a fourteenth-century chancel, though the rest is nineteenth century. Be sure to find the excellent memorial to Frances Durdoe (died 1733) with a relief panel of three standing female figures.

Memories to John Warren

Marnhull church is one of Blackmoor's best and has good, late sixteenth century brass and some fine memorials. Note the one to John Warren, the parish clerk who died in 1752:

.... who smoked all his life
And so did his wife
And now there's no doubt
But their pipes are both out

SHERBORNE AND THE SURROUNDING AREA

Abbey Church

Abbey Close
Sherborne
Open: May-September, daily 9am-6pm, October-March, daily 10am-4pm
☎ 01935 812452

Almshouses

Trendle Street
Sherborne
Open: Easter-September, Monday and Wednesday 2-4pm
☎ 01935 813245

New Castle

Sherborne
Open: Castle: April-October, Tuesday, Thursday, Saturday, Sunday and Bank Holiday Mondays 12.30-5pm. Grounds: April-October, Thursday-Tuesday 12.30-5pm
☎ 01935 813182

Old Castle (English Heritage)

Sherborne
Open: April-September, daily 10am-6pm; October daily 10am-5pm; November-March, Wednesday-Sunday 10am-4pm. Closed Christmas Day and Boxing Day.
☎ 01935 812730

Sandford Orcas Manor House

Sandford Orcas
Open: May-September, Monday 10am-6pm, Sunday 2-6pm. Also open Easter Monday 10am-6pm
☎ 01963 220206

Town Museum

Abbey Gate House
Church Lane
Sherborne
Open: All year, Tuesday-Saturday 10.30am-4.30pm, Sunday and Bank Holiday Mondays 2.30-4.30pm.
☎ 01935 812252

Worldlife Butterflies and Lullingstone Silk Farm

Compton House
Over Compton
Open: Easter-September, daily 10am-5pm. Also open at Autumn half-term.
☎ 01935 474608

Blackmoor Vale

Fiddleford Manor (English Heritage)
Nr Sturminster Newton
Open: April-September, daily 10am-6pm, October-March, Daily 10am-4pm. Closed 25, 26 December and 1 January.
☎ 01258 453731

Newton Mill

Sturminster Newton
Open: Easter-September, Saturday, Sunday, Monday and Thursday 11am-5pm
☎ 01258 473760

Purse Caundle Manor

Purse Caundle
Open: By appointment only.
☎ 01963 250400

Town Museum

Chantry Fields
Gillingham
Open: All year, Monday, Tuesday, Thursday and Friday 10am-5pm, Saturday 10am-12noon
☎ 01747 822173 or 823176

Continued overpage

Town Museum

Bath Road
Sturminster Newton
Open: April-September, Thursday
and Sunday 2.30-5pm
☎ 01258 473506

Longleat and Stourhead

Longleat
Nr Warminster
Wiltshire
Open: House: April-December, daily
11am-4pm (5.30pm from Easter to
October). Guided tours only at set
times between 10am-4pm from
October to December. Closed
Christmas Day.
Safari Park and other attractions:
April-October, daily 10am-5pm
☎ 01985 844400 (9am-6pm daily)
☎ 0891 884581 (for general informa-
tion 24 hours daily)

Stourhead House and Gardens (National Trust)

Sourton
Nr Warminster
Wiltshire
Open: House: April-October, Satur-
day-Wednesday 12noon-5.30pm or
dusk
Garden: All year, daily 9am-7pm or
sunset
King Alfred's Tower: April-October
Tuesday-Friday 2-5.30pm or dusk,
Saturday, Sunday and Bank Holiday
Monday 11.30am-5.30pm or dusk.
☎ 01747 841152

To return to Sherborne, head south-west to Buckhorn Weston which stands at the very edge of Blackmoor Vale, then turn south to **Kington Magna**. From the church in this pretty village there is a marvellous view across the Vale. Beyond the village, the minor road joins the A30. Turn right, crossing into Somerset, then turning left along the A357 to re-enter Dorset and reach **Stalbridge**, a large village with a very fine market cross (at its northern end) raised in the fifteenth century, but refurbished, and over 30 ft (9m) high.

Turn right in the village, following a minor road to **Stourton Caundle** where the church has a fine memorial tablet to Aylen Fernandez by Eric Gill and a fifteenth-century alabaster effigy said to be of Agnes Fauntleroy. Go west, then north to **Purse Caundle**, a pretty village with a lovely manor house, built in the late fifteenth century on the site of an earlier one in which kings hunting in local royal forest left their injured dogs for treatment and recuperation. The manor house has a Great Hall from its earliest building and some excellent later rooms and furnishings. Now head west along the A30 to return to Sherborne.

STOURHEAD AND LONGLEAT

To the north of Gillingham on the other side of the A303 lies **Stourhead**, a house and park that now belongs to the National Trust. The house was one of the first of the great Georgian houses, designed by Colin Campbell and completed in 1722. It was built for Henry

Hoare, a banker. Hoare bought the estate from the Stourton family who had owned it since the Norman conquest. The house was badly damaged by fire in 1902, but rebuilt in fine style. One of the parts most seriously damaged was the library where in 1751, legend has it, Edward Gibbon, then aged 14, was inspired to write the *Decline and Fall of the Roman Empire*. The house is superbly furnished, with carved woodwork by Grinling Gibbons, statues by Michael Rysbrack and a fine collection of paintings.

About 20 years after completion of the house Henry Hoare's son laid out the gardens, adding lakes and temples – a copy of the Roman Pantheon and the Baalbeck Temple of the Sun among others – statues and bridges. The whole is one of the finest eighteenth-century gardens in Britain, especially pleasing in spring when the azaleas and rhododendrons are in bloom, and in autumn when the beech trees turn to gold.

The entrance to the estate is marked by a late fourteenth- century High Cross brought here from Bristol. The lower niches of the Cross hold original statues of Kings John, Henry II, Edward III and Edward IV. The upper statues, of Henry VI, Elizabeth I, James I and Charles I were added in 1663. To the east of the estate, Alfred's Tower, a well-known landmark, was raised in 1772 on the traditional site of Alfred's raising of his standard in 878 to form an army to fight the Danish invaders.

Longleat stands on the site of an Augustinian (later Carthusian) Priory. At the Dissolution the estate was bought by Sir John Thynne for £53. It is still in the hands of the Thynne family, now the marquis of Bath. Sir John lived in the monastery buildings, but gradually rebuilt and extended: what the visitor now sees is mostly from the mid-sixteenth century. The huge house is in fine Elizabethan style, with a uniform design on all four façades, an unusual feature for the time. The interior is as grand as the exterior with beautiful furnishings and priceless artwork. Longleat is the home of the Needlecraft Centre, and there are excellent collections of costume and Flemish tapestries.

Longleat's gardens are in formal, Italian style, but the parkland was the work of Capability Brown who spent five years here, from 1757 to 1762. Later the park was remodelled by Sir Humphrey Repton.

Today the grounds are more famous for the **Safari Park**, Britain's first. Vehicles are required to enter the big cat, wolf, rhinoceros and elephant enclosures, but visitors can walk among giraffes, zebras, camels and llamas. The park also accommodates sea lions and gorillas, and a tropical house with stunning butterflies. At the pets' corner, children can get much closer to the animals.

To complete the attractions there is the world's longest hedge maze, a railway and a collection of dolls' houses.

T he Isle of Purbeck is, of course, nothing of the kind, but in ancient times the area must have appeared island-like to those living in it and to those living north of the River Frome. The Frome is a broad river and at its mouth is a wide area of marshland which gradually becomes Poole Harbour. This broad marsh and the wide valley seem to separate Purbeck from the rest of Dorset. To the east and south lie the sea. Only to the west was there land access on to, and off, the Isle. But it was steep, deeply folded country, a sparsely populated area that must have seemed as difficult to cross as the river or sea.

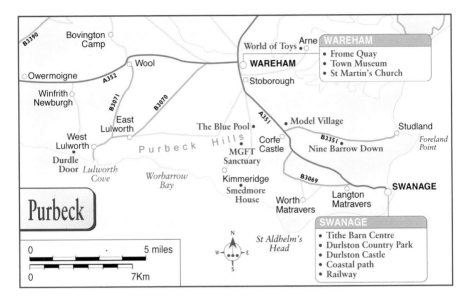

Today the western edge of the Isle is loosely defined. Most folk agree that it follows the coast to Lulworth Cove, perhaps even Durdle Door, then follows the Luckford Lake stream from East Lulworth to the Frome. Of course the less romantic would follow the B3070. Here, for no very good reason, we push the western border further west, beyond Chaldon Down to the A353 and Osmington.

Purbeck has one of the most extraordinary geologies of any similarly-sized area in Britain, a fact that adds an extra dimension to a visit, producing a contrasting range of scenery within a journey rather than within a day or so. The Kimmeridge rocks, the Isle's oldest, contain layers of bituminous shale which are exploited for the oil. To the east the hard Purbeck limestone creates dramatic cliff-scapes and was once quarried. Within the limestone beds are thin seams of a close-grained rock composed almost entirely of freshwater snail shells, with colours from pale grey to pale green, that could be polished – Purbeck marble.

To the north of the limestone is a band of clay and then the Purbeck Hills, chalk hills that end with the spectacular cliffs of the Foreland Point. North again there is sandy heath, but even here there is a peculiarity – ball clay of such quality that it was extracted to form fine china: much of Wedgwood's china was made of Purbeck clay, including the most famous order, the 1,000-piece service for Catherine the Great of Russia.

To explore this remarkable Isle we shall start at Wareham, its 'capital', then move on to Corfe Castle and Swanage, before heading west to the tortured cliffs of Lulworth.

WAREHAM

The site between the rivers Frome and Piddle, bounded to the east by the sea, was recognised for its defensive qualities early, there being evidence of an Iron Age settlement. Certainly by the seventh century there was a Saxon town, Bishop Aldhelm founding a church (probably where St Martin's sits today) in 698. In 876 Guthrum, a Viking leader took the town, recognising both its local defences and its strategic importance – his fleet could reach it safely, and the Frome Valley offered a route westward. In 877 King Alfred moved against the Vikings: in a sea battle off Swanage it is said that the Norsemen lost 120 ships. Deprived of his supply route Guthrum had to leave Wareham: by 879 he had also left Wessex, and the stage was set for a leap in Wareham's prosperity. Alfred decided to defend the south coast, setting up fortified towns *(burhs)* not more than 20 miles (32km) apart. Wareham was one of these towns, three-sides of a square of defensive walls, topped by a wooden fence, being erected around it. The fourth side was protected by the Frome. The town walls (reinforced by the Normans) can still be seen and walked, offering fine views of the town.

As peace returned to Wessex, Wareham's special position made it an important trading centre, the more so after it was granted a royal mint and King Athelstan decreed that all trade had to take place in the *burhs*. As Wareham was also a port its fortunes rose sharply. The town remained prosperous when the Normans arrived, but the wars between Stephen and Matilda, in which Wareham sided with Matilda

and was besieged by Stephen's army, caused a decline. This was heightened when the Normans, who had built a castle at the town, poured their resources into the Corfe Castle. As if these things were not enough, Wareham's harbour also began to silt up. As ships grew larger this silting became ever more of a problem and led to the development of Poole.

During the Civil War Wareham changed hands several times, narrowly escaping total destruction at the hands of the Parliamentarian commander Sir Anthony Ashley Cooper. Cooper wanted to burn the town to the ground to stop its potential use by Royalists. The town was saved (though Cooper was proved right when the Royalist retook it, but only for a few weeks) but in 1762 it was razed anyway when fire roared through it. The fire is said to have started when ashes were emptied on to a dung heap. In just a few hours on a hot July day, almost 75 per cent of the town was destroyed.

A TOUR ROUND WAREHAM

Wareham was rebuilt in fine eighteenth- and nineteenth-century style and is a delight. To explore it, start at the **Frome Quay** at the southern end of the town. Once Wareham's trading heart, the Quay is now used mainly by pleasure craft and, with the eighteenth century bridge crossing the river, is very picturesque.

On its eastern side are the **Priory**, now a hotel, which incorporates part of a sixteenth-century monastic building. Legend has it that there was a nunnery on this site in Saxon times and there was certainly a Benedictine house in Norman times. This became a Carthusian Priory, which was dissolved in 1536. The nearby Lady St Mary Church had a Saxon nave until 1842 when it was demolished and the present church built. St Edward's Chapel dates from a Norman church of about 1100.

Leave the quay into South Street. Across the road is Abbot's Quay. This can be followed to Tanners Lane (bear right) and Pound Lane (turn left) where the remains of Wareham Castle (an earth mound and some ditches) lie on private land. Continuing along Pound Lane reaches the old walls at a point known as Bloody Banks, so called because here three 'rebels' were hanged, drawn and quartered after one of Judge Jeffreys' Assizes. The rebels' heads were placed on spikes, but on the first night a local man, Thomas Delacourt, removed the heads, hid them (under his bed, legend has it) and later buried them secretly.

From the quay, turn right along South Street. **The Black Bear Hotel,** on the left, has a life-sized bear above the door. It is said that if the bear falls from its position the world will end. Further along the street is The Cross, with the overpowering and rather ugly Town Hall on the right. Turn right into East Street, passing the **Streche Almshouses** on the right. These were originally built by John Streche (who died in 1418), but have been rebuilt since. The belfry and cupola were taken from the Old Town Hall. Further along East Street, on the left, is the **Town Museum** with displays on local history and a very good collection on TE Lawrence. To the left (along West Street) at The Cross, a detour is worth-while to see the **Rex Cinema.** This dates from the 1910s and is the only remaining gas-lit cinema in Britain. Films are shown by means of carbon arc projectors.

St Martin's Church

From The Cross, continue ahead along elegant North Street to reach **St Martin's Church**. This, too, has Saxon origins. Indeed it is one of Dorset's best surviving Saxon churches, dating from the early eleventh century. The Saxon work is the nave and chancel arch. The north aisle is twelfth century and the tower sixteenth. Inside, pride of place is taken by the full-size marble effigy of TE Lawrence in Arab dress. The effigy, by Lawrence's friend Eric Kennington, was supposed to lie in Salisbury Cathedral, but the Dean declined to accept it and it was placed here. It is a superb work and should not be missed.

FROM WAREHAM TO CORFE CASTLE

To the south of Wareham a turn to the left from the A351 leads to **Arne**, crossing Hartland Moor, one of Purbeck's two finest sections of heath, the other being at Studland. Also at Arne is **A World of Toys**, a museum devoted to childhood, with collections of toys – trains, cars, lead soldiers – together with collections of teddy bears, dolls, dolls' houses and musical boxes. A fascinating place.

Further along the A351, at Stoborough Green, a right turn leads to the **Blue Pool**, a pretty pool surrounded by 25 acres of heathland with heather, gorse and pine. The pool is an old clay pit (used for the

North Street, Wareham

• PURBECK HEATH'S RARE WILDLIFE •

The **Dartford warbler** has not been seen for many years near the site of its discovery near Dartford. It is now to be found almost exclusively on the Dorset heaths, specifically Studland, Hartland and Arne. It is an inactive bird and therefore vulnerable to bad weather, so its numbers depend on the degree of severity of the previous winter. A handsome bird, it has a wine-coloured breast, grey head and long tail, boldly cocked. The birds feed low in the heathland scrub and are rarely in view for long, particularly if the wind is blowing, so the visitor who wishes to see them must be very quiet and patient.

The **smooth snake**, so called because its scales lack the ridge characteristic of the adder and grass snake and thus is velvety smooth, is the rarest of British reptiles, occurring only on the southern heaths. It is long and sleek, beautiful in silver with small dark markings. Ironically, its chief food was the **sand lizard**, itself now restricted to the southern heaths and so rare that the smooth snake has had to change its diet. The sand lizard is longer than the common lizard which its resembles, and the male turns bright green on its sides and belly during the mating season in May and June.

Even if you are not lucky enough to see any of the rarer species, a visit to the heath is worthwhile. The dominant plant is the common heather or ling, but other species of heather occur, as do gorse and a few stunted trees. In places where drainage is poor, there is bogland and even the occasional pond where dragonflies will be seen. The wetlands support not only these fine insects, the falcons of the insect world, but rare plants as well such as bog asphodel, pimpernel and sundew. The heaths are also home to rare insects including the large marsh grasshopper, several smaller grasshoppers, bog bush crickets and butterflies such as the silver-studded blue. In winter, the visiting bird life includes merlins and hen harriers.

extraction of Purbeck's fine china clay) and changes colour with the angle of view and with temperature, both as a result of clay particles in suspension. In warm weather the particles settle and the water turns green. In colder weather they rise and the water turns blue. Paddling and swimming are not allowed in the pool. The site also has a museum exploring the history of the Purbeck clay industry: there is a remarkable collection of clay pipes and some porcelain from a wrecked Dutch East Indiaman. There is also a tea shop.

Continuing south the visitor will soon reach Corfe Castle, but before reaching the town, take the left turn along the B3351 to visit Studland and Foreland Point. **Studland** is a notoriously difficult village in which to park. When you have, the church is worth visiting: it is a virtually complete twelfth-century Norman building and is very beautiful. From

Studland, most visitors head east to Foreland Point, but there is a fine walk to the west, crossing heath to reach the Agglestone, a huge single stone estimated to weight 400 tons and standing over 16 ft (5m) high. It was reputedly thrown here from the Isle of Wight by the Devil – he was aiming at the 'skittles' of Old Harry and his wife, but missed.

The best walk to **the Agglestone** is from the car park just beyond the Knoll House Hotel. From the same car park, a nature trail follows the shore line of Studland Bay and then explores a section of the Studland Nature Reserve. Studland Heath (which extends beyond the Agglestone and covers the area up to the sand dunes of the shore), Hartland Moor and Arne Heath are the last stronghold of three of Britain's rarest species – the Dartford warbler, the smooth snake and the sand lizard.

Visitors to Studland walk to Old Harry for the most dramatic view of the chalk Purbeck Hills, but the hills are worth exploring along their length. From Corfe Castle a path traverses the long chalk ridge, starting with a climb of East Hill. Eastward the chalk ridge changes name frequently – Rollington Hill, Brenscombe Hill, Ailwood Down, Nine Barrow Down, Godlingston Hill. In the past these hills supported Dorset Horn sheep, a small animal with the remarkable ability to breed twice yearly. Efforts to make it a bigger sheep by cross-breeding created the Dorset Down breed, but lost the abundant lambing. The chalk grasslands were created and are maintained by such grazing: if the land is ungrazed it returns to scrub. It is an interesting contradiction that this apparently natural land-scape is maintained by farming.

To the north of Brenscombe Hill, at Brenscombe Farm, the Romans built a villa at the spring line of the slope, sheltered from the prevailing weather by the ridge. Beyond Brenscombe Hill is **Nine Barrow Down**, a name correct in terms of

Ballard Down

Ballard Down is probably the best place for butterflies in Dorset, and one of the best spots in England because it receives influxes of migrants. These may only be red admiral, peacock or painted lady, but they are found in such numbers as to produce a breathtaking spectacle. Rarer species also occur, mostly notably the clouded yellow. To these migrant swarms are added the 'ordinary' English butterflies – brimstone, orange tip and small tortoiseshell, the last named clinging on to each head of the abundant carline thistle.

At the end of Ballard Down are the steep chalk cliffs that are the target of walkers from Studland. At their highest the cliffs plunge over 350 ft (100m) into the sea, the chalk dazzlingly white in the sun. The cliffs are as distinctive as the White Cliffs of Dover, and more attractive – giant bites taken out of the chalk, leaving pinnacles, natural arches, narrow headlands and spectacular coves.

structure if numerically inaccurate. Purbeck's Neolithic folk set a single 100ft (30m) barrow on the ridge, but it is named after their Bronze Age successors who added 17 round barrows to the cemetery, mostly grouped around the original tomb, but two offset on Godlingston Hill where they have been given fanciful names: Giant's Grave and Giant's Trencher.

At the western end of Nine Barrow Down is the highest point of the ridge and of Purbeck, 654 ft (199m) above the sea. On again is another small gap in the ridge, not as steep or as wide as that at Corfe. Beyond, an obelisk tops Ballard Down, a granite needle erected by George Burt of Swanage to commemorate, as the inscription says, 'the introduction of pure water from the chalk formation to Swanage'. It notes, grandly, that the granite was brought from near the Mansion House, London, without actually mentioning that it was then a gas-lamp post.

At **Foreland Point** (also occasionally called Handfast Point) are the twin stacks of Old Harry and Old Harry's Wife. **Old Harry** was made a virtual widower in the gales of 1896 when his wife was almost destroyed, and he too has been undermined and will eventually go the same way. The point was described by Thomas Hardy as a 'windy, sousing, thwacking, basting, scourging Jack Ketch of a corner'. In rough weather that is true, but it can also be a tranquil spot to sit and watch the cormorants on the stacks and view the Needles over on the Isle of Wight. To the south of the Point, the cliff has been undermined to form a cave called the Parson's Barn. The name derives from the time when tithes were demanded from the peasant folk – a time when nothing was as large as the parson's barn!

The walk along the cliffs of Foreland Point is magnificent, but please be cautious: in wet weather chalk becomes slimy and very slippery, and in dry weather, particularly if the sun is shining, the surface at the cliff edge can become glazed.

This fine walk along the Purbeck Hills started at **Corfe Castle**, the next place along the A351 south of Wareham. Corfe Castle stands at a cleft in the Purbeck Hills, a gap several hundred yards wide roughly half-way along the range. Within the gap there is a natural mound, an outlier from the hills. The advantages of fortifying the mound were obvious, and the Saxons certainly appreciated them, there being a castle of some sort on the mound by the tenth century. Today the remnants of a later castle stand on the mound. The site is one of the most dramatic in Dorset. From the north, the Purbeck Hills stand like a green wall along the horizon except for this one gap. In that gap is the castle on its mound, the stump of an old tooth spoiling the perfect symmetry of Purbeck's smile.

It is not clear when the first castle was built, but there was certainly one here in 978 when the **young King Edward**, son of King Edgar, came after hunting to visit his stepmother Elfrida and step-brother Ethelred. The young king, probably 15 years old at the time, was no stranger to the castle and would have thought little of being met outside by servants of Elfrida who offered him wine. He drank and, as he did so, was stabbed in the back. His horse bolted, the boy staying in the saddle until loss of blood caused him to fall. His foot snagged the stirrup and he was dragged some distance until his body was released, to lie in a stream at the foot of the hills. Elfrida's servants hurriedly gathered up the body and hid it in a nearby cottage, taking and burying it a few days later in an unmarked grave near Wareham.

St Edward's Well

One story has it that the body of Edward was placed not in a grave but in a well, and that the well was lit by a shaft of light so that those searching for the body could find it. The well water had miraculous curative power and was known as St Edward's Well. After it had been found, the body was taken to Shaftesbury Abbey, and as the funeral procession left Wareham, Elfrida tried to join it, but each horse she mounted refused to move and she was left behind.

Following the murder, St Dunstan, Archbishop of Canterbury, crowned Ethelred king, noting that no good could come of a reign that started in so bloody a fashion. As if to prove him right, Ethelred became the Unready, and the Danes plundered his kingdom. Elfrida, the new king's mother, is believed to have been behind the murder, but the boy's death was badly received everywhere and she was overcome with guilt. To atone for her sin she retired to a nunnery she built at Bere Regis.

As the years went by the stories

of the boy king's goodness spread and legends sprang up around the tale of his murder. The hut in which he lay was owned by a blind woman, and on the night the body lay there a heavenly light filled the hut and her sight was restored.

The castle that now lies in ruins on top of the mound in Corfe Gap is not the one that brooded over the death of Edward the Martyr. The ruin is of a **Norman castle**, initially built by William the Conqueror, but greatly improved by King John who used it as a royal prison. Here he imprisoned the wife and son of William de Braose, a Marcher lord infamous for his treacherous dealings with the Welsh in and around Abergavenny. De Braose fled the king's wrath to France, his family being held against his surrender. The bargain was straightforward – come back or they starve to death. De Braose did not return, John did not relent, the wife and son did not survive.

Since the castle had its own well it was virtually impregnable. Any direct assault faltered on the steep mound and beneath the walls, and the Purbeck ridges were too far away for missiles to create much more than an annoyance. Even in the early days of cannon this was true, for Corfe Castle held out as a Royalist stronghold against a Parliamentarian siege for almost two years towards the end of the Civil War. The castle was held for the king by Lady Bankes, wife of Sir John, whose small garrison – apparently just five men supported by Lady Banks' maids – defied all efforts to dislodge it. They were resupplied at one stage by a small troop under a Royalist officer called Cromwell (an unfortunate name for a king's man), who

Above: Corfe Castle Below: Abbot's Quay, Wareham

brought with him the recently captured Roundhead governor of Wareham.

The Dungeon

As a prison the castle was formidably set, and the dungeon, at the extreme west of the site, is every schoolboy's dream. It was reached by a trap door in the ceiling: if the prisoner survived the fall, there was little chance of escaping. The unfortunate inmates sat in darkness and their own rising filth waiting for the trap to move bringing a shaft of light, some less foul air, food and water. And if the trap did not open they could shout themselves hoarse for all the castle guard cared. Twenty-two French knights lay here once and starved.

Unfortunately the governor was smooth-tongued and persuaded one of the garrison to betray the castle in exchange for safe conduct. The Parliamentarian commanders decided the castle should never again be a threat and ordered it to be slighted: the walls were undermined and blown up with gunpowder. In the early days of the siege the lead was stripped from the church roof and used for shot. The unprotected church decayed quickly and was also soon in ruins.

The town of Corfe grew up around the castle, taking its name. It was a prosperous place in the early years of the stone trade, having a monopoly on the shipment of stone through Ower Quay on Poole Harbour. An interesting tradition from that time is that, on Ash Wednesday, Corfe's most recently married man supplies a football which is kicked from the town to Ower, the lord of the manor (who 'owns' the road) being given a pound of pepper for allowing the 'procession'. This most unlikely event is great fun and draws crowds from all over.

The town is worth exploring for its beautiful houses. West Street especially is lovely. In it are the town museum, exploring its history, and the model village, a one-twentieth scale model of the village in authentic Purbeck stone. The Square, the open area below the castle, is also delightful. Close by is the church – dedicated to St Edward, of course – with a fifteenth century tower: the rest is nineteenth century and has some good internal features in Purbeck marble. There are also some very attractive buildings in East Street.

Having explored Corfe Castle, follow the main road to reach Swanage.

SWANAGE

The history of Swanage is the history of Purbeck stone quarrying, for although there was a small fishing village here before the stone was first worked, most of the houses in the town owe their existence to the quarries. At first the stone was gathered by anyone willing to land a boat near the cliffs, but a more regulated trade was soon established, using Corfe Castle as a trade centre and Ower Quay (to the north of Corfe) as a dock.

The poor tracks that led from Swanage to Corfe were the only connection between the town and the outside world at that time and, as a result, most of Swanage's supplies came by ship. It seems strange, in view of these imports, that it took the Civil War, the destruction of Corfe Castle and the decline of the town beside it, to persuade Swanage that being its own port would increase its prosperity. Even then it was not until the early 1800s that Swanage really took off.

John Mowlem was born in Swanage in 1788. He trained as a quarryman, then went to London where he worked as a stone mason. Soon he started his own company, at first chiefly building roads, taking on his nephew, George Burt, to assist. Mowlem and Burt were clearly hard working and imaginative. They bought a quarry in Guernsey and several ships to transport stone. They demolished buildings in London, shipped the stone back to Swanage as ballast in the company ships before re-erecting the buildings. The stone they collected from Swanage was hauled to the quay by horses and 'banked' (stacked) by the shore at a place still known as **Bankers**.

When the ships arrived the stone was loaded on to large-wheeled carts which were hauled into the water. The stone was transferred into lighters and rowed to the stone-carrying ships. Only when John Mowlem returned to Swanage in 1844 was a stone quay built. Mowlem also built the town's first proper roads, a real bonus as the stone carts turned the earth roads to mud in winter and threw up choking dust in summer. Mowlem and Burt also built a town hall, a library and a museum, and gave the town piped water. In 1868 Mowlem died, leaving Burt as the unofficial lord of Swanage. Burt responded by building Durlston Castle and the Great Globe, and Purbeck House.

Burt also sought to develop Swanage as a seaside resort. After several years of lobbying the railway arrived in 1885, bringing visitors and also linking the town with the outside world by means other than sea. The railway also exported some stone. George Burt died in 1894, having seen his vision for Swanage fulfilled. The railway closed in 1972, but has recently been reopened between Norden and Swanage, adding an extra attraction to the glorious coastal scenery that lies north and south of Swanage Bay.

An exploration of Swanage should start at the **Mill Pond**, the most picturesque spot in town. The pond, and the spring that fed it, was the town's water supply for many years, but the cattle and horses that also used it stirred up the mud causing annoyance to the locals. John Mowlem solved the problem by building the enclosing walls. The bubbles rising from the spring can be seen by looking hard at the pond's centre. Close to the pond is the town **church**. The oldest part, the bottom part of the tower, is fourteenth century and was originally a defensive tower. The tower had no door at ground level, the locals climbing a ladder to a single floor 33ft (10m) high and then hauling the ladder up behind them: the tower was necessary because of frequent raids by French pirates in the thirteenth and fourteenth centuries. The tower was incorporated into the church in a major rebuild of 1620. There was a further remodelling in the nineteenth century.

North of the church is the railway

station. When the railway closed in 1972 the track was lifted, but in 1975 a local group of enthusiasts took over the old station and laid new track. The railway, which uses steam locomotives, currently reaches Norden, just beyond Corfe Castle, but the aim is to reach the BP terminal at Furzebrook and so connect with the mainline station at Wareham.

From the Mill Pond go south, then turn left along High Street, soon reaching **Purbeck House** on the right. This was George Burt's house, built in 1875 on the site of a Georgian house which he demolished. Both the house and gardens have items salvaged from London demolitions: an arch from Hyde Park Corner, with columns and panels from Billingsgate Fish Market; even tiles and stone chips from the Houses of Parliament and Albert Memorial. These have been blended into a rich tapestry of a house with an octagonal tower and a wall gazebo, a truly delightful building.

Further along High Street, on the left, is the **Town Hall**. This, too, is an amalgam, its façade once gracing Mercer's Hall in London's Cheapside, and is equally attractive. Behind the hall is the town's old lock-up. The 'Blind House', as it was known locally, has a tablet above the door noting that it was 'Erected for the Prevention of Vice and Immorality'.

Bear right with the High Street: soon, on the right at 2 Victoria Terrace, is **John Mowlem's house**. The curious turret on the roof is where Mowlem had a telescope to observe the stars at night, and stone loading during the day. Further along High Street, also on the right, is the old Royal Victoria Hotel (now private apartments) renamed when

Princess Victoria spent one night in it in 1835.

Now head for the sea front where the old rails for the stone trucks can still be seen. There is also a memorial to King Alfred's sea victory over the Vikings. Heading east, towards Peveril Point, the old stone quay is passed. The next landmark is the Wellington clock tower, also brought here from London (it stood at the southern end of London Bridge) where it had been dismantled in 1854 as a hazard to traffic. The two Ionic pillars also came from London.

DURLSTON COUNTRY PARK AND THE COASTAL PATH TO KIMMERIDGE

To the south of Swanage is **Durlston Country Park**, an area of unspoilt country covering the coast from Durlston Head to Anvil Point.

Durlston Castle was built by George Burt in 1887 and is as curiously eccentric as many of his other works. One of Burt's original intentions, that it be a restaurant, was – and still is – realised, but his second, that Lloyds use it as a signal station, was not. Below the castle is **Burt's Great Globe**, with the continents and rivers picked out. The Globe is a 10-ft (3-m) diameter sphere of Portland stone weighing 40 tons. It was constructed in 15 segments at Greenwich and pieced together here – using granite dowels – at the same time as the castle was being erected.

Behind the globe are slabs of stone with the most surprising information – there are more on the wall of the castle. The relative sizes of the sun (1090 ft – 332m) and the moon (2 ft 9 ins – 84cms) to the 10-foot

Above left: Purbeck Cliffs Above right: The Great Globe at Durlston Country Park Below: The bay at Swanage

globe, and other items reflect Burt's own preoccupations. The common black swift does not fly at a rate of 200 miles per hour, despite the tablets of stone!

Below the Globe the visitor reaches information boards on the bird life often seen, and the dolphins occasionally seen, off Durlston Head. From here the Coastal Path offers a magnificent walk – all the way to Devon of course, but a walk of just a mile or two – a few kilometres – is worthwhile. Soon reached are the **Tilly Whim Caves**. The caves are named after the owner, Mr Tilly, who used a whim, a wooden derrick, to lower blocks of stone directly into barges for transport to Swanage. Next comes Anvil Point and its lighthouse.

Beyond the lighthouse, on the **Coastal Path** to St Aldhelm's Head, the visitor is alone with the sea and the gulls. The cliff is not as high here and is generally left by the rock climbers to the kittiwakes; there are no houses or close villages, making the Coastal Path remote and less frequented. The limestone has been weathered to impressive shapes, angular blocks and ledges, with occasional evidence of man's involvement with the sea.

There are quarry caves above Dancing Ledge, where barges were loaded. The ledges are so called because the strata, pushing out into the sea at a low angle, cause the sea water to dance around the rocks. Here the seabirds include puffins – now, sadly, reduced to just a handful of pairs – while in winter the spot is well-known for black redstarts. On the top of the cliffs here early spider orchids thrive, one of the few places in Britain where they are found.

At **Hedbury** there are more caves and a Georgian cannon facing out to sea, a dim reminder of an enemy who never came. The Seacombe Quarries are the best of all, with cave entrances shored up by columns of Purbeck stone. Above are the metal cocoons that were machine-gun posts built for a more recent invasion scare.

Next is the level ground of **East Man** where some of the 170 people who drowned when the East Indiaman *Halsewell* was wrecked in January 1786 are buried. The sea mangled the bodies of the dead, but tossed up on shore, untouched, the hourglass that kept the watch on the ship. Some of those who survived the wreck clung to the cliffs at Seacombe until help arrived from Worth Matravers. The village can be reached from each end of East Man

The cliffs now rise higher as **St Aldhelm's Head** is approached. The head is windswept, impressively sheer and shows the weird architecture that quarrying and weathering bring to limestone. On its flat top are the ruins of a radio station, the whitewashed coastguard cottages and the massive, buttressed fortress that is **St Aldhelm's Chapel**, dedicated to Aldhelm of Sherborne and dating from the twelfth century. But is it really a chapel? Its huge walls, a yard thick, reduce the inside to an almost perfect 26ft (8m) square, hardly the usual ground plan for a Norman church. And who worshipped here?

But chapels can be built for more than one reason, and there is a legend that a Norman knight stood here one day in the mid-twelfth century, to wave goodbye to his child, son or daughter, on the day of his or her wedding. The newly-weds left

Purbeck by ship, perhaps for a honeymoon in Normandy, and before the knight's eyes the ship was torn apart by the treacherous waters below the Head. The helpless man watched his child die and swore that all future travellers would know of the Head. He built his chapel landmark and gave it a turret roof so that a light could burn to guide ships at night.

Beyond St Aldhelm's Head the Coastal Path undulates its way westwards. It falls steeply below the rugged crags of Emmetts Hill, and goes down to the sea itself at **Chapman's Pool**. This is more the seaside of childhood: safe bathing in an enclosed cove, a couple of small boats on the water, rocks and rock pools – and the rocks are packed with ammonites as a bonus. Beyond the pool, **Hounstout Cliff** rises steeply, giving a sharp climb, with an easier descent to the even ground above the Kimmeridge Ledges. At **Clavell's Hard** a water-fall drops 30 ft (9m) to the beach below, and here, as if to prove the point that there is oil in the shale rock, the cliff caught fire in 1973 and burned for several months.

The next landmark is Clavell Tower, now a dangerous ruin, built by the Reverend John Richards of Smedmore House in 1820 and named after the Clavell family who had owned the house and were Richards' ancestors. The tower could have been an observatory, but may have been a folly. Beyond the tower is Kimmeridge Bay.

SWANAGE TO KIMMERIDGE

Returning from Swanage to Corfe Castle, bear left on the B3069, going through **Langton Matravers** where the Coach House Museum tells the story of the local stone industry. Here, too, is the **Putlake Adventure Farm** where children can meet farm animals and pets, perhaps feeding the calves and lambs. There is also a farm trail, and the farm has a tea shop.

Worth Matravers churchyard

In Worth Matravers church yard lies Benjamin Jesty, a local farmer. His epitaph notes that he died in 1810 aged 79, and that 'he was born at Yetminster in this County and was an upright honest man particularly modest for having been the first person known that introduced the Cow Pox by inoculation and who from his great strength of mind made the Experiment from the Cow on his wife and two sons in the Year 1774'. The story is true, Jesty 'inventing' inoculation before Jenner at Berkeley, Gloucestershire, though it is the latter who is remembered for having done so.

Jesty's local reception was the same as Jenner's, however: both men were hated and ridiculed for their experiments by a superstitious folk who believed they would be turned into cows by the procedure and who, in any case, felt that smallpox was a judgement from heaven and not to be trifled with.

The village duck pond at Worth Matravers

Lulworth Cove

From Langton, a minor road leads north-west to **Worth Matravers**, a prettier village, its stone cottages grouped around a duck pond. The village inn, the Square and Compass, takes its name from old quarrying tools, Worth once being a centre for stone quarrying – on the coast at Winspit, just a short walk away. The village church is a Norman building, almost as good as that at Studland. The thirteenth-century tympanum shows the Coronation of the Virgin, but it is sadly weathered.

Continue along the B3069, from where there are marvellous views, to the right of Corfe Castle, to reach **Kingston**, a pretty village dominated by its church built, of local stone, by GE Street for the Earl of Eldon. It is a magnificent building, but far too large for the village. The B3069 rejoins the A351: turn left to Corfe, then left again along a minor road to **Church Knowle**, a very attractive village. Here the MGFT (Margaret Green Foundation Trust) Animal Sanctuary is devoted to the rescue and care of horses and other animals.

Just beyond the village a turn to the left leads to **Kimmeridge**, a nicely positioned, neat village. To the east is **Smedmore House**, a very beautiful, tree-shrouded building. It was built of Portland stone in 1761, incorporating an earlier house of Sir William Clavell. Inside there is a wealth of period furniture, an eighteenth-century kitchen and a museum with a collection of dolls and some historical items.

From the village a road leads down to a car park at **Kimmeridge Bay**. The Kimmeridge clays are dark grey bands of clay and bituminous shale formed when muddy waters overlaid coral reefs. From earliest times the shale has been recognised as a fuel, but the technology to extract oil from the beds did not exist until quite recently. Now on the cliff edge there is a nodding donkey extracting 40,000–60,000 barrels of oil daily. Off shore is the **Purbeck Marine Wildlife Reserve**, set up to preserve the unique flora and fauna of Kimmeridge Bay. The Reserve covers habitats from the shore to a depth of 66ft (20m) and includes a marked trail for divers. Snorkellers will also be able to enjoy parts of the trail. The plant life includes a number of species of wrack, anemone and sponge, with many crabs and shellfish as well as fish. The Reserve covers the Bay as far west as Mupe Rocks, but the western section falls within the Army's Lulworth range and access is restricted in exactly the same way as it is for walkers.

THE COASTAL PATH TO LULWORTH COVE

Beyond the oil well is the boundary of the army's firing range. When attempting to walk the ranges, which extend from here to Lulworth Cove and inland to the Purbeck Hill ridge, it is absolutely necessary to obey certain rules that are posted at the range boundaries. **Do not enter if the gates are locked; stick to the paths and do not let children or dogs stray; do not enter buildings, pick anything up, camp or light fires; do not walk in mist or at night; and always obey the range wardens.**

Within the range, the cliff scenery is as fascinating as ever: the broad rock ledge skirt of Broad Bench; Brandy Bay, so named because of its its smuggling associations, and the mighty overhang of

Gad Cliff. Inland from Gad Cliff is **Tyneham**, the famous range village over which there has been so much dispute. The army evacuated the villagers in 1943, apparently just for the duration of the war, but the villagers have never been allowed to return. It is a moot point as to whether the army's presence has conserved the area, but it is true that the wild flowers on this section are superb: the army has no use for herbicides and nature runs the plant life.

Beyond Gad Cliff is Worbarrow Tout, rising like a whale's back from the sea and sheltering the popular bathing spot of **Worbarrow Bay**. At the far end of the sickle-shaped bay is Flower's Barrow the inappropriate name given to the Iron Age fortress on Rings Hill. The fort must have been one of the most impressive of Dorset's many, the only one to use sea cliffs as a natural barrier. But this is where the Purbeck Hills meet the sea and, in time, the cliffs were undermined, dumping the seaward side of the fort on to the beach. It is said that a phantom Roman army tramps across the fort (the idea that the ghostly marchers are Romans is at odds with history, but then so too the very existence of a phantom army).

During the Popish plots of the late seventeenth century an army was seen, not just heard, at Rings Hill, marching inland. Over a hundred people saw it and the local squire, John Lawrence, raced to Wareham. The local militia was mobilised, the town fortified, the Frome bridge barricaded, messengers were sent to London. And the Rings Hill army vanished into the air.

Beyond Worbarrow Bay is the delightfully named Arish Mell, then Mupe Rocks and the most famous of the Purbeck coves, Lulworth.

Napoleon at Lulworth

A local legend claims that one night a local woman heard voices in the cove while walking and, fearing for the safety of her smuggler husband (a Frenchman now living in Dorset) she crept towards the sea. A longboat had landed from a ship just off shore and Napoleon himself was on the beach with a number of men pouring over a map. Napoleon stared at the cliffs, shrugged and said *'C'est impossible'*. The men climbed back into the longboat and rowed away. The lady lived until 1884 when, at 104 years of age, she died, still insisting that it was indeed Napoleon.

WEST PURBECK

To the west of Church Knowle lies **Steeple**. In the church here are several depictions of the 'Stars and Stripes' coat-of-arms of the Lawrence family. George Washington, first President of the USA, was a descendant of the family and is said to have used the coat of arms as a basis for the flag of the newly-independent United States. From Steeple the road westwards crosses the Purbeck Hills, with several magnificent viewpoints along the way. From the first (at Grid Reference 903816, just before the road junction) a walk eastwards along the Hills reaches Grange Arch, an

Blue Pool

Furzebrook
Open: Pool: March-November, daily
9.30am-5.30pm
Museum: April-October, daily
9.30am-5.30pm
☎ 01929 551408

Children's Summer Farm

East Lulworth
Open: May-September, daily 10am-
4.30pm
☎ 01929 400352

Coach House Museum

St George's Close
Langton Matravers
Open: April-September, Monday-
Saturday 10am-12noon, 2-4pm
☎ 01929 423168

Corfe Castle
(National Trust)

Open: March-November, daily 10am-
5.30pm (4.30pm in March). November-February, daily 11am-3.30pm.
☎ 01929 481294

Lulworth Castle
(English Heritage)

East Lulworth
Open: April-October, Sunday-Friday
10am-6pm. October-March, Sunday-
Friday 10am-4pm.
☎ 01929 400352

MGFT Animal Sanctuary

Church Knowle
Open: All year, daily 11am-4pm
☎ 01929 480474

Model Village

West Street
Corfe Castle
Open: Easter-September, daily 10am-
6pm
☎ 01929 481234

Putlake Adventure Farm

Langton Matravers
Open: Easter-October, daily 11am-
6pm
☎ 01929 422917

Town Museum

West Street
Corfe Castle
Open: April-October, daily 9am-6pm;
November-March Saturday and
Sunday 10am-5pm.
☎ 01929 552740 for information

Town Museum

East Street
Wareham
Open: All year, Monday-Saturday
10am-1pm, 2-5pm
☎ 01929 553448

Smedmore House

Kimmeridge
Open: Infrequently May-mid-
September, usually on Wednesday
2.15-5.30pm. Also open by appointment.
☎ 01929 480719

Swanage Railway

Open: Steam trains run daily from
Easter to mid-November, and at
weekends throughout the winter.
There is a timetable, subject to
annual change, but usually offering
15 trains daily in July and August, 6
from April-June and in September,
and 4 on winter weekends.
☎ 01929 425800

Places to Visit

Tithe Barn Museum and Art Centre

Church Hill
Swanage
Open: Easter-September, Daily except Saturday and Sunday morning 10.30am-12.30pm, 2.30-4.30pm (open until 9.30pm on weekends from June to August)
☎ 01929 423174

A World of Toys

Arne
Open: April-June and September, Tuesday-Friday and Sunday 1.30-5pm. July and August, daily 10.30am-5.30pm
☎ 01929 552018

---

eighteenth-century folly constructed by one of the Bond family who owned Creech Grange. The family also built Bond Street in London. Soon the road divides: to the left is Tyneham, while straight on is Lulworth.

LULWORTH

Lulworth is divided into two villages, East and West, separated by a few miles and the army's Lulworth Camp. East Lulworth is a pretty, tiny village in which stands Lulworth Castle. The castle is an early seventeenth-century hunting lodge built in romantic style by Viscount Bindon. The castle was gutted by fire in 1929 but is being restored by English Heritage. It is worth visiting for the view from the tower and the lovely parkland.

Close to the castle is St Mary's Chapel, the first free-standing Catholic church to be built in England since the Reformation when it was erected in 1786 by the Weld family. The family were given permission for the chapel by George III on condition that it did not look like a church. Externally it certainly

does not.

West Lulworth is less pretty than its neighbour, and a good deal more crowded in summer with visitors being attracted to the marvellous Lulworth Cove.

The Cove is almost totally enclosed, its rocks tortured by the earth's forces.

To the east of the Cove, and within the army's range, is a fossil forest. To the west is Stair Hole where the sea has carved its way through the cliffs, and Durdle Door where it has done the same thing but in much more spectacular style. The name 'durdle' is apt: in the Dorset dialect it meant a barn, and the doorway created by the sea is certainly large enough for a barn. On the cliffs between the Cove and the Door, look out for the rare Lulworth Skipper butterfly. The butterfly was first found at Durdle Door in 1832 and is still local to the area.

North of Lulworth the B3071 reaches Wool, a town with a modern feel despite its old and pretty centre. At the centre, Spring Street is especially attractive, with a stream running beside the road and several beautiful old cottages. Close by is

Holy Rood Church which has a finely carved stone pulpit.

To the west of Wool, occasional steep roads explore the **Chaldon Downs**, though few make it to the sea, the coast here being very remote, visited by few apart from walkers on the Coastal Path. One of the roads reaches Chaldon Herring. Also known as East Chaldon, this is a pretty village famous for having been the home of author TF Powys for over 30 years until 1940, and his brother Llewelyn who lived here for 15 years. The third brother, John Cowper Powys, was also a frequent visitor. In TF Powys' most famous book, *Mr Weston's Good Wine*, the village is renamed Folly Down.

The three brothers are commemorated by three curious memorials – sculpted fossils in stone boxes – on the ridge to the south of the village. There is also a memorial to Llewelyn Powys by the sculptress Elizabeth Muntz. Ms Muntz, who was buried in the churchyard, was also responsible, in collaboration with the village children, for the collage in the church which depicts the village in 1940. The collage includes the prominent group of six Bronze Age round barrows to the north of the village. With the standard accuracy of such names the barrows are known as the Five Marys.

Wool Bridge

To the north of Wool is Wool Bridge, a sixteenth-century stone bridge. As at Sturminster Newton there is a notice threatening transportation to anyone damaging the bridge. It is said that a ghostly coach crosses the bridge when misfortune is about to befall a member of the Turberville family, though the coach can only be seen by members of the family. Perhaps with this legend in mind, Thomas Hardy had Tess spend her honeymoon in nearby Woolbridge Manor. The sleepwalking Angel Clare carried Tess to an open coffin in Bindon Abbey, to the east. The coffin is apparently still there, but the abbey is closed to the public at present.

ACTIVITIES FOR CHILDREN

The main theme parks/fun parks for children are mentioned within the text and listed in Places to Visit in the relevant chapter. In addition to these there are numerous small amusement/entertainment centres and more are being added all the time.

Younger children will also enjoy the llama treks offered by Brit Valley Llamas, while older children will enjoy the quad bike and Mini Mavrik rides offered by the Henley Hillbillies. The Henley site also offers evening badger watches.

Bruit Valley Llamas
New House Farm
Beaminster
☎ 01308 868674

Henley Hillbillies
Old Henley Farm
Buckland Newton
☎ 01300 345293

ARCHAEOLOGICAL AND HISTORICAL SITES

All the sites listed below are open at any reasonable time. Those with specific opening times are detailed in Places to Visit for the appropriate chapter.

**Abbotsbury Abbey
(English Heritage)**

Ackling Dyke
Cranborne Chase

Bockerley Dyke
Cranborne Chase

The Cross and Hand Stone
near A37 at Break Heart Hill

The Cursus
Cranborne Chase

The Grey Mare and Her Colts
near Abbotsbury

**Jordan Hill Roman Temple
(English Heritage)**
near Weymouth

**Kingston Russell Stone Circle
(English Heritage)**
near Abbotsbury

**Knowlton Church
and Earthworks
(English Heritage)**
near Gussage All Saints

**Maiden Castle
(English Heritage)**
near Dorchester

**The Nine Stones
(English Heritage)**
near Winterbourne Abbas

St Aldhelm's Chapel
Isle of Purbeck

**St Catherine's Chapel
(English Heritage)**
Abbotsbury

CRAFT AND ART CENTRES

Many of the towns and villages of Dorset have thriving craft centres and art galleries. The most important of these are mentioned in the text and noted in Places to Visit in the relevant chapter, but many of those not mentioned are very worthwhile.

MARKETS

Several of Dorset's larger towns have markets. The best are at:

Dorchester, Wednesday 8am–3pm
Weymouth, Thursday 8am–3pm
Wimborne Minster, Friday 7am–2.30pm, Saturday 8am–1pm and Sunday 9am–4pm

NATURE RESERVES

There are many Nature Reserves within Dorset. Some of the most important are mentioned in the text, but information on all the sites can be obtained from the following organisations:

Dorset Wildlife Trust
Brooklands Farm
Forston
Dorchester
DT2 7AA
☎ 01305 264620

Royal Society for the Protection of Birds
South-West Office
10 Richmond Road
Exeter EX4 4JA
☎ 01392 432691

OPENING TIMES

The details in Places to Visit are correct at the time of publication, but are subject to revision and should be checked beforehand if there is any doubt. This is particularly true for opening times at Bank Holidays. Most sites are open at Easter, but few are open at Christmas/New Year.

SPORTS

General Sports

The main towns, and particularly Bournemouth, have facilities for bowls, tennis and squash.

Golf
Ashley Wood Golf Club
Wimborne Road,
Blandford Forum
☎ 01258 452253/480379/450190

**Bournemouth Golf Range
(9-hole and Floodlit Golf Range)**
Parley Green, Parley (opposite Bournemouth Airport)
☎ 01202 593131 (range) and 01202 591600 (course)

Bournemouth and Meyrick Golf Club
Meyrick Park
☎ 01202 290307

Bridport and West Dorset Golf Club
East Cliff, West Bay
☎ 01308 421095/422597/
421491

Broadstone (Dorset) Golf Club
Wentworth Drive
☎ 01202 692595/693363/
692835

Came Down Golf Club
Higher Came
☎ 01305 813494/812531/
812670

**Canford Magna Golf Club
(Two 18-hole courses)**
Knighton Lane
☎ 01202 592555

Crane Valley Golf Club
West Farm, Romford
☎ 01202 814088

Dudsbury Golf Club
64 Christchurch Road, Ferndown
☎ 01202 593499/594488

East Dorset Golf Club
Hyde, nr Bere Regis
☎ 01929 472244/471294

Ferndown Golf Club
Golf Links Road, Ferndown
☎ 01202 876096/872022/
874602

Highcliffe Golf Club
Lymington Road
☎ 01425 272210/272953

Iford Bridge Golf Club
Barrack Road, Christchurch
☎ 01202 473817

Isle of Purbeck Golf Club
Corfe Road, Studland
☎ 01929 450361/450354

Kingston Heath Golf Club
Francis Avenue, Northbourne,
Bournemouth
☎ 01202 572633/577870/
578275

Lyme Regis Golf Club
Timber Hill
☎ 01297 442043/442963/
443494/443822/444988

Lyons Gate Golf Club
Lyons Gate Farm, Buckland
Newton
☎ 01300 345239

**Moors Valley Country Park Golf
Course**
Nr St Leonards
☎ 01425 479776

Parkstone Golf Club
Links Road, Parkstone
☎ 01202 707138/708025

Queens Park Golf Club
Queens Park West Drive,
Bournemouth
☎ 01202 396198/396817/
394466/302611

Sherborne Golf Club
Higher Chatcombe
☎ 01935 812274

Sturminster Marshall Golf Club
Moor Lane
☎ 01258 858444

Wareham Golf Club
Sandford Road
☎ 01929 554147/554156

Wessex Golf Club
Radipole Lane
East Chickerell
☎ 01305 784737

Weymouth Golf Club
Links Road, Weymouth
☎ 01305 773981/773997

Wolfedale Golf Club
Charminster
☎ 01305 260186

Riding

Though Dorset is not a recognised centre for riding and trekking, there are several places in the county where horses can be hired or treks joined.

Skiing

Christchurch Ski and Leisure Centre
Matchams Lane
Hurn
☎ 01202 499155

Skiing, snowboarding and ski bobbing are available. Gloves are essential.

Swimming Pools

Bournemouth Leisure Pool and Fitness Centre
Bournemouth International Centre
☎ 01202 456400

Clayesmore School Sports Centre
Iwerne Minster
☎ 01747 811810

Dolphin Swimming Pool
Kingland Road
Poole
☎ 01202 677217

Gillingham Leisure Centre
Hardings Lane
Gillingham
☎ 01747 822026

Purbeck Sports Centre and Swimming Pool
Worgret Road
Wareham
☎ 01929 556454

Stokewood Road Swimming and Fitness Centre
Bournemouth
☎ 01202 510436/529658

Weymouth and Portland Swimming Pool
Knightsdale Road
Weymouth
☎ 01305 774373

Sports Centres

Ashdown Leisure Centre
Adastral Road
Canford Heath
☎ 01202 604224

Blandford Leisure Centre
Milldown Road
Blandford Forum
☎ 01258 455566

Bridport Leisure Centre
Brewery Fields
Bridport
☎ 01308 427464

**Christchurch Ski and
Leisure Centre**
Matchams Lane
Hurn
☎ 01202 499155

**Clayesmore School
Sports Centre**
Iwerne Minster
☎ 01747 811810

David Lloyd Leisure plc
5 Knole Road
Bournemouth
☎ 01202 394333

Gillingham Leisure Centre
Hardings Lane
Gillingham
☎ 01747 822026

Gryphon Leisure Centre
Bristol Road
Sherborne
☎ 01935 814011

**Haven Sports and
Leisure Centre**
Banks Road
Sandbanks
☎ 01202 700211

Littledown Centre
Chaseside
Bournemouth
☎ 01202 417600

Lytchett Manor Sports Hall
Post Green Road
Lytchett Manor
☎ 01202 632765

Kemp Welch Leisure Centre
Kemp Welch School
Herbert Avenue
Parkstone
☎ 01202 738787

Poole Sports Centre
Dolphin Centre
☎ 01202 777788

**Purbeck Sports Centre
and Swimming Pool**
Worgret Road
Wareham
☎ 01929 556454

Queen Elizabeth Leisure Centre
Blandford Road
Wimborne Minster
☎ 01425 888208

Shaftesbury Leisure Centre
Salisbury Road
☎ 01747 854637

Thomas Hardy Leisure Centre
Cobury Road
Dorchester
☎ 01305 266772

Two Riversmeet Leisure Centre
Stoney Lane South
Christchurch
☎ 01202 477987

Verwood Leisure Centre
Chiltern Drive
☎ 01202 826560

Water Sports

As might be expected, Dorset has enormous potential and facilities for water sports. All the main resorts offer hire and tuition for most water sports. The main centre is Poole, Poole Harbour offering sheltered conditions which are ideal for those learning a new sport as well as experienced practitioners. Poole also offers the hire of large yachts for day sailing.

TOURIST INFORMATION OFFICES

The principal county tourist office is:

Dorset Tourism
County Hall
Dorchester
DT1 1XJ
☎ 01305 221001

Other main offices can be found at:

Blandford Forum
Marsh and Ham Car Park
☎ 01258 454770

Bournemouth
Westover Road
☎ 0906 802 0234

Bridport
32 South Street
☎ 01308 424901

Christchurch
23 High Street
☎ 01202 471780

Dorchester
Antelope Yard
Trinity Street
☎ 01305 267992

Lyme Regis
The Guildhall
Bridge Street
☎ 01297 442138

Poole
The Quay
☎ 01202 253253

Shaftesbury
8 Bell Street
☎ 01747 853514

Sherborne
Digby Street
☎ 01935 815341

Swanage
White House
Shore Road
☎ 01929 422885

Wareham (Easter-September only)
Trinity Church
South Street
☎ 01929 552740

Weymouth
The King's Statue
The Esplanade
☎ 01305 785747

Wimborne Minster
29 High Street
☎ 01202 886116

LANDMARK VISITORS GUIDES

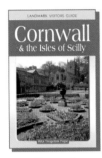

Cornwall
ISBN: 1 901522 09 1
256pp, Full colour
£9.95

Devon
ISBN: 1 901522 42 3
224pp, Full colour
£9.95

Dorset
ISBN: 1 901522 46 6
240pp, Full colour
£9.95

Somerset
ISBN: 1 901522 40 7
224pp, Full colour
£10.95

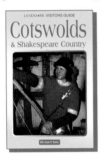

Cotswolds
ISBN: 1 901522 12 1
224pp, Full colour
£9.99

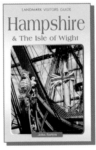

Hampshire
ISBN: 1 901522 14 8
224pp, Full colour
£9.95

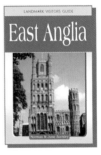

East Anglia
ISBN: 1 901522 58 X
224pp, Full colour
£9.95

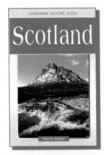

Scotland
ISBN: 1 901522 18 0
288pp, Full colour
£11.95

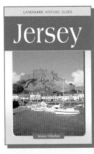

Jersey
ISBN: 1 901522 47 4
224pp, Full colour
£9.99

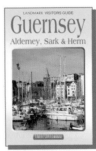

Guernsey
ISBN: 1 901522 48 2
224pp, Full colour
£9.95

Harrogate
ISBN: 1 901522 55 5
96pp, Full colour
£4.95

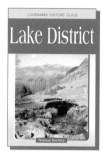
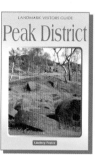
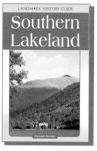
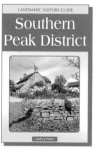

Lake District	Peak District	Southern Lakeland	Southern Peak
ISBN: 1 901522 38 5	ISBN: 1 901522 25 3	ISBN: 1 901522 53 9	ISBN: 1 901522 27 X
224pp, Full colour	240pp, Full colour	96pp, Full colour	96pp, Full colour
£9.95	£9.99	£5.95	£5.95

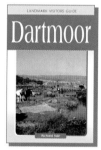

West Cornwall	South Devon	Dartmoor
ISBN: 1 901522 24 5	ISBN: 1 901522 52 0	ISBN: 1 901522 69 5
96pp, Full colour	96pp, Full colour	96pp, Full colour
£5.95	£5.95	£5.95

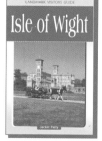
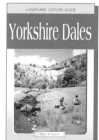

New Forest	Isle of Wight	Yorkshire Dales
ISBN: 1 901522 70 9	ISBN: 1 901522 71 7	ISBN: 1 901522 41 5
96pp, Full colour	96pp, Full colour	224pp, Full colour
£5.95	£5.95	£9.95

Pack
2 months
into
2 weeks
with your
Landmark
Visitors
Guides

Fact File

TRAVEL AND ACCOMMODATION

Dorset is easily reached. From the east the M3/M27 motorways extend almost to the county's eastern border, while several fine roads head south from the M4/M5.

The county has an abundance of accommodation ranging from the plain and simple to luxury class hotels. Lists of accommodation are available form the main tourist offices.

WALKING

The Dorset Ranger Service offers an annual programme of day walks at various places throughout the county. The programme can be obtained from local tourist information centres and libraries or by obtaining a copy of the Dorset Countryside Book, published annually. This is also available at tourist information centres and libraries, or directly from:

Dorset County Council
Environmental Services Directorate
County Hall
Dorchester
DT1 1XJ
☎ 01305 224214

For details of the walks programmes for particular areas of the county, ring the Rangers Service on:

Central Dorset	☎ 01929 424443
Eastern Dorset	☎ 01425 478082
Western Dorset	☎ 01305 266920

The county's Environmental Services directorate (address /telephone number as above) also offers a range of walks exploring Dorset's archaeology and architectural heritage. Details are available at tourist information offices or from the address/telephone number above.

The National Trust also offers a full programme of short walks around its numerous properties in the counties. For full details contact:

The National Trust
Dorset Area Office
Hillbutts
Wimborne Minster
BH21 4DS
☎ 01202 882493

The Dorset Coastal Path is a National Trail following the coast from Sandbanks to Lyme Regis (where it links with the South Devon Coastal Path – these two paths, together with the coastal paths of Cornwall, North Devon and Somerset form the South-West Peninsula Coastal Path, Britain's longest National Trail.) The Dorset Coastal Path is a magnificent route, following the county's entire coast – apart from a section near Abbotsbury where it moves inland to avoid Chesil Beach: the Beach can be walked, but requires ankles of steel and a desire for personal suffering which would do justice to a medieval monk.

The Wessex Ridgeway is an 'unofficial' long-distance footpath which links the (official) Ridgeway National Trail to Lyme Regis by traversing Cranborne Chase and the North Dorset Downs.

Before walking in the army's Lulworth Range, for your own safety you must ensure that the range is open to visitors. The ranges are open most weekends and during school holidays. For full information contact:
☎ 01929 462721

LANDMARK
VISITORS GUIDES

US & British VI*
ISBN: 1 901522 03 2
256pp,
UK £11.95 US $15.95

Antigua & Barbuda*
ISBN: 1 901522 02 4
96pp,
UK £5.95 US $12.95

Bermuda*
ISBN: 1 901522 07 5
160pp,
UK £7.95 US $12.95

Barbados*
ISBN: 1 901522 32 6
160pp,
UK £7.95 US $12.95

St Lucia*
ISBN: 1 901522 82 2
144pp,
UK £6.95 US $13.95

Cayman Islands*
ISBN: 1 901522 33 4
160pp
UK £7.95 US $12.95

Jamaica*
ISBN: 1 901522 31 8
160pp
UK £7.95 US $12.95

Orlando*
ISBN: 1 901522 22 9
256pp,
UK £9.95 US $15.95

Florida: Gulf Coast*
ISBN: 1 901522 01 6
160pp
UK £7.95 US $12.95

Florida: The Keys*
ISBN: 1 901522 21 0
160pp,
UK £7.95 US $12.95

Dominican Republic*
ISBN: 1 901522 08 3
160pp,
UK £7.95 US $12.95

Gran Canaria*
ISBN: 1 901522 19 9
160pp
UK £7.95 US $12.95

Tenerife
ISBN: 1 901522 17 2
160pp,
UK £7.95

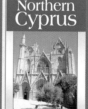

North Cyprus
ISBN: 1 901522 51 2
192pp
UK £8.95

Madeira
ISBN: 1 901522 42 3
192pp,
UK £8.95

To order send a cheque (check)/Visa/MasterCard details to: **Landmark Publishing,**
Waterloo House, 12 Compton, Ashbourne, Derbyshire DE6 IDA England
Tel: 01335 347349 Fax: 01335 347303 e-mail: landmark@clara.net
web site: www.landmarkpublishing.co.uk

* In USA order from **Hunter Publishing**
130 Campus Drive, Edison NJ 08818, Tel (732) 225 1900 or (800) 255 0343
Fax: (732) 417 0482 www.hunterpublishing.com

Provence*
ISBN: 1 901522 45 8
240pp,
UK £10.95 US $17.95

Côte d'Azur*
ISBN: 1 901522 29 6
144pp,
UK £6.95 US $13.95

Dordogne
ISBN: 1 901522 67 9
176pp,
UK £9.95

Vendée
ISBN: 1 901522 76 X
160pp,
UK £7.95

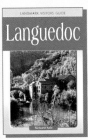

Languedoc
ISBN: 1 901522 79 2
144pp,
UK £6.95

Bruges*
ISBN: 1 901522 66 0
96pp,
UK £5.95

Ticino
ISBN: 1 901522 74 1
192pp
UK £8.95

Italian Lakes*
ISBN: 1 901522 11 3
240pp,
UK £10.95 US $15.95

Riga*
ISBN: 1 901522 59 8
160pp,
UK £7.95

Cracow
ISBN: 1 901522 54 7
160pp,
UK £7.95

Iceland*
ISBN: 1 901522 68 7
192pp,
UK £12.95 US $17.95

New Zealand*
ISBN: 1 901522 36 9
320pp
UK £12.95 US $18.95

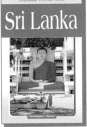

Sri Lanka
ISBN: 1 901522 37 7
192pp,
UK £9.95

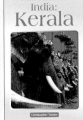

India: Kerala
ISBN: 1 901522 16 4
256pp,
UK £10.99

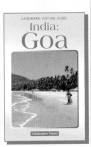

India: Goa
ISBN: 1 901522 23 7
160pp,
UK £7.95

Prices subject to alteration from time to time

INDEX

INDEX

Published by
Landmark Publishing Ltd,
Waterloo House, 12 Compton, Ashbourne, Derbyshire DE6 1DA England
Tel: (01335) 347349 Fax: (01335) 347303 e-mail: landmark@clara.net

ISBN 1 84306 001 9

Print: Gutenberg Press Ltd, Malta
Cartography: Mark Titterton
Design: Mark Titterton

Front cover: Cottages at Piddletrenhide
Back cover top: West Bay
bottom: Antelope Walk, Dorchester

Picture Credits:
All photography provided by Richard Sale and Lindsey Porter